TO PROTECT AND SERVE

TO PROTECT AND SERVE

How to Fix America's Police

Norm Stamper

NATION
BOOKS
New York

Published by Nation Books, A Member of the Perseus Books Group
116 East 16th Street, 8th Floor
New York, NY 10003

Nation Books is a co-publishing venture of the Nation Institute and the Perseus
Books Group

Books published by Nation Books are available at special discounts for bulk
purchases in the United States by corporations, institutions, and other organizations.
For more information, please contact the Special Markets Department at the
Perseus Books Group, 2300 Chestnut Street, Suite 200, Philadelphia, PA 19103, or
call (800) 810-4145, ext. 5000, or e-mail special.markets@perseusbooks.com.

Designed by Timm Bryson

Library of Congress Cataloging-in-Publication Data
Names: Stamper, Norm, author.
Title: To protect and serve: how to fix America's police / Norm Stamper.
Description: 1 Edition. | New York: Nation Books, 2016. | Includes index.
Identifiers: LCCN 2016000403| ISBN 9781568585406 (hardback) | ISBN
9781568585413 (ebook)
Subjects: LCSH: Police—United States. | Law enforcement—United States. |
Police misconduct—United States. | Community policing—United States. |
BISAC: POLITICAL SCIENCE / Political Freedom & Security / Law
Enforcement.
| SOCIAL SCIENCE / Criminology. | POLITICAL SCIENCE / Political
Freedom &
Security / Civil Rights.
Classification: LCC HV8139 .S675 2016 | DDC 363.20973—dc23 LC record
available at http://lccn.loc.gov/2016000403
10 9 8 7 6 5 4 3 2 1

To the survivors:
Those who have lost loved ones through wrongful acts of law enforcement
Those who have lost police officers to on-the-job violence

CONTENTS

PREFACE

It's a quiet Saturday morning, a pleasant 82°F in Ferguson, Missouri. Patrol officer Darren Wilson, who began work at 6:30 a.m., responds to a midshift 911 call from a woman at Park Ridge Apartments: a man is out to shoot her. By the time the twenty-eight-year-old patrol officer arrives, the suspect is gone, and the complainant declines to pursue charges.

Wilson clears the call, ready for whatever crops up next in the 911 queue. He is dispatched right away to the Northwinds Apartment complex. A two-year-old is having difficulty breathing; emergency medical personnel will soon be on scene. Wilson gets there quickly, sticks around, reassures the mother before watching the ambulance drive off with its little patient.

Back in his marked Chevy Tahoe, Wilson motors down Canfield Drive, where he spots a couple of young black men strolling down the middle of the street. Not safe for them, plus they're interfering with traffic. The officer stops about twelve yards away, gets out of his car and approaches. "Hey, Mike."

"Yeah?" the bigger of the two says. He is eighteen-year-old Michael Brown, his companion twenty-two-year-old Dorian Johnson. "What you want?" Brown asks.

"Just wondering why you're walking in the middle of the street. Why don't you try the sidewalk? Safer there."

"Fuck what you have to say," Brown says. He doesn't shout it, but he doesn't whisper it, either.

Wilson calls for backup, then smiles at Brown. "Really, I'm not here to cause any problems."

And he isn't. He loves working the Canfield Green community, enjoys the diversity of the area. As a white cop in a black neighborhood, he gets it. He understands the chip-on-the-shoulder attitudes, especially among young black men. His fellow cops have labeled Canfield Green "anti-police," their most charitable pet name. They stop and frisk everything that moves and write traffic tickets by the bucketful—generating revenue, safeguarding their salaries, adding to the economic hardship of the area's low-income residents. They make "skinny" arrests, most for low-level, nonviolent drug offenses and a panoply of constitutionally shaky municipal code violations, often fabricating "probable cause"—if they bother with it at all. They misuse their batons, their dogs, their Tasers. And they pepper their speech and e-mails with racial slurs, ridiculing the nation's first black president and his wife, and the nation's first two black attorneys general. But Wilson, one of the department's fifty white cops (four others are black, in a city whose population is over two-thirds African American), works hard to get along with the residents, forging positive relations, aiming to build trust. In fact, he believes a big part of his job is to create a partnership with the people on his beat, to work collaboratively with them to solve problems. More than anything, he wants to put an end to the deep-seated, historical animosity between the community and his police department.

"Seriously, I just want you guys to be safe."

"Then why you always hassling us?" Brown says, his tone softening. "We ain't done nothing wrong."

Wilson notices that Brown is clutching a fistful of cigarillos. During his last call, the officer overheard other units being dispatched to a theft from Ferguson Market and Liquor, a convenience store not far from Canfield. The loot? Cigarillos. The crime report has been upgraded from misdemeanor shoplifting to strong-arm robbery, a felony. Wilson plays it cool. Alert, fully aware of his surroundings, he nevertheless assumes a nonthreatening stance and speaks in calm, soothing tones. "Last thing I'm gonna do is hassle you guys. You got my word."

They chat like that briefly, Brown continuing to goad Wilson, the officer refusing to get sucked in. Ninety seconds after his request, a backup unit pulls in, followed immediately by another. Wilson briefs his fellow cops, one of whom had taken the report at the convenience store. "Our guy?" Wilson says, glancing over at Brown.

The officer nods.

When Wilson informs Brown what he's learned about the crime, that it was captured on CCTV, the youth shakes his head and sighs. He surrenders the cigarillos and puts his hands behind his back. Wilson cuffs him without incident.

THE COP AND THE prisoner talk on the way to jail. "Seriously, Mike. What's it like out here for you? I mean, dealing with your police department?"

"*My* police department? That's some crackass bullshit." He pauses. Wilson says nothing. "Truth is, it's messed up, man. You guys jack us around all the time, for nothing. It's 'nigga' this and 'nigga' that. Always stopping us for no reason, throwing us to the ground, busting us for 'failure to comply . . . '"

"Tell you what," Wilson says as he removes the cuffs inside the new sally port of the city jail at police headquarters. "I'll have a talk with the prosecutor. Not making any promises, but it might help. But, you gotta know: what you did in that store was bad, real bad. You gotta promise, no more. Word?"

Brown hesitates for the longest time, then nods. "Word, Officer Wilson. No more."

Wilson has heard it before, but he believes the kid.

The next day, Wilson chats up the prosecutor, puts in a good word for the young defendant. Originally charged with robbery, Brown cops a negotiated plea to misdemeanor theft. He pays a small fine, gets credit for time served, and is assigned three weekends of community service.

In the fall, on probation for the theft, Michael Brown starts classes at St. Louis's Vatterott College, where he studies HVAC. He goes on to graduate and becomes a technician in his community, specializing in keeping his neighbors' homes warm in the winter, cool in the summer.

Officer Darren Wilson continues his career as a Ferguson police officer and earns praise from the African American community for his spirit of cooperation, his sensitivity and compassion.

And life goes on in Ferguson, a small town in the middle of the country that few have, or ever will, hear about.

SADLY, AS WE ALL know, this rosy "what might have been" scenario is far removed from what actually happened in that Missouri city of 21,000 on August 9, 2014, when Darren Wilson shot and killed Michael Brown.

Simply put, Darren Wilson did not appear to be the tactful, community-oriented, safety-conscious cop one would hope for in such a tense situation—tension the officer could have avoided. In fact, in his grand jury testimony, Dorian Johnson quotes Wilson, shouting at the young men from his SUV as he passed them going the opposite direction, "Get the fuck out of the street!"[1] Wilson in his own grand jury testimony denies this.

According to Officer Wilson's testimony, after he had passed the men, Brown shouted at him, "Fuck what you have to say!" Wilson backed up at high speed, tires screeching. (Johnson testified that had they not heard the tires, they would have been struck by the police vehicle.) As he caught up to the two men, Wilson cut the wheel sharply and came to a rest just inches from Brown and Johnson, close enough that he couldn't open the driver's side door without hitting them. The officer was, in his own words, "trapped" inside his police car. Wilson testified during the grand jury hearing that Brown reached into the car and struck him, twice. He grabbed Brown's arm but he "felt like a five-year-old holding on to the Hulk."

"I'd already taken two to the face," he told the jurors. He thought a third blow "might be fatal." So he pulled his duty weapon, a .40-caliber Sig Sauer P229, and shouted at Brown, "I'll shoot!"

Brown responded with "the most intense, aggressive" expression on his face, grabbed the barrel of the handgun, and allegedly said, "You're too much of a pussy to shoot me."

During the struggle, Wilson attempted to shoot Brown but the gun "misfired," twice. Actually, with Brown's hands on the barrel, it threw the weapon "out of battery." (In other words, it did what a gun in that condition is supposed to do, namely, "click" each time as Wilson pulled the trigger—it's a mechanical effect, and a safety feature.) Finally able to wrest the gun away and operate the slide of the semiautomatic handgun, Wilson fired two rounds, the first missing Brown, the second striking him. Brown staggered back, then took off running, yelling at his friend Johnson to "keep running, bro."

Wilson got on the air, informed the dispatcher that shots had been fired, and requested backup. He got out of the car and began running toward the fleeing Brown. At a disputed distance (35 feet, according to Wilson's estimate; 148 or 153 feet, according to where the body was found), Brown stopped, turned around, and took a "shuffle step" as though preparing to run back at the officer. According to Wilson, one of Brown's hands was balled into a fist, the other "hidden in his waistband." As Brown advanced toward him, the officer fired, twelve times. Six of the rounds missed, six struck the teenager, including one to the forehead and one to the top of the head, the latter suggesting that Brown was falling to the ground when the last shot struck him. Contrary to some reports, Wilson did not shoot Brown in the back. As to whether Brown had his hands up, in a sign of surrender, the record is unclear. What is clear is that Brown was unarmed.

It is not a stretch to conclude that Wilson's behavior, from beginning to end—the average cop knows, or should know, never to conduct business from the front seat of a police car—all but guaranteed a lethal outcome.

Had the officer known Michael Brown beforehand, as in our hypothetical scenario (it was not until the day after the fatal encounter that Wilson would even learn the names of the two young men); had he treated Brown respectfully; had he employed sound safety procedures; and, of course, had young Brown chosen not to physically confront the officer—it is highly unlikely the encounter would have produced a fatal outcome.

There would have been no mass protests, no looting, arson, or rock- and bottle-throwing incidents. Nor would the Ferguson Police Department's overly aggressive, militaristic tactics have been on display for the whole world to see. And the nation would have been spared the drama of St. Louis County prosecutor Robert McCulloch's biased, eccentric decision-making and a St. Louis County grand jury's verdict, each of which fueled additional outrage.

The death of Michael Brown, combined with a fraught preexisting relationship between police and community, and the decision to leave the teenager's body in the street for hours—angered, saddened, and galvanized citizens in Ferguson and beyond to demand fundamental changes in the way our cities are policed. (Throughout, I refer to "citizens" or "the citizenry." In this context, these terms have nothing whatsoever to do with citizenship. Instead, they are used here exclusively as synonyms for inhabitants: the "citizens of New York City," for example, or "the citizenry" of Ferguson. My intent is to help retire the word "civilian" in drawing a distinction between police and community members. Why? Because, if those served by police are civilians, that makes cops, ipso facto, a military force.)

To the dismay of the Ferguson Chamber of Commerce and local boosters, "Ferguson" has become shorthand for police aggression, racism, profit-motivated policing, trigger-happy cops, and unrestrained militarism. Chiefs and elected officials in other parts of the country are often quoted: "We can't afford another 'Ferguson' here."[2]

To that extent we can thank the Ferguson Police Department—it could have been *any* police force—for setting in motion the wheels of desperately needed institutional reform.

WHAT WOULD POSSESS A South Carolina cop to shoot a fleeing, unarmed man in the back? Why would a police officer drive his van like a madman through the streets of Baltimore, Maryland, as his soon-to-be-dead, handcuffed prisoner is tossed about like a sack of potatoes? How could a New York City cop apply greater and greater, ultimately fatal, pressure to the neck of a man in medical distress while ignoring repeated cries of, "I can't breathe! I can't breathe!"? Why are police officers taking the lives of so many unarmed black men, teenagers, and preteens, the homeless, the mentally ill?

Do these lives matter to our police officers?

Americans are insisting on answers to these questions. They are also calling for an explanation for what they see as an excessively aggressive, militarized response to mass protests, almost always sparked by these same controversial police actions.

Above all, they are demanding accountability for official misdeeds, and an end to what they see as a pattern and practice of unlawful police violence.

ADDING TO THE VOLATILITY of current affairs is the reaction of America's police officers themselves. Rank-and-file cops of the biggest city in the nation are making a habit of turning their backs on their mayor; there's been talk of "de-policing," or the "blue flu" (withholding services or not showing up for work), in such cities as New York, Baltimore, Seattle, Chicago, Cincinnati, Philadelphia; and we have witnessed within the ranks an increasingly ugly, often blatantly racist echo chamber of chatter about blacks, Latinos, "welfare moms," the president, the attorney general.

And each day's news seems to bring a fresh report of the ambush of a police officer or, much more often, yet another controversial police shooting or in-custody death.

ACCURATE, THOROUGH, TIMELY INVESTIGATIONS—RESULTING in sanctions, as appropriate—are vital in every case, of course. But an examination of the underlying, systemic causes of police misconduct and seemingly permanent community-police tensions is also critically important. What structural, political, and workplace-cultural forces have combined to create such a sad and sorry state of community-police relations?

Friends—graying former colleagues who, like me, spent their entire adult lives in police work—point to disturbing changes in the policies and practices of today's law enforcement, especially since 9/11. Some believe we may have passed a point of no return, that the community-police relationship has been ruptured beyond repair. It's a legitimate line of speculation: Has the institution entered an irreversible spiral of increasing polarization and hopelessness?

REGRETTABLY, LOST IN THE maelstrom is an appreciation of the many cops who work hard, treat people with respect, honor the constitution, and save lives. These police officers deserve better.

It's hard to imagine a more taxing, difficult role in society. Police officers work the streets at all hours—nights, weekends, holidays, sometimes under extreme conditions—wielding the coercive power of government, enforcing unpopular laws, encountering people at their worst, confronting in one moment an armed assailant and in the next trying to comfort a dead child's parents. All this against a backdrop of persistent, systemic social and economic ills: racism and discrimination, homelessness, unemployment, inaccessible health care, failing schools, inadequate child care, and so on. And the job is particularly demanding today, given the proliferation of firearms (every other car stop, every other 911 call seems to produce a gun), the images of a cop behaving badly in a particular city replayed countless times online, the disintegration of "community." Nevertheless, we expect, indeed we demand of today's police officers that they meet the letter of the law in their everyday work, satisfy the dictates of procedural justice, treat all people with empathy and compassion, and exercise great discipline and restraint in the face of the most intense provocation, including threats to their lives.

POLICING HAS NEVER ENJOYED universal acceptance, much less esteem. Its history as a formal institution, dating from the mid-nineteenth century, has been tainted by corruption, discrimination, and excessive force. Pointing to the seeming intractability of these problems, a small but growing number of observers from both the left and the right have recently challenged the very authority of organized policing. Eloquent critics, from Mychal Denzel Smith to Radley Balko, have raised the question of whether policing as we know it rests on solid constitutional footing, or whether the institution should be abolished altogether.

Given these conditions, what can be done to restore trust in policing—or to build confidence in the police where it has never existed?

The "few bad apples" theory is not enough to explain police misconduct. The kind of behavior widely questioned and condemned today is, in reality, part of a deeply ingrained, historically dysfunctional structure, that is, a moldering orchard, or, if you prefer, a rotten barrel. A fresh, healthy apple will quickly turn in such an environment.

As a beat cop, as an undercover detective, and through promotions up the ranks to the position of police chief, over the course of thirty-four years, I had the privilege to work with exceptionally fine police officers in two big-city departments. I saw, firsthand, countless examples of compassion, competence, and heroism—good cops getting the job done in spite of the system, not because of it.

In these pages, I will focus on how the institution is organized, and how that structure—anachronistic, paramilitary, rigidly bureaucratic—

produces a workplace culture that serves as a breeding ground for racism, corruption, sexual predation, brutality, unjustified lethal force, and excessive militarism. I will explain how today's cop culture guarantees a toxic, "diseased" workplace that no amount of careful screening or academy training—or body cams, or legal reforms, or tweaked policies and procedures, or recalled mayors or "replacement" police chiefs, or even the cloning of a thousand good cops—can hope to reverse.

Given that the pathology of American policing is embedded in the very structure of the institution, radical surgery, in the form of a fundamental transformation of our federal and local law enforcement agencies, is the only logical and sustainable remedy.

THE FERGUSON OFFICER WHO shot Michael Brown now belongs to a fraternity of police and ex-police officers whose members include the plainclothes cop who choked the life out of New Yorker Eric Garner; the rookie whose bullet ended the twelve-year-old existence of Cleveland's Tamir Rice; the Seattle officer who shot and killed a partially deaf, chronically inebriated wood-carver, John T. Williams; the Atlanta officer who took the life of a naked, unarmed, mentally ill Anthony Hill; the Pasco, Washington, and Albuquerque, New Mexico, cops who shot to death, respectively, Antonio Zambrano-Montes and James Boyd, homeless men; the Brooklyn rookie who took the life of an unarmed Akai Gurley as he stood on a stairwell landing, talking with his girlfriend; the North Charleston, South Carolina, patrol officer who fired eight times at a fleeing Walter Scott, striking him in the back and killing him; the Baltimore officer whose wantonly reckless operation of a prisoner van severed the spine of Freddie Gray; the Texas Department of Public Safety trooper whose shrieking, out-of-control arrest of Sandra Bland would lead to her in-custody death in the Waller County Jail; the Chicago cop who pumped bullet after bullet, sixteen slugs in all, into the body of seventeen-year-old Laquan McDonald; and the University of Cincinnati police officer who shot an unarmed Samuel DuBose after stopping him for having no front license plate on his car. Like countless others throughout the nation, these citizens posed either no risk or a manageable threat to the officers.

All of that is a way of saying that every one of these deaths could and should have been prevented, sparing each family survivor, each community, and, yes, each police officer, a lifetime of heartache.

TO BE CLEAR, THE officers responsible for these incidents are also victims of the system of American policing.

That New York City Police Department (NYPD) officers Rafael Ramos and Wenjian Liu were executed at the height of anti-police fervor on the streets of New York should come as little surprise. Mental illness may help explain that particular shooter's motive for the December 20, 2014, ambush, but there can be no denying that millions of Americans have had it with their cops. Social networks teem with expressions of rage toward my former colleagues.

And, as noted, many of America's police officers, feeling deeply misunderstood and unappreciated, are equally angry, in direct and steadily mounting proportion to the criticism they continue to receive. They don't all express their anger in mature fashion: each day, through a variety of online feeds, I receive accounts, often vivid and graphic, often racially tinged, of the fierce hostility many cops feel toward their critics. Of course, my electronic in-basket also includes plenty of bombastic anti-police sentiment.

This is not a good thing—polarization never is. Yet, each "side" seems content to talk past the other, which happens when honest conversation is confined to one's own family of interests, when any "reaching out" to the other side takes the form of attacks.

America's police officers perform tasks of the utmost importance and sensitivity, often under urgent, sometimes life-threatening conditions: suspects holding innocent hostages at gunpoint; violent family abusers threatening to kill the people they purport to love, along with any cop who tries to stop them; human traffickers armed with AK-47s; school and workplace shooters; and, of course, all the drug-war bloodshed, played out in home-invasion robberies and drive-by shootings. Even terrorism. The killings of political satirists at the *Charlie Hebdo* offices in Paris; the more recent, wide-scale terrorist attacks in that same city; the slayings of free-speech advocates at a Copenhagen public event; the murders of a police officer and a mother and a father during a shootout at a Planned Parenthood facility in Colorado Springs; and the attacks that left fourteen dead at San Bernardino's Inland Regional Center—such incidents could happen anywhere in the world at any time, as Americans know all too well.

And, almost always, the first responder is a uniformed police officer of the local police department.

IN LIGHT OF ALL this, and to underscore the humanity behind the badge, I believe it's essential for critics to understand the risks our police officers take, the sacrifices they make. And I do hope my fellow critics can find it in their hearts to cultivate a genuine appreciation of this reality.

It's not only self-defeating for protesters to dehumanize police officers, it is dangerous. For everyone. No matter how righteous the protest, for some to chant, "Pigs in a blanket, fry 'em like bacon!" is not only silly and self-sabotaging, it's disgusting. Or to put it differently, *I* was disgusted when I saw news coverage of just such a display at the Minnesota State Fair in August 2015.

I think most people get the self-defeating part: if your tactics turn off the very people you're trying to win over—fence-sitters, passive, nondemonstrative allies, and, yes, the police—it just doesn't make a whole lot of sense to employ those tactics.

As to the dangerous part? A message urging violence against cops (however cute, witty, or rhetorical) is bound to prompt certain members of the public to take extreme action against police officers. It also bears noting that threatening members of an armed, organized force, trained in the efficient use of violence, is not a smart move.

I believe Officers Ramos and Liu of the NYPD, Harris County sheriff's deputy Darren Goforth, and other ambushed officers would be alive today but for the inflammatory "the only good cop is a dead cop" thread of some fringe protest messages. I would like to believe—hell, I do believe—that only a small fraction of police critics want to see officers shot in the head as they pump gas or sit in their patrol cars.

This is not a plea to end demonstrations against police violence and other abuses—far from it. In fact, a strong, sustained citizens' movement against police brutality and racism is the cornerstone of any viable reform effort. Moreover, by design, protest demonstrations are intended to disrupt and bedevil the status quo—and that has never been more pertinent or more urgent than it is today.

But I do make an appeal here and now for critics to embrace nonviolence, in word and deed.

UNDER THE BEST OF circumstances, police work is delicate and demanding. Done well, it is a thing of beauty. But it requires of its practitioners an uncommon blend of skills and qualities. I will spell out these requisite skills and qualities, and describe how communities can restructure policing to ensure that both current and prospective cops are physically, mentally, psychologically, emotionally, and ethically up to the task.

My inclination, however, is not toward a psychology of police work but rather toward organizational and political theory. This more sociological (albeit studiously nonacademic) approach recognizes that a given individual can bring to the job substantial maturity—cognitive skills, patience, judgment, empathy—and exhibit the potential to do quite well as a police officer. But the cop culture has a way of chewing up even strong-willed, well-intentioned young officers and spitting them out. Or co-opting them, and taking special pleasure in doing so. If we are going to change all that, we need to understand how today's police departments operate in the here and now, behind the scenes.

I propose, in these chapters, a fundamentally new way for police to operate, in full partnership with the citizenry, under a transformed role of the federal government, and in a manner that would make today's calm, disciplined professionals of the cop world the norm, not the exception. I also argue for broad and sustained grassroots opposition to the status quo, a willingness of activists, politicians, academics, everyday Americans, and sympathetic cops and police executives to act boldly in support of a new, *community-driven* system of policing. The stakes are too high to do otherwise.

1

FROM FERGUSON
TO NEW YORK

I THOUGHT I UNDERSTOOD the "quota system" when I was a rookie beat cop in San Diego. The year was 1966. It seemed every motorist I stopped for a violation had something to say on the subject: "Yeah, yeah. I know. You gotta meet your quota. Just give me the damn ticket, I'm late for work!" Often followed by a mumbled version of, "God, I hate you guys." I didn't realize then that it wasn't just "bad PR" that was wrong with the quota system, nor was it merely the dishonorable revenue-driven incentive behind it. It was something else entirely. Something bigger, more insidious.

Cops on the beat never called it the "quota system." It was the "numbers game," and our sergeants, with pressure from on high, made it clear, explicitly: We were to write two "movers" a day. Warnings didn't count, equipment violations didn't count, parking tickets didn't count—only moving citations counted. We understood the money motive, realized the city council and the numbers-crunchers in city hall had put pressure on the city manager to put pressure on the police chief, who in turn pressured his command staff to generate the requisite number of revenue-producing traffic citations.

Two a day, and it didn't matter whether they were for speeding, busting a red light, veering over a lane line, making a questionable right turn, or driving too slowly. Or whether our traffic enforcement had any effect at all on public safety. What mattered was that we got those two a day. (Typical response to a disgruntled motorist? "I don't have a quota, ma'am," my fellow cops and I would reply. "Chief says we can write as many as we want.") In fact, exceed the minimum, and there just might be a seat for you in Detectives.

And it wasn't just tickets.

It was all about "productivity." A "productive" beat cop returned to the station at the end of shift, shuffled over to the report sergeant's desk, and deposited, every night, a healthy handful of source documents. Onto the designated piles went field interrogation (FI) slips, arrest reports, and, of course, those movers. There were other stacks on the desk as well, smaller ones, for the occasional parking ticket (usually in response to a citizen's complaint of a blocked driveway), crime reports, property and narcotics and vehicle impound slips, fender-bender accident forms, and the like. But the Big Three—arrests, FIs, and traffic tickets—those were the ones that counted.

Tickets were important, of course. But to many, especially detectives and their bosses over in the Investigations Bureau, field interrogations were especially valued. Known variously as "field interview" or "stop and frisk" or "Terry stop," or by numerous unfortunate colloquialisms such as "shakedown" (San Diego) or simply "shake" (Seattle), the activity refers to the practice of stopping individuals on the street to ascertain their identities and the "occasion of their presence" in an area—with or without the constitutional nicety of "reasonable suspicion" that pointed to involvement with some form of criminal activity. (The pressure to "produce" was such that some cops resorted to the phone book or the local cemetery to harvest names and "pad the daily" with "FIs.") Needless to say, FIs were, and steadfastly remain in many cities, a major source of key information for detectives (following up on crimes in a geographical area, for example)—and a major source of conflict in the community-police relationship, especially in communities of color.

IN A BUREAUCRACY, WHAT gets counted counts. And therein lies the larger, more insidious problem alluded to earlier. The real problem with a quota system is that the more you produce, the "better" the cop you are—in the eyes of the system. Once you made probation, your performance evaluations were essentially reduced to "activity recaps," a summary of the numbers you harvested over a given period of time. The numbers game shaped us as police officers, indeed it defined us as police officers. As I observe in my current consulting, training, and expert-witness work and note in federal investigations into police departments like Ferguson, there is abundant evidence that the numbers game survives to this day.

In fact, many supervisors believe that counting and recapping activity is the only way to evaluate police performance.

At no time did a boss ever question or counsel me as a rookie cop about the conditions on my beat. How many burglaries, robberies, rapes, auto thefts, car prowls, assaults, or vehicle accidents, injuries, fatalities, hit-and-runs, had taken place in my assigned geographical area of the city while I was on duty? When and where were these incidents taking place? Were there more of them this year than last year? This week over last week? And what of the nature of these incidents?

Of course, behind every crime statistic was a victim, and a suspect or suspects: people hurting other people, frightening them, affecting their quality of life, their property values, the safety and welfare of their children. And nowhere was this more heartbreaking than in economically disadvantaged neighborhoods.

How was I going about collecting my numbers; how was I treating people?

Didn't matter.

There was zero assessment of the quality of my relations with the citizens I'd been hired to protect and serve. The people on my beat were, in a word, irrelevant. As long as I stopped enough of them, handed them enough tickets, arrested enough of them, I would, at a minimum, keep the sergeant off my back. And, optimally, get him (there were no "hers" at the time, in any of the supervisory, much less managerial or executive ranks, or, for that matter, in uniform) to support my aspirational career track.

Of course, it was understood that a "productive" beat cop would generate heat from time to time. A citizen's complaint or two during a particular rating period? No cause for concern, possibly even justification for praise. It showed I was out there "working," being "productive." Being a cop.

Which brings us to Ferguson.

ANYONE WHO WANTS TO understand just how bad policing can get, and how it can get that bad, must read the March 4, 2015, Department of Justice (DOJ) report on the Ferguson Police Department (FPD).[1] The 102-page document is a searing indictment of a Midwest police agency whose cops—aided and abetted by their chief of police, the city prosecutor, the municipal court judge, the court clerk, and virtually every elected official in town—systematically violated the constitutional rights of its citizens. And did so in the most blatant, public, unapologetic way imaginable. It was almost as if they didn't know any better—a theory worth pursuing.

Justice Department investigators, acting under authority of the "pattern or practice" provision of the Violent Crime Control and Law Enforcement Act of 1994, the Omnibus Crime Control and Safe Streets Act of 1968, and Title VI of the Civil Rights Act of 1964, conducted a thorough investigation.

As noted in the DOJ report, investigators interviewed the city manager, mayor, police chief, municipal court judge, municipal court clerk, finance director, and "half of FPD's sworn officers, and others." They went on ride-alongs with the cops, reviewed "35,000 pages of police records as well as thousands of emails and other electronic materials provided by the police department." They put statistical experts to work on FPD's "stops, searches, citations, and arrests, as well as data collected by the municipal court." They did some court watching, and they interviewed dozens of defendants. They examined previous, independent studies of court practices in both Ferguson and St. Louis County. And they "sought to engage the local community, conducting hundreds of in-person and telephone interviews of individuals who reside in Ferguson or who have had interactions with the police department." They spoke with neighborhood associations, other community groups, and "advocacy" organizations. Finally, they brought along two outside police chiefs who reviewed FPD's policies and incident reports and conducted their own interviews.

What they found confirmed "a pattern or practice of unlawful conduct within the Ferguson Police Department that violates the First, Fourth, and Fourteenth Amendments to the United States Constitution, and federal statutory law." Not that this surprised many in the black community of Ferguson—or, for that matter, viewers of CNN, MSNBC, the networks, the BBC, Al Jazeera America, and readers of US and global news organizations, which by the time the Justice Department report hit the streets, had exposed many of these disturbing practices. No, the astonishing news was the extent to which official Ferguson "copped out," freely admitting wholesale trespasses against the constitution. The system's players were doing what came naturally, what they had been taught.

This normalized, indeed routinized official behavior resulted in thousands of Ferguson residents—disproportionately black, disproportionately poor—suffering physically, economically, and emotionally for decades. It's enough to break your heart, and piss you off.

Speaking personally, the anger comes from a realization that these government officials knew or should have known that not only were they harming the very people they'd been hired to help, they were methodically breaking the law—and destroying any chance to nurture respect for it. Where did the cops, the attorneys, the judge get their education? Did criminal law, criminal procedures, constitutional law mean nothing to them?

And what of those who exchanged repugnant, racist e-mails or laughed at criminal defendants (many of whom had committed no crimes at all)?

As I have acknowledged previously, I behaved badly as a rookie cop, sometimes spectacularly so, especially in my disregard of civil liberties.[2] Nevertheless, I amassed a personnel file full of brownie points and other accolades, and I was rewarded with plum assignments and promotions. As I moved up the ranks in San Diego and came to occupy, from 1994 to 2000, the top-floor, corner office of the Seattle Police Department (SPD), I met plenty of police officers who toiled quietly, and who treated both fellow officers and citizens with civility and courtesy.

And that makes me wonder about the "silent" men and women of official Ferguson, those singled out for praise in the Department of Justice investigation:

Notwithstanding our findings about Ferguson's approach to law enforcement and the policing culture it creates, we found many Ferguson police officers and other City employees to be dedicated public servants striving each day to perform their duties lawfully and with respect for all members of the Ferguson community. The importance of their often-selfless work cannot be overstated.

The question we must ask ourselves is whether it is enough to be a "dedicated public servant," to strive each day to perform one's job "lawfully and with respect" for all people. Is our "selfless" work really enough if the person we work alongside routinely violates the constitution and denigrates his or her fellow citizens? While we do nothing about it?

This conversation is not about farming. Or cosmetology, or food service, or retail sales. It is about life-and-death, peace-and-freedom decision-making. About enforcing the law of the land, and ensuring justice.

WHAT, EXACTLY, DID THE investigators find wrong in Ferguson? Buckle your seatbelt:

FOCUS ON GENERATING REVENUE

THE DOJ FOUND THAT virtually every branch and tributary of the city's bureaucracy—the mayor, city council, city manager, finance director, municipal court judge, municipal court prosecutor, court clerk, assistant clerks, police chief—all were enmeshed in an unending race to raise revenue through municipal fines and fees:

> City officials routinely urge Chief [Tom] Jackson to generate more revenue through enforcement. In March 2010, for instance, the City Finance Director wrote to Chief Jackson that "unless ticket writing ramps up significantly before the end of the year, it will be hard to significantly raise collections next year. . . . Given that we are looking at a substantial sales tax shortfall, it's not an insignificant issue." Similarly, in March 2013, the Finance Director wrote

to the City Manager: "Court fees are anticipated to rise about 7.5%. I did ask the Chief if he thought the PD [police department] could deliver 10% increase. He indicated they could try." The importance of focusing on revenue generation is communicated to FPD officers. Ferguson police officers from all ranks told us that revenue generation is stressed heavily within the police department, and that the message comes from City leadership. The evidence we reviewed supports this perception.

Let's assume for a moment that in a traditional "good government" (corruption-free) municipality, the town's beat cops conscientiously respond to 911 calls. They self-initiate inquiries into suspicious activity; investigate crimes and motor vehicle and industrial accidents; write reports; keep an eye on the beat's schools, parks, and recreation centers; and, oh yes, write traffic citations to drivers going 40 mph in a 20 mph school zone, or racing to beat a passing freight train through an intersection, or texting while driving. They're not "community-oriented" cops per se, but they're hardworking people doing a fair day's work.

Now, let's assume that, hurting for revenue, the city's leaders (and their number crunchers), unmindful of or unconcerned about their cops' relations with the community, put the squeeze on the police department. "More tickets," says the finance director. "More tickets," says the city council, the mayor, the city manager, the police chief. "More tickets," says everyone in the chain of command, right down to the sergeant who tells her officers, "More tickets."

"Why?" her officers ask.

"I don't know, because I told you so?" answers the sergeant. (Of course, she could say, "Because the lieutenant told me.") No matter what she says, the cops will see through it. Five minutes after the order comes down, the rank and file will have sussed out the truth of this new mandate. Including its motive. And from that point on, this "good government" city is no more. The cops will be doing the wrong thing for the wrong reasons. And that has a way of changing a police officer's self-concept, and behavior. Let's say a young cop has joined the local PD to give back to her community, to make a positive difference in the lives of her fellow citizens. But pressure for "more tickets" (or more FIs, more arrests) transforms her into a hunter, and the citizens on her beat into prey. The young, idealistic cop, yielding to pressure from her boss, wanting to get ahead, starts targeting motorists and pedestrians. Soon, she is pulling over cars with flimsy or no justification, writing bad tickets; stopping people without reasonable suspicion; arresting them without probable cause. And, if you're the one being cuffed or cited, don't even try to explain yourself to her. She's too busy, she has other numbers to collect.

An officer trained in a system where people are reduced to numbers is very likely to dehumanize the people on his or her beat, and once that happens there's little hope for decency, mercy, or even something resembling objectivity. The people are simply a means to a self-centered end: good performance appraisals, choice assignments, a succession of stripes, bars, and stars and other insignia or rank as one advances up the rungs of the hierarchical ladder, taking home fatter and fatter paychecks.

Governments need money to operate, of course. Fair and equitable taxation, reasonable service fees, other irreproachable, transparent sources of revenue make sense. Excessive reliance on fines, fees, and forfeitures wrung from the criminal justice system does not. The former has legitimacy; the latter—policing for profit—lacks it.

There's an axiom in organizational life: the minimum expected becomes the maximum achieved. If, in plotting budget costs and projecting revenues, the numbers don't add up, the word goes out. And it's not merely "more tickets," it's *X number* of additional citations. Cops who collect the minimum are rewarded with satisfactory performance evaluations. Those who, like me, back in the day, far exceed the quota? Well, let's just say, these cops can virtually write their own ticket, careerwise.

POLICE PRACTICES

VARIABLES TOO NUMEROUS TO count affect the development, and durability, of the cop culture. Each police department is different but only, I submit, in minor, usually cosmetic ways: the cut of the uniforms, the color scheme of the cars, the argot, jargon, and patois of cops on the beat. A

Camden, New Jersey, beat cop, with his rich Jersey accent, his Sam Brown belt and "fifty mission crush" headwear bears little obvious resemblance to his flat-toned, hatless, plain-belted counterpart in Boise, Idaho. But they're both cops, which means they are much more alike than different.

Renowned sociologist Jerome Skolnick wrote the definitive academic book on police culture. *Justice Without Trial: Law Enforcement in Democratic Society* (1967, latest edition 2015) provides foundational wisdom about the extent to which danger and authority combine to produce a cop's "working personality" and foster social isolation and solidarity within the ranks. In fact, Skolnick maintained that any job description that called on a person to exercise sensitive discretionary decision-making authority in the face of physical danger (think police officer) was simply demanding way too much of the practitioner. Add to the mix certain organization pressures, like the numbers game, and you have the makings of a department whose members are all but guaranteed to act with indifference if not hostility toward "outsiders," namely, the people they've been hired to protect and serve. Taken together, these agency and psychological realities help explain why so many cops form such strong bonds with one another, socialize exclusively with one another, keep silent for and lie for one another—and why they believe no one else understands them, or *can* understand them.

I know of no law enforcement agency, certainly no local PD or sheriff's department, whose members have escaped these influences—and their behavioral manifestations and consequences.

In Ferguson, for example, the DOJ investigation found that "the City's emphasis on revenue generation has a profound effect on FPD's approach to law enforcement. Patrol assignments and schedules are geared toward aggressive enforcement of Ferguson's municipal code, with insufficient thought given to whether enforcement strategies promote public safety or unnecessarily undermine community trust and cooperation." Further:

> Officer evaluations and promotions depend to an inordinate degree on "productivity," meaning the number of citations issued. Partly as a consequence of City and FPD priorities, many officers appear to see some residents, especially those who live in Ferguson's predominantly African-American neighborhoods, less

as constituents to be protected than as potential offenders and sources of revenue.

A cop playing the numbers game in earnest will inevitably develop tunnel vision, along with a distorted understanding of the limits of his authority: the "sanctioned right to order the actions of others." From the report:

> This culture within FPD influences officer activities in all areas of policing, beyond just ticketing. Officers expect and demand compliance even when they lack legal authority. They are inclined to interpret the exercise of free-speech rights as unlawful disobedience, innocent movements as physical threats, indications of mental or physical illness as belligerence. Police supervisors and leadership do too little to ensure that officers act in accordance with law and policy, and rarely respond meaningfully to civilian complaints of officer misconduct. The result is a pattern of stops without reasonable suspicion and arrests without probable cause in violation of the Fourth Amendment; infringement on free expression, as well as retaliation for protected expression, in violation of the First Amendment; and excessive force in violation of the Fourth Amendment.

The report relates the story of a thirty-two-year-old African American man who'd been playing basketball in one of the city's public parks. Seated in his car, cooling off, he noticed a police vehicle pull in behind him, blocking his own car. The officer got out, demanded ID, accused the man of being a pedophile, ordered him from the car, and patted him down—not one discrete action of which was justified, legally or otherwise. The cop asked for permission to search the car. The man, asserting his constitutional rights, declined—which evidently, in the officer's mind, now justified an arrest. At gunpoint, reportedly. The man was charged with eight violations of the Ferguson Municipal Code, including "making a false declaration" (for telling the officer his name was Mike when it was actually Michael), not wearing a seatbelt (even though he was in a parked car), having no driver's license, and having an expired license.

The man told federal investigators he lost his long-term job as a contractor with the federal government because of those charges.

MUNICIPAL COURT PRACTICES

ONE OF THE MANY disturbing scenes to come out of Ferguson was incidental video footage of dozens of local residents, overwhelmingly black, spilling out of the courthouse and waiting. And waiting. They were there, late at night to be "processed" by the court—not for any alleged violations tied to the protests but for a ticket each had gotten weeks or months before Darren Wilson shot Michael Brown. From the report: "The court primarily uses its judicial authority as a means to compel the payment of fines and fees that advance the City's financial interests. This has led to court practices that violate the Fourteenth Amendment's due process and equal protection requirements."

I can hear cops all over the land exclaiming, "Hey, do the crime, do the time! We did our jobs, the court is doing its job. It's called accountability." What that sentiment fails to take into account are the thousands of citations and arrests of the questionable nature and dubious quality described above. That, plus a Kafkaesque system that piles on additional fees and conditions that make it all but impossible for the city's poor to meet those obligations.

And it's not just in Ferguson. All states make provisions for the suspension of a driver's license for a variety of reasons such as failure to pay a traffic fine, driving under the influence of alcohol or other drugs, lack of insurance, or liability in a motor vehicle accident. In California alone, 4 million drivers have had their driving privileges suspended. Say a cop catches you on radar doing 45 mph in a 35 mph zone. You're unemployed, undereducated, have a language difficulty, haven't a spare dime to your name, and now you're facing a $180 fine. The date for your court case comes and goes. Your license is suspended, a warrant issued for your arrest. Your troubles are just beginning. Say you find a job, start earning wages. Driving home from work one day, you get pulled over for a minor traffic violation. The officer runs your ID through the system. He busts you for the warrant, writes you up for the additional violation, plus driving on a suspended license. And he impounds your car. At this point you're probably looking at $1,000 or more to set yourself straight with the courts. You're also looking at the possibility of license revocation. And, depending on the state, you may never get your car back.

Returning to Ferguson. The DOJ report states that in just one year (2013), the court issued over 9,000 warrants for minor violations such as traffic and parking tickets and housing code violations (another big money-maker for the city). "The court's practices . . . impose unnecessary harm, overwhelmingly on African-American individuals, and run counter to public safety."

RACIAL BIAS

THE EVIDENCE IS IN. The Ferguson Police Department has engaged for decades in systemic racial discrimination.

The city's African American population stands at roughly 67 percent, but, as the department's own statistics show, from 2012 to 2014, African Americans accounted for 85 percent of vehicle stops, 90 percent of all citations, 93 percent of all arrests. Blacks were more than twice as likely as white motorists to be searched during traffic stops, even though such stops were 26 percent less likely to yield contraband (than for traffic stops of white motorists). During that same period, the department wrote four or more citations to blacks on seventy-three occasions; only twice did non–African Americans receive four or more citations. On one occasion an officer wrote an individual fourteen citations. There was an acknowledged, ongoing contest to see who could write the most tickets, and tallies were posted on a stationhouse wall to spur officers to ever-increasing heights of "productivity."

The statistical picture for the court system was equally dismal—no surprise, given that the court itself is actually located inside police headquarters and that, incredibly, the court clerk and the assistant clerks, all part of the profit-driven machine, report directly to the chief of police. The judge (there is a new one now, and he's taken steps to end this sweeping miscarriage of justice) is nominated by the city manager, elected by the city council—a structure and practice that undermines the independence of the judiciary.

Police use-of-force figures are equally problematic. Almost 90 percent of documented force was applied against African Americans. And topping them all at 100 percent, in all fourteen documented dog-bite cases (there are four canines on patrol), the person on the receiving end was an African American.

COMMUNITY DISTRUST

MANY CITY OFFICIALS AND police officers, along with some (mostly white) Ferguson residents, maintain the public outcry against their police department was caused by "outside agitators"[3]—a woeful defense heard often during civil rights demonstrations of yesteryear in the South (though the same claim was made by many cops and some segments of New York City's population in the aftermath of the Eric Garner killing).[4]

In point of fact, as expressed by local residents as well as visiting protesters, Ferguson's city hall and its police department earned every moment of negative air time, every drop of angry ink.

As the Justice Department concluded its report, "Our investigation has shown that distrust of the Ferguson Police Department is longstanding and largely attributable to Ferguson's approach to law enforcement. This approach results in patterns of unnecessarily aggressive and at times unlawful policing; reinforces the harm of discriminatory stereotypes; discourages a culture of accountability; and neglects community engagement."

The report documents numerous examples of unlawful stops, unlawful arrests, unlawful force, unlawful discrimination. It chronicles ticket fixing for friends and relatives. It describes neglectful police practices, including a slow, apathetic, occasionally abusive response to victims of crimes, particularly domestic violence. It enumerates racist, sexist, and other offensive e-mail exchanges between department supervisors and court personnel, one depicting President Obama as a chimpanzee, another referring to bare-chested dancers, presumably in Africa, as "Michelle Obama's High School Reunion."

The Department of Justice investigation leaves little doubt why most citizens were not prepared to believe what their police department told them about Michael Brown's death. Or pretty much anything else it had to say. The Ferguson Police Department had lost its legitimacy.

I HAVE ONE CRITICISM of the Justice Department's findings, namely, its assertion that the FPD "has moved away from the modest community policing efforts it previously had implemented." This assumes that true community policing had *any* kind of pre–Mike Brown foothold in the policies and practices of the Ferguson Police Department.

Too many police agencies claim to operate in accordance with the values and principles of "community policing," when in reality, their operations remain under the exclusive control of the local agency. That's not community policing. If the Ferguson Police Department sufficiently valued "positive police-community interactions" and "familiarity with African-American neighborhoods," as the DOJ asserts, there's a good chance Michael Brown would be alive today. Further, the DOJ report puts all the responsibility for "community policing" on the bureaucracy. It paints the community as a passive victim of the city's unfortunate movement "away from . . . modest community policing efforts."

But authentic community policing doesn't just evaporate because the cops believe they have better things to do. The community doesn't allow that to happen. We can only hope that citizens' outrage at the Michael Brown killing, and at the police department's deep-seated, institutionalized abuses, now thoroughly exposed, has empowered local residents to claim their rightful place as "co-owner" of the FPD. Indeed, by mounting the protest, by saying "enough," the community has done just that.

AT BOTTOM, THE QUESTION is this: Is Ferguson an anomaly, a statistical outlier on the national policing scene? Or is it symptomatic of the broader institution—from the smallest, rural police departments of America to the nation's biggest, most urbanized department?

"THE BRUTAL, THE CORRUPT, THE RACIST, THE INCOMPETENT"

IN OCTOBER 2014, NEW York City police commissioner Bill Bratton stepped up to the microphone at the city's brand new police academy and, speaking to his eight hundred commanders, lashed out at "the brutal, the corrupt, the racist, the incompetent" within the ranks of the NYPD.[5]

It was a singular moment in the life of at least one big-city police department: the top cop—not "anti-police" activists—openly admitting, in plain language, the presence of brutality, corruption, racism, and incompetence in his organization. Most police leaders, when their departments come under fire, circle the wagons, defend the "professionalism" of the "vast majority" of their officers, and perhaps admit to the occasional presence of a cop or two whose aberrant behavior "does not meet our high standards" (the old "bad apples" platitude).

That "vast majority" response has been worked to death, yet it gets trotted out every time a police officer shoots an unarmed teenager or a fleeing adult in the back. Or chokes or beats a man to death. Or, on the way to jail, subjects a handcuffed prisoner to a "rough ride" or a "screen test" (propelling the prisoner, cuffed behind his back, into the steel screen separating front and back seats). Or rapes a motorist. Or steals drugs. Or plants drugs on an innocent person or a "throw-down" gun on a deceased suspect. Or kidnaps and tortures suspects and witnesses—with impunity, as in Chicago (where, as will be described in Chapter 10, a sadistic commander was allowed to lead his band of rogue cops in a decades-long reign of terror).[6]

Yet even Bratton, in that same speech to his command staff, felt compelled to overdo the overdone by saying, "The vast, vast, vast majority of our officers" (99 percent, in his estimation) do their city proud.[7]

It *is* important, of course, to celebrate cops who get the job done, play by the rules, make their cities safer, lend comfort to confused, injured, frightened citizens. But it's also time to admit: at any given moment, in any given city or county, odds are the local PD is being sued or assailed for precisely the kind of behavior condemned by Bratton. It's been going on for a long time, since the days of the early-eighteenth-century slave patrols. The problem of police abuse in this country is systemic, it runs deep and wide, and it is getting worse.

And when the people in charge cling to that "vast majority" sound bite they advance a solitary diagnosis, and a sole prescription: bad cops? Fire them. Why bother with costly, systemic reform if "inappropriate" behavior is merely an anomaly?

I'm not saying all cops are unfit for the job. Most are well suited to the work—especially when they first sign on. For the rookie, however, exposure to "anti-community" cops, and every department has them, is all it takes. These "real cops"—the police department's ass-kicking, knuckle-dragging "tough guys," who are rude, arrogant, callous, and cynical, if not corrupt— become powerful role models for young, impressionable newbies.

Even Bratton in his book, *The Turnaround: How America's Top Cop Reversed the Crime Epidemic* (with Peter Knobler, 1998), estimated that a full 30 percent of the officers assigned to the 30th Precinct in the early to mid-1990s had been tainted by a corruption scandal—stealing and dealing drugs, extortion, excessive force, civil rights violations, and more. This was during Bratton's first "tour of duty" as NYPD commissioner in 1994; he personally led an early morning raid on the "Dirty 30," removing a captain and personally seizing the badges of two officers, never to be reissued.[8]

Further, reinforcing the distance between NYPD cops and the citizens they serve, Bratton pointed to focus groups and surveys revealing that during this same period, 90.8 percent of his cops believed that the public "has no understanding of police problems" and that only 23 percent felt the community had a "good relationship with the police." This was years before the controversial death of Eric Garner, and it led NYPD's top cop to ask, "How do we get our cops to understand that citizens are entitled to respect, while cops need to earn it?"[9]

BACK IN THE EARLY 1970s, a handful of starry-eyed police reformers, me among them, predicted that because of community policing, our nation's cops would soon come to understand that police in America belong to the people, not the other way around; that an ethic of treating people respectfully would eventually become embedded in police culture; that an intended effect or at least a byproduct of community policing would be decreased reliance on the archaic paramilitary model of police work; and that cops would work in authentic partnership with the citizenry, putting an end to imperious, unilateral decision-making. As a result, the nation would see increasing sensitivity, openness, and accountability within the ranks. Along with lower crime rates. And safer, happier, well-behaved cops.

As a young, idealistic lieutenant in the San Diego Police Department (SDPD), I believed these improvements, led by both internal and external reformers, were just around the corner, relatively speaking, certainly not more than a generation or two away.

I could not have been more wrong.

Today's law enforcement agencies, including Bratton's, are even more distant and disengaged from the communities they serve. They are certainly more militarized, coming across as soldiers rather than domestic peacekeepers, with almost everything about them being military—their uniforms, vehicles, weapons, jargon, tactics, and so on. Reflecting the reality that increased militarization does not represent progress, American law enforcement today is arguably as corrupt, bigoted, brutal, and trigger-happy as it was during the 1960s and 1970s, not to mention earlier eras.

How do we know this?

Over three years ago, the libertarian Cato Institute developed the National Police Misconduct Reporting Project (PoliceMisconduct.net). Using primarily local news sources, the project gathers specific, credible case data from around the country and publishes updates as the cases make their way through both administrative and judicial processes. Public policy makers and critics alike can examine both current and archived information on the website. CATO acknowledges incomplete data (only a handful of states allow public release of police disciplinary actions), but there is no other single source that provides such comprehensive information on trends and patterns of police misconduct. Rarely does a day go by that six or more entries are not added to the list. For example, here are the entries for November 24, 2015:[10]

- El Paso County, Colorado: A deputy was arrested on an assault charge for actions against a jail inmate in September.
- Panola County, Mississippi: A deputy was arrested for DUI.
- Update: Fullerton, California (First reported 07–28–11): The City agreed to pay $4.9 million to the family of Kelly Thomas, who was

beaten to death by police in 2011. Two officers were fired because of the incident but were ultimately acquitted of criminal charges.

- Chicago, Illinois: Officer Jason Van Dyke was charged with first-degree murder for the shooting death of seventeen-year-old Laquan McDonald in October 2014. Video of the shooting was released to the public Tuesday evening. Protests were largely peaceful.
- Hidalgo County, Texas: A deputy was arrested for DUI.
- Del Rio, Texas: An officer was arrested for DUI.
- Blue Island, Illinois: An officer was arrested for sexual assault.
- Lyon County, Kansas: A deputy was suspended after his arrest for involuntary manslaughter and other charges as a result of [a] 2012 automobile crash.
- Port St. Lucie, Florida: An officer was fired for actions at a bar and being untruthful about those actions later.
- Pittsburgh, Pennsylvania: An officer pled guilty to participating in a mortgage fraud scheme. He allegedly prepared and submitted false documents.

This random, "day in the life" glimpse at police misconduct cases represents, with a couple of notable exceptions, a collection of relatively mild examples, especially when compared to more celebrated cases of false arrest, perjury, bribery, reckless pursuits, drug rip-offs, drug dealing, ticket fixing, rape and other sexual assaults, stalking, domestic violence, child abuse and child rape, robbery, burglary, beatings, extortion, mob protection, murder-for-hire, and, of course, unjustified police shootings and in-custody deaths.

Other organizations keep tabs on specialized police actions. The *Guardian*, for example, monitors all US police shootings in a project called The Counted. Its website traces the number of people killed by police (regardless of justification), year-to-date. The regularly updated site breaks down shootings by ethnicity. In August 2015, the rate of blacks shot and killed by police was 4.26 per million incidents. For the Hispanic/Latino population, the rate was 1.87, and for whites, 1.71. The site also provides photographs of the deceased, maps, and an up-to-date, state-by-state recap of all incidents.[11] (The *Washington Post* also began a monitoring project in 2015, keeping an up-to-date tally of police shootings and calling for improved reporting of police shootings throughout the states.)[12]

StoptheDrugWar.org, founded by fellow drug-policy reformer David Borden in 1993, has featured a weekly compendium of corrupt police activity for many years in its highly regarded *Drug War Chronicle*. Assembled by writer-editor Phil Smith, the column "This Week's Corrupt Cops Stories" highlights police scandals, typically several per day, such as bribery, drug smuggling, sexual assaults, even murder.

Scandal visits infrequently in some jurisdictions, but in others it's taken up more or less permanent residence. As in the arcade game Whack-A-Mole®, the insidious creature lurks below the surface. Just when police and city officials think misconduct has been eradicated (through discipline, arrest, or dismissals from the force), it pops up again.

The history of the NYPD provides a good case study. Roughly every twenty years, the NYPD has been battered by sustained allegations of deep-seated, far-ranging corruption. An investigation by a "commission" or a committee is the historically preferred response.

In 1894, the future president of the United States, then NYPD Commissioner Theodore Roosevelt, was moved to form the Lexow Committee. Headed by clergyman and police critic Charles Henry Parkhurst, the committee found evidence of police "extortion, bribery, counterfeiting, voter intimidation, election fraud, brutality, and scams."[13]

More recent examples include the Knapp Commission in 1972—famous for drawing a distinction between herds of "grass eaters" (the numerous cops who would accept free meals and bribes) and "meat eaters" (those who would openly solicit bribes and shake down gambling, prostitution, and narcotics operations).[14] Then came the Mollen Commission in 1992, which found that nothing much had changed.[15]

And so it goes in police work, as it has since its inception.

2

DOOMED FROM THE START

THE HISTORY OF AMERICAN police work begins in London, in 1829. Earlier "policing," from biblical times forward, took the simple form of neighbors watching out for neighbors.

Next came the more formal "hue and cry," a practice in early English law (the Statute of Winchester, 1285), which provided, mandatorily, that all able-bodied men of villages and towns would shout out, clang a bell, or sound a trumpet if they witnessed a felony, for example, a robbery. They would chase down and, if fast enough, lucky enough, and tough enough, capture the robber. By law, the pursuers could not be held liable for "damages" resulting from the pursuit or apprehension. Also by law, it was a crime to raise a false hue and cry.

This approach to policing was abolished in the early nineteenth century, giving way to a more formal arrangement whereby "watchmen" were hired to keep an eye on their town or village through the night. Often old and feeble, frequently drunk, and not above taking bribes or extorting their fellow citizens, the watchmen were authorized and obligated to arrest any stranger who happened to pass through town during hours of darkness (absent evidence of a crime, the hapless stranger was released when the sun came up). In the quieter areas of town, the most glamorous and exciting part of the job was to call out the hour, ignite the gas lamps at night, and snuff them out in the morning.

In America, prior to the Industrial Revolution, public order was maintained through use of "night watches." The northern colonists, for example, typically established local ordinances that required able-bodied men to take a turn on night patrol. Larger towns often raised money to pay for a constable or two whose job was to keep an eye out, maintain order on the streets, and report and put out fires. The southern colonies, on the other hand, embraced slave patrols, the first "modern" police organization in America. Larger than the watches of the North, the slave patrols maintained the economic order of the southern colonies by controlling slaves, capturing fugitives, and administering punishment.

Rural areas embraced the sheriff (a term derived from the "shire-reeve") concept, borrowed from the British. Sheriffs were largely tax collectors and writ servers (a perilous occupation: the first known fatality of an American lawman was Cornelius Hogebloom of Columbia County, New York, shot on October 22, 1791, as he attempted to serve a "writ of ejectment").[1]

Law enforcement on the western frontier was very much a hit-and-miss proposition, with vigilantes holding sway in the earliest days. In time, settlers from the northern colonies generally opted for appointment of a "marshal" with "watchers," whereas settlers from the South favored election of a sheriff and a posse system.

In general, the Western world found the specter of a uniformed, military-like domestic police force anathema to the dual causes of freedom and democracy (some might argue, given the extent to which today's police resemble the military, that these early skeptics were prescient).

But with burgeoning economic injustices, monarchical abuses, and general lawlessness—precipitated by the Industrial Revolution and the transformation from an agrarian to an urban society—Great Britain, in the early 1820s, began seriously to entertain the idea of a formal, uniformed, paid, civil-service police force. Sir Robert Peel led the process. He was a natural for the job as he had pulled off complicated and impressive legal renovations during his first term (1822–1827) as home secretary, overhauling and liberalizing the criminal law.

After years of cagey, intense political maneuvering, Peel persuaded a wary Parliament to consider a policing act. Why the reluctance? As noted, the lawmakers feared that an organized police force would inevitably lead to corruption, tyranny, and "militarization," with police officers treating the populace as enemy combatants. But Peel, promising assurances of scrupulous accountability, prevailed. And Parliament passed the Metropolitan Police Act of 1829.

Of course, not every supporter of the act was driven by the same public-spirited motives of crime prevention and the greater civic good. The wealthy, propertied class exerted substantial pressure on Parliament, too. How else but through organized policing could its special interests be "protected and served"? Some things never change.

Peel insisted that his nation's peace officers stand tall, literally as well as figuratively. He put them in crisp blue tailcoats and top hats, which later gave way to the eponymous "bobby" helmets. And, through his police chiefs, he set and enforced the highest standards of honor and efficiency. In the early years of its existence, the Metropolitan police force fired 2,200 of the first 2,800 it hired—individuals who evidently felt at liberty to continue to conduct themselves as they had in the free-wheeling, pre-Peelian days when there was little or no accountability for constabulary misconduct.[2]

US CITIES SUCH AS Boston, New York, and Philadelphia, reeling like Britain from the same social ills caused by the Industrial Revolution and recognizing the woeful inadequacy of their "watchmen" system, began studying the Metropolitan Police Act of 1829.[3]

They were not good students.

In transplanting the British system to American soil (Boston in 1838, New York in 1845, Philadelphia in 1854), the emissaries ignored many of the safeguards that Peel had assiduously labored to include in the act. From the time the NYPD was formed, ward bosses, commissioners, and chiefs presided over a political spoils system in which cops bought beats and the upwardly mobile purchased promotions (by the 1870s, an NYPD captaincy, for example, went for $15,000).[4] Hiring standards were nonexistent; supervision and discipline, hit and miss. It helped, of course, if your father, grandfather, brother, uncle, or cousin worked for the city.

The same or similar systemic deficiencies spread like a contagion to other American cities as they, too, haphazardly adopted a version of the "British model": St. Louis Metropolitan Police Department in 1846, Chicago PD in 1854, Los Angeles PD in 1869 (same year as Seattle), and many others. My old department in San Diego was established in 1889,[5] its new cops donning derby hats, high-collared coats, and seven-point stars. They worked twelve hours a day, seven days a week, a common police schedule throughout the country, from San Francisco to Boston, providing plenty of time to rake in the spoils of the job.

AMERICA'S LOVE AFFAIR WITH "home rule" denied the country the kind of consistent national standards—and consistent enforcement of those standards—that Peel had worked so hard to embed in the English system.

The US Constitution is silent on the matter of "cities" ("counties," too, for that matter). Yet local governments—because of their closeness to the people, their knowledge of local conditions, their putative grasp of the "public good"—believed they should have the right to create their own governance structures, to levy taxes and finance local services, and to enact and enforce municipal and county laws. The idea gained great popularity starting with the Progressive Era (1890–1920). This, despite a 1903 Supreme Court case (*Atkins v. Kansas*) that held that cities are "creatures, mere political subdivisions, of the State for the purpose of exercising its powers." Yet even after another high court case (*City of Trenton v. New Jersey*, 1923) affirmed *Atkins*, the movement toward home rule was unstoppable.

Those living both in cities and in rural America during the 1930s grew more and more suspicious of and antagonistic toward the "feds"—a product, in part, of the national government's inability to address neighborhood services (streets, sewers, water quality, utilities, law enforcement). And, there was growing opposition at the local level to federal oversight and regulations. Local businesses, civic officials, and the National League of Cities (founded in 1926) began to exert substantial pressure on the national government to return (or to keep) power at the local level. This dissatisfaction continued, until by 1990, thirty-seven states had embedded constitutional authority for home rule in their cities, and twenty-three states had done likewise for their counties.[6]

As home rule rooted itself in the structural and ideological psyche of American life, politicians, especially those who leaned right, cooperated fully. President Richard Nixon, for example, provided no- or few-strings-attached block grants to local communities for everything from transportation to law enforcement. President Ronald Reagan, ideologically averse to federal rules in the first place, cut "red tape" and regulations—even as he gutted funding for social programs, including mental health. And, though the courts have occasionally blown the whistle on some local governments' willingness to cut programs intended to advance or at least honor constitutional guarantees, home rule remains a pillar of American governance.

And that makes certain police reforms, of the type Sir Robert Peel would surely have supported, a formidable challenge.

To THIS DAY, PEEL, who went on to serve twice as prime minister, remains an iconic figure to many in modern law enforcement throughout Europe and North America. Commissioner Bratton listed Peel's Nine Principles on his NYPD blog—four months before the Eric Garner choking death—saying, "In my long police career I have often drawn inspiration from a great hero of mine, Sir Robert Peel." Bratton reports that he carries a copy of the principles everywhere he goes, on a folded piece of paper. "My bible," he told a reporter.[7]

Peel's principles are the cornerstone of community policing; they have been invoked in the campaign to "professionalize" police behavior; and they have become a rallying point in nascent US efforts to reverse the trend toward militarized policing.

Presented here, each of Peel's Nine Principles is followed by what I am convinced would be a common reaction of today's police officers, Bratton (and other Peel acolytes) excepted:

Principle 1: "The basic mission for which the police exist is to prevent crime and disorder."

The Supreme Court has made it more and more difficult for cops to catch and convict the bad guys. Furthermore, many people—the liberal establishment in particular—believe the basic mission of the police is to protect and advance the interests of "social justice," of "multiculturalism," of ethnic and sexual minorities over native-born, able-bodied, straight, white men. More and more, police officers are being exploited to help carry out this agenda of political correctness and social reengineering at the expense of crime fighting and the prevention of disorder.

Principle 2: "The ability of the police to perform their duties is dependent upon public approval of police actions."

Which public are we talking about? There is no clear definition of "the public," so in the meantime, cops decide on their own whose "approval" they seek.

Principle 3: "Police must secure the willing cooperation of the public in voluntary observance of the law to be able to secure and maintain the respect of the public."

Achieving "voluntary observance of the law" is beyond the capacity of the country's police officers. They are not educators, Sunday-school teachers, or social workers. They did not raise the law breakers they are expected to deal with. And when's the last time "the public" showed police officers respect?

Principle 4: "The degree of cooperation of the public that can be secured diminishes proportionately to the necessity of the use of physical force."

Like it or not, police officers are empowered to use coercive force against their fellow citizens—a necessity of the profession. Were Peel around today, cops would ask him, "Do you, sir, go to work every day knowing that sudden, violent death is an occupational hazard? We do." True, cops are not permitted to use force that is, well, unnecessary. Nor are they allowed to use more force than is "reasonably necessary," regardless of the circumstances. But here's the rub: Who defines these terms? Who decides whether force, to whatever degree, is necessary? Not in a courtroom decision, or one made in a judge's chambers, but in the real world? The police do. Always have, always will. Of course, they know they will be *judged* . . . after the fact. But, as they like to say, "Better to be judged by twelve than carried by six."

Principle 5: "Police seek and preserve public favor not by catering to the public opinion but by constantly demonstrating absolute impartial service to the law."

"Absolute impartial service"? Sounds good, but "the public opinion" tends to get defined by the preferences and priorities of a city's squeaky wheels, and its "leaders": the mayor, city council, city manager, and, too often, a politically correct police chief. Many officers are fond of those few politically incorrect leaders with the cojones to stand up to the powers that be in city hall. (See, for example, Joe Arpaio of Maricopa County. True, he's an elected county sheriff, but what city cop wouldn't want him at the helm of his local PD? You can be sure Sheriff Joe's "Nine Principles" don't look anything like Peel's.)

Principle 6: "Police use physical force to the extent necessary to secure observance of the law or to restore order only when the exercise of persuasion, advice and warning is found to be insufficient."

"Persuasion, advice, and warning"? These are the tools of timorous teachers and proselytizing preachers. The last thing you want showing up at your door when you call the cops is a social worker or a counselor. Police officers are not above trying persuasion, but when that fails, they look to M4 assault rifles, stun grenades, and MRAPs [mine resistant ambush protected vehicles]. That's necessary force when hitting a fortified drug house, or facing rock- and bottle-chucking protesters, agitators, and other miscreants.

Principle 7: "Police, at all times, should maintain a relationship with the public that gives reality to the historic tradition that the police are the public and the public are the police; the police being only members of the public who are paid to give full-time attention to duties which are incumbent on every citizen in the interests of community welfare and existence."

The "police are the pubic and the public are the police"? What is that but an awkward way of saying the police are not special, not exceptional? Well, police officers are special. They have been taught to stand apart from "the public," in order to form, explicitly, that famous thin blue line between them and the bad guy. They believe the moment that line dissolves, society will be looking at decaying cities, chaos, and anarchy.

Principle 8: "Police should always direct their action strictly towards their functions and never appear to usurp the powers of the judiciary.

Officers have been told: you're not judge, jury, and executioner. But try living by that credo at three in the morning with an armed and dangerous fugitive pointing a blue-steel .45 at your cranium and threatening to blow you away.

Principle 9: "The test of police efficiency is the absence of crime and disorder, not the visible evidence of police action in dealing with it."

A cop will tell you, police work is highly visible activity, no matter how you slice it. Why do you think they wear uniforms? Drive conspicuously marked automobiles? They are armed, equipped, and trained to go after the bad guy. Most cops are not into subtle. Not into *blending in* with the community.

So, HERE STANDS THE institution, almost two centuries removed from Sir Robert Peel's vision of virtuous, accountable police work, and steadily moving further and further away from it.

It's not that the country hasn't tried to achieve Peel's ideals. In fact, the United States has undergone several waves of "police reform" since the nineteenth century: establishment in the early twentieth century of state and city civil service merit systems to combat police nepotism and a political spoils system; creation, for better or worse, of a military command structure (often mislabeled a "professional" structure) in the 1930s, a response to border-to-border, coast-to-coast police brutality and corruption (the thinking was that a military structure is stricter, that it provides greater control over police actions when, paradoxically, it does the opposite; more on this in Chapter 12); adoption in the 1960s and 1970s of various "community relations" and "community policing" models, a reply to social- and human-rights insurrections—labor, antiwar, civil rights, and campus unrest; and, in the 1990s, implementation of a variety of training and disciplinary reforms in response to high-profile police abuse incidents, such as the Rodney King (Los Angeles) and Abner Louima (New York City) cases.

But, owing to the work of investigative reporters, social media, cellphone moviemaking, and ubiquitous YouTube footage, the American people have witnessed abundant evidence of the quality and caliber of contemporary local law enforcement. And though their information is sometimes incomplete, and not always accurate, they are emphatically not happy with what they see.

A *USA Today*/Pew Research Center poll of August 26, 2014, conducted in the aftermath of the Michael Brown shooting in Ferguson, shows that by a two-to-one margin, Americans believe that:

> police departments nationwide don't do a good job in holding officers accountable for misconduct, treating racial groups equally and using the right amount of force. While most whites give police low marks on those measures, blacks are overwhelmingly negative in their assessment of police tactics. More than nine of 10 African Americans say the police do an "only fair" or poor job when it comes to equal treatment and appropriate force.[8]

As noted, rank-and-file police officers are also feeling betrayed—by their critics, from across the political spectrum, as well as by some of their own bosses. There is defiant talk among the rank and file, as cops feel stymied, believing the next action they take (if indeed they take it at all), no matter how justified, will get them in trouble.

As we can see, corruption and misconduct have been an integral part of the structure and culture of American policing from the very beginning. Although some agencies have shown halting progress, the institution itself has failed to make necessary, lasting changes. And the American people, particularly young people, poor people, and people of color—those most in need of fair, equitable, and caring police work—are making their discontent known.

So, we're at an impasse of sorts. And of all the barriers that stand in the way of Peel's Principles of effective, humane policing, one towering sociolegal obstacle, addressed in the next chapter, stands out.

3

SAVE MONEY, SAVE LIVES: END THE DRUG WAR

IN THE 1960s, WHEN I became a beat cop in San Diego, manufacturing, selling, possessing, or using "dangerous drugs" or "controlled substances" were all violations of the law. But there was no "war," per se, on drug-law violators. We made the occasional pot bust, less frequently a heroin or cocaine pinch. Drug enforcement was viewed by many of us almost as an ancillary duty. You'd stumble across an offender on a traffic stop or at a loud-party call. Mostly, you were on the prowl for non-drug-related crime: a gas station or liquor store stickup series, a burglary-fencing ring, an auto theft "chop shop" operation. Undercover narcs, of course, worked dope full time, chasing users and dealers. They played their snitches, sat on open-air markets, interrupted hand-to-hand dealing, and squeezed small-time street dealers in the climb up the chain to "Mister Big."

But because most local police forces devoted only a small percentage of personnel to *French Connection*–worthy cases, and because there were no "mandatory minimum" sentences (passed by Congress in 1986 to strip "soft on crime" judges of sentencing discretion on a host of drug offenses), and because street gangs fought over, well, streets—as in neighborhood turf (and cars and girlfriends)—not drug markets, most of our jails and prisons still had plenty of room for violent, predatory criminals.

The point is, although they certainly did not turn their backs on drug offenses, the country's police were not at "war" with users and dealers. And though their government-issued photos may have adorned the wall behind the police chief's desk, a long succession of US presidents stayed out of the local picture.

But in 1971, Richard Nixon, reeling from the public's dissatisfaction with the war in Southeast Asia and looking for a handy, politically attractive, powerless target, famously proclaimed drug abuse "Public Enemy Number One," then declared an all-out "War on Drugs."

And that changed everything.

WARS AREN'T FOUGHT WITHOUT foes, so with the stroke of the presidential pen, millions of Americans were transformed from local lawbreakers into enemy combatants threatening our nation.

Still, until the early 1980s, the War on Drugs was mostly about propaganda (every war also needs a marketing campaign), convincing the American people that not only traffickers but those who abused or simply used drugs were criminals. Those addicted to heroin, for example, didn't need help so much as containment, in order to keep them away from the nation's kids. Nixon's "silent majority" and evangelist Jerry Falwell's "moral majority" did not need convincing of the "jail 'em" strategy, nor did many otherwise intelligent, socially aware people. They bought into the Big Lie. *Reefer Madness*, the 1936 cult hit, was dusted off in the 1970s and found a fresh (mostly amused) audience; Hanna-Barbera animated a frenetic, thirty-second psychedelic anti-drug public service announcement (PSA); Peter Falk narrated Arnold Shapiro's 1978 *Scared Straight!*, a documentary about deterring juvenile crime (mostly drug-related offenses); Jackson Browne starred in an anti-heroin PSA in which the singer furnished voiceover to the tune "Doctor My Eyes." The national propaganda was designed both to educate (or panic) people and to justify greater levels of funding, greater numbers of drug enforcers, and additional enforcement machinery, most of which began finding their way to local jurisdictions.

(Oddly enough, Richard Nixon devoted a larger percentage of his anti-drug budget to prevention and rehab than has any president since, with the possible exception of Jimmy Carter.)[1]

All-out war arrived with the 1980s as President Ronald Reagan went out of his way to out-law-and-order Nixon, to claim title to the toughest-on-drugs leader. To that end, Reagan rolled out his own war declaration, on October 14, 1982:

> Thirty-seven federal agencies are working together in a vigorous national effort, and by next year our spending for drug law enforcement will have more than tripled from its 1981 levels. We have increased seizures of illegal drugs. Shortages of marijuana are now being reported. Last year alone over 10,000 drug criminals were convicted and nearly $250 million of their assets were seized by the DEA, the Drug Enforcement Administration.[2]

From that point on, in each year of Reagan's two-term presidency he added more resources to wage the growing war on his own people. Sounds like a lot of money, a lot of seizures, and a lot of "drug criminals" going to jail. But those figures pale against the costs—financial, environmental, geopolitical, and social—that mounted during his administration, and which have since exploded. Following are just a few examples of what the War on Drugs has wrought:

> From the time of Nixon's announcement on June 17, 1971, the United States has spent over $1.3 trillion prosecuting the drug war.[3]
> Tens of millions of Americans, disproportionately poor and of color, have been incarcerated for low-level, nonviolent drug offenses, their families fractured, their futures jeopardized if not ruined.[4]
> The drug war has made the United States the world's biggest jailer: we have roughly 5 percent of the planet's population, but our prisons are home to almost 25 percent of all inmates in the world; a staggering 2.3 million Americans spent last night behind bars.[5]
> The average cost of incarcerating an inmate: $30,000; to educate a public-school student: $11,665 (in California, the contrast is much greater: $62,000 per inmate, $9,200 per student).[6]
> Growth in the corporatization of American prisons continues apace, with profits driving private companies to build, and fill, often to well

beyond capacity, as many cells as possible, an unconscionable practice thoroughly documented by the American Civil Liberties Union
(ACLU) in its incisive 2011 report, "Banking on Bondage."[7]

"Mandatory minimum" sentencing, begun in earnest during the Reagan years, has resulted in millions of nonviolent offenders being ware-
housed in federal prison, with states following suit through enactment
of their own "three-strikes" and similar mandatory-minimum legislation, and laws aimed at a host of drug offenses, including possession
of small quantities of marijuana.[8]

The UN Office on Drugs and Crime, a strong supporter (and follower)
of US drug policy, has determined that American efforts to wipe out
drug sources abroad are responsible for far-flung deforestation and
pollution—a major "unintended" environmental consequence of the
US-led global war on drugs.[9]

Most experts acknowledge US drug policy (and Americans' appetite for
prohibited drugs) as the single-greatest driving force behind the tens
of thousands of deaths resulting from the Mexican cartels' barbaric
wars.[10]

Political and economic destabilization has been a direct result of both
drug-based capitalism and drug enforcement throughout Latin
America (targeting, for example, left-wing guerrillas and tolerating
right-wing paramilitary forces) and the Middle East (for example, fostering record trafficking and money-laundering profits for drug lords,
as well as strong indications of CIA involvement in drug dealing and
in tolerating drug operations.)[11]

Credible estimates of the value of global illicit drug trafficking range
from $320 billion to $500 billion, a compelling incentive to engage
in the commerce, and to protect market share by whatever means
necessary.[12]

Then there is this: if current illicit drugs were legalized and taxed at
rates comparable to those of alcohol, the United States would realize almost $88 billion in law enforcement savings *and* annual tax
revenue.[13]

THE LOGIC, AND THE organizing mechanism that drives these costs, financial and otherwise, is rooted in prohibition. Prohibit drugs and we'll end addiction. Prohibit them and we'll keep dangerous substances out of the hands, and bodies, of our kids. Prohibition means we'll see fewer impaired drivers on our roads; those addicted to them will no longer shoplift, or commit burglaries and robberies, or prostitute themselves, or sell drugs in order to finance their next fix. Prohibit drugs and our neighborhoods will be safer and healthier, the world a better place to live and to raise our children.

The fallacy of this logic is self-evident. Prohibition does exactly the opposite of what its proponents intend, something we learned during the days of alcohol prohibition when the country opted to ban something that had for centuries been popular, and legal.

What exactly did alcohol prohibition accomplish? For starters, the country's thirst for booze did not abate, and crime of all sorts skyrocketed—including one rarely seen before 1920: the drive-by shooting.

Cue the theme from *The Untouchables*. Envision a gun barrel poking out the back window of a shiny black Ford as its wheelman whips the vehicle around a corner on two tires. Picture the muzzle fire, hear the distinctive rat-a-tat-tat of a Thompson submachine gun scattering innocent pedestrians with bullets meant for rival bootleggers, snitches, nosy or disloyal cops.

Getting caught in the cross fire of mobster shootouts wasn't the only hazard during Prohibition. Extortion, liquor and cash rip-offs, even overdose deaths (in the form of bad bathtub gin) proliferated. Our neighborhoods, our children were distinctly less safe. And more than a few police officers, hired to protect and serve "the people," worked instead for syndicate bosses, pocketing considerably more than their civil service salaries. They collected protection money, served as personal bodyguards, and employed "selective enforcement" tactics against the competition.

Then, in 1933, recognizing the folly of prohibition, the American people repealed the Volstead Act, the constitutional authority behind the booze ban, and replaced thirteen years of prohibition with a regulatory system. The nation soon saw major reductions in crime, violence, and other social problems. The government began collecting taxes on alcohol. Police were freed up to concentrate on real crimes, and crooked cops were dealt a sub-stantial blow.

Then we did it all over again, with drugs.

THE TWO REPUBLICAN PRESIDENTS, Nixon and Reagan, backed by conservative lawmakers, positioned themselves as uncompromising on drugs, cheerleaders of a moralistic, "zero tolerance" mentality. But many would be surprised to learn that in the 1980s such liberal luminaries as Democratic senators Barbara Boxer, Paul Wellstone, Patrick Leahy, and Tom Harkin endorsed proposed legislation by Phil Gramm, a Republican, that would have denied welfare, including food stamps, to anyone con-victed of even a misdemeanor drug offense. The version that ultimately passed had a felony threshold, which meant that in those many states where small-quantity marijuana possession remained a felony, tens of thousands of otherwise law-abiding Americans went to jail, losing not only their free-dom but their post-incarceration access to jobs and careers, public hous-ing, student loans, welfare, and food stamps. And, of course, they lost the right to vote. To most politicians, these setbacks were the price one paid for choosing the life of a drug user.

This fervid "anti-drug" mentality, and the initiatives born of it, have given rise to a nation that is bankrupting its criminal justice system, mor-ally and financially—even as it continues to imprison disproportionate numbers of blacks, Latinos, and the poor, as documented in Michelle Al-exander's must-read, *The New Jim Crow: Mass Incarceration in the Age of Colorblindness*.

In addition to the deep, structural racism at the heart of the drug war, the US Constitution, especially the presumptively color-blind Fourth Amend-ment, has taken a stupefying hit.

In New York City, until very recently, patrol officers, with direction from on high, routinely violated the Constitution's stop-and-frisk authority as outlined in the landmark Supreme Court case *Terry v. Ohio* (essentially granting police officers the right to stop and question a person on the basis of a reasonable suspicion that the individual has committed, is committing, or is planning to commit a crime). According to the NYPD's own figures, police made 191,558 such stops in 2013. Of those stopped and frisked, 169,252 (88 percent) were "totally innocent." Of those, 56 percent were black, 29 percent Latino, and 11 percent white.[14] The cops' most frequent target? A pocketful of weed or crack cocaine.

On August 12, 2013, a federal court judge found in *Floyd, et al. v. City of New York, et al.* that the NYPD was liable for racial profiling and unconstitutional stop-and-frisk policies and practices.[15]

It was about time. According to a 2013 study by Harry Levine, Loren Siegel, and Gabriel Sayegh, the NYPD spent 1 million police hours making 444,000 pot-possession arrests between 2001 and 2012.[16] The study further revealed that whites, who use marijuana at roughly equal rates, are far less likely than blacks to be busted for possession. This is where many of my police colleagues would pipe up and say that's because, unlike black consumers, white users generally don't hang out on street corners. And that, of course, is a nod to both race and class bias. Moreover, skeptics like me would ask those police officers to take a look at the frisk side of the stop-frisk equation (or the stop-*question*-and-frisk formulation preferred by the NYPD brass). Whether it's, "Empty your pockets!" or "You don't have anything in that coat you wouldn't want me to see, do you?" police officers in New York and other cities across the country regularly use the coercive power of their badges, guns, and words to conduct questionable if not blatantly illegal searches.

Worse, in order to "discover" these drugs some cops plant them on innocent people.

Cops like Philadelphia narcotics officer Jeffrey Walker. A fellow officer, Thomas Liciardello, had suspected Walker of talking to Internal Affairs about the widespread practice of planting drugs on Philadelphians. He texted Walker, "Your [sic] now a rat I hope you die. I will have you locked up by midnight. Goodbye loner." Walker replied, "You will be in jail before me." In 2015, Walker went to prison for stealing $15,000 from a suspect and planting drugs in his car. Two months later, Liciardello went to prison. Other drug squad members on trial include Brian Reynolds, Michael

Spicer, Perry Betts, Linwood Norman, and John Speiser. Walker, testifying
in his corruption trial, admitted that he "stole drug money, planted evidence and lied on police paperwork too many times to count."[17]

In Inkster, Michigan, a suburb of Detroit, in January 2015, one William
"RoboCop" Melendez stopped a black motorist, fifty-seven-year-old Floyd
Dent, ostensibly for a traffic violation. Later, Melendez would admit that
he'd stopped the car because Dent, a man with no criminal record, a retired
autoworker employed by the Ford Motor Company for thirty-seven years,
was in an area of known drug trafficking. After one officer pulled Dent
from behind the wheel of his Cadillac, Melendez grabbed him around the
neck, drove him to the ground, choked him, and hit him—a total of sixteen
times—in the head, as a fellow officer applied a stun gun to Dent's leg and
stomach. The beating took place within full, unobstructed view of a police
car's dash cam. At no time did Dent appear to offer any physical resistance.
Finally, having told Melendez, "I can't breathe," Dent went limp.

With his "bad guy" in custody, and no longer in view of the video recorder, Melendez conducted a search of the vehicle. He came out of the car
empty-handed. But a moment later, as can be seen on the video, he removed
a plastic baggie from his pocket. The baggie appears to contain a white
powder. He returned to the Cadillac. A moment later the video ended. Dent
was charged with possession of cocaine.

According to his attorney, Dent passed a polygraph and tested clean for
any drugs. He claimed the cocaine had been planted by the police. A reasonable suspicion, given Melendez's actions. And his record.

As a Detroit cop in the 1990s and 2000s, Melendez was accused repeatedly of brutality, conspiracy, falsifying reports, and planting drugs.
In 2004, he was indicted on multiple charges brought by the US Attorney
following an investigation by the FBI. Although he was acquitted of those
charges (recall that juries have a hard time convicting cops), Detroit has
paid out millions of dollars to settle civil suits brought against Melendez
and the city.[18]

Now, the city of Inkster has agreed to a $1.4 million payment to Dent,
who spent three days in the hospital being treated for broken ribs, blood on
his brain, and other injuries. Melendez, fired after criminal charges were

filed against him, was convicted of the beating in Wayne County Circuit Court on November 19, 2015.[19]

And in New York, Justice Gustin L. Reichbach, who in 2011 presided over a bench trial of NYPD cops accused of planting drugs, had this to say: "I thought I was naïve. But even this court was shocked, not only by the seeming pervasive scope of misconduct but even more distressingly by the seeming casualness by which such conduct is employed." The justice went on to say, "Anything goes in the never-ending war on drugs, and a refusal to go along with questionable practices raise[s] the specter of blacklisting and isolation."[20]

If you're a character-challenged cop, the Narcotics Detail is the place to be. But you don't have to be a crooked cop, or working for a crooked agency, to build a "money making machine" for your local PD.

PRIOR TO 1990, IF a law enforcement agency wanted to convert to its own use assets seized during a drug raid, the agency had to petition the court to have the assets declared "forfeited," but only if those assets were valued at more than $100,000. Then, the law was amended to allow administrative (versus judicial) forfeitures of cash and "monetary instruments" without regard to value. And if the agency had its eye on "other property" (cars, guns, boats, "hauling conveyances") valued at $500,000 or less, there was no longer a need for the agency to take its case to court.[21] State and local law enforcement agencies simply went after these "instruments" or "fruits" of illicit drug commerce.

Between 1989 and 2010, US attorneys seized $12.6 billion in forfeited assets, at an annual growth rate of 19.4 percent.[22]

As is so often the case in criminal justice matters, an analysis of state-by-state applications of local and federal forfeiture laws reveals both major reporting inconsistencies and proof of official corruption.

Any American who values this country's freedoms should read Sarah Stillman's article in the August 12, 2013, issue of the *New Yorker*. In it, she provides harrowing accounts of citizens' encounters with police officers, one in particular, in Tenaha, Texas, bent not on arrest but on seizing cash, cars, jewelry, and other property. Cars there were stopped for little or no reason, their drivers and passengers—disproportionately black and Latino, disproportionately poor—searched and relieved of personal items, like a tiny gold cross and money earmarked for the purchase of dental work. Other seizures included a used car, real estate for a church parish, restaurant equipment at a local auction. I was a cop for thirty-four years, and I remain an ardent student of policing. Rarely have I reached such heights of rage or depths of despair as when I read Stillman's piece. For some law enforcers, reasonable suspicion for a stop is simply unnecessary: just make it up. The same goes for probable cause for a search.[23]

And, lest there be any misunderstanding, law enforcement's practice of seizing citizens' assets is not confined to the US 59 corridor from Houston to Tenaha. It happens all over the country.[24]

An officer doesn't even have to make an arrest in order to seize his fellow citizens' property. Fully 80 percent of forfeitures occur without a charge being filed. And if those citizens want their belongings back? They must go to court, at no small expense, and with no guarantee that their property will be returned to them.

Even the British comedian John Oliver, citing numerous examples of the practice, expressed concern over his adopted country's misuse of civil seizures and forfeitures. In October 2014, he devoted a sixteen-minute segment of his HBO show to a rousing exposé of civil-asset abuses, concluding, "Public trust in the police is one of *the* most vital elements in a civilized society. But for many Americans that trust has been undermined by . . . civil forfeiture."

It's not hard to understand why thousands of cash-strapped cities and towns, like Ferguson, Missouri, experience "seizure fever" and turn their attention from actual crime fighting to policing for profit. Or why these laws were enacted in the first place: to give law enforcement another tool with which to make life difficult for racketeers, major-volume money launderers, and other nefarious types. But it's the unemployed, the working poor, and blacks and Latinos who are being hurt most.

The most significant effort at reform to date, the Civil Asset Forfeiture Reform Act of 2000, has fallen far shy of the mark. Law enforcement agencies are more dependent than ever, some might say addicted, to the revenue stream that is seized and forfeited assets.

As DEVASTATING AS THE drug war has been—and I believe it is the country's worst public policy since slavery and Jim Crow—there is another intolerable consequence. I refer here to damage done to the integrity and trustworthiness of American law enforcement.

It's tempting to romanticize the "good old days" of Officer Friendly, the cop on the beat who was always there to lend a helping hand (even if he was more gruff than cordial). I can't tell you the number of times I've heard from older citizens who all but mist over when talking about what it was like to have a cop on the beat who provided directions if you were lost; helped steer a wayward kid onto a healthier path; came to your aid if you found yourself on the losing end of a street fight or in an automobile collision; offered practical tips for crime prevention; and always seemed to "get his man" when the neighborhood was being terrorized by daytime burglars or nighttime hot prowlers. They miss those days, these citizens, and so do I.

But they're not coming back, not so long as we insist on pressing our cops into a military mold and deploying them as foot soldiers on the front lines of a bankrupt, no-win drug war.

PRESIDENT OBAMA'S SECOND-TERM initiatives—the commutation of a handful of sentences for low-level, nonviolent federal drug offenders; his visit to a federal prison in Oklahoma (the first ever for a sitting president); and a call for an end to mass incarceration, while laudatory, will have little effect unless the people, and their elected representatives, demand changes to the vastly larger state prison system, and to our drug laws.

Of course, "the people" *have* spoken in Washington state, Colorado, Alaska, Oregon, and Washington, DC, by legalizing recreational marijuana. Voters in a dozen other states are likely to do the same in the near future.

It's a start.

But we need to finish the work. How? By ending the drug war. By legal-izing, regulating, and taxing *all* drugs. By treating drug use by adults as an individual right and as a public health issue (becoming a criminal justice issue only if, as with alcohol, an individual decides to drive impaired, furnish to a minor, or commit any other offense while under the influence). And by treating drug abuse, including addiction, as the medical matter we know it to be: as with the incarceration of the mentally ill, the jailing of drug-sick people is both a pervasive and an utterly shameful practice.

My brothers and sisters in Law Enforcement Against Prohibition (LEAP), an organization whose members advocate the legalization, regulation, and control of all drugs, have "taken point" in the drug war, meaning in military parlance they've assumed the first and most exposed position in confronting "the enemy." Some of them, armed to the gills, have smashed down doors on those predawn, "shock and awe" drug raids. Some, like Jack Cole, have worked "deep cover" assignments.

Cole spent fourteen of his twenty-six years with the New Jersey State Police in Narcotics, mostly in an undercover capacity. During that time, he worked street drug users and "billion-dollar" international drug traffickers. He spent the last two years of the assignment living in Boston and New York City, posing as a fugitive drug dealer wanted for murder.

A detective lieutenant when he retired, Cole co-founded LEAP in 2002. The global organization of current and former cops and federal agents, judges, prosecutors, probation officers, prison wardens, and supporters is inspiring current and former drug warriors to rethink the wisdom of waging war against our own people.

For his part, Cole pulls no punches in talking about the harm he believes he caused during his fourteen years as a narc. In fact, his compelling antiprohibition activism is one of the ways he confronts the "emotional residue" of having helped to perpetuate a war that is "steeped in racism, that is needlessly destroying the lives of young people, and that is corrupting our police."[25]

According to Harvard economist Jeffrey Miron, ending the drug war would save the country $41 billion annually.[26] Imagine those dollars being spent to finance the transition from prohibition to regulation, from a criminal justice to a public health model, from busting sick people to helping them.

A January 11, 2016, article in the *Los Angeles Times* notes that by the end of 2016, Seattle's needle-exchange program, the largest in the United States, will have "given out more than 4 million syringes to drug users, helping to protect them [and their fellow citizens] against HIV, hepatitis C, and other needle-borne threats."[27] In that same article, King County sheriff John Urquhart was asked to comment on plans to expand, mobilize, and—against existing state and federal laws—help heroin users with the safe administration of the drug. "As long as there was strong, very strong, emphasis on education, services, and recovery," replied Urquhart, "I would say that yes, the benefits outweigh the drawbacks." In fact, said the sheriff, "We will never make any headway in the war on drugs until we turn the war into a health issue."

JACK COLE BELIEVES, AS do thousands of other current or former drug warriors, that ending the drug war would have a dramatic side benefit, namely, reversing the growing tide of police militarization—while, at the same time, improving the relationship between America's police and millions of disaffected citizens.

4

COPS AND MENTAL ILLNESS

PICK A BIG CITY, or a small one. Odds are, its police department has shot and killed at least one mentally ill person.

Like on Bainbridge Island, here in my home state of Washington. Situated across Elliott Bay, a thirty-five-minute ferry ride from Seattle, Bainbridge Island is verdant and rural, with thriving small-town businesses, a wealthy population, and diverse tourist attractions. It enjoys majestic views of the Olympic Mountains to the west and Seattle's skyline across the bay to the east. There is a palpable live-and-let-live ethic among the roughly 23,000 residents. It's lovely, artsy, serene.

But its serenity was shattered on the night of October 26, 2010.

Bill and Joyce Ostling knew their son was different, even from his toddler days. According to *Seattle Times* reporters Jonathan Martin and Ken Armstrong, "One expert diagnosed Doug with schizophrenia. Another suspected Asperger's, a form of autism associated with repetitive behavior and a lack of social skills."[1] Either way, Bill and Joyce, who came to favor the second diagnosis, had found ways over the years to work with their son. When they realized he couldn't change, they changed their behavior toward him. And it made life better for all.

Often, "mental illness" calls to 911 come from frantic parents: a beloved family member is in distress, a danger to oneself or others. This particular call, in October 2010, however, came from Joyce and Bill's son himself.

Then forty-three years old, Douglas yelled into the phone, "What are you?" "What is that?" "Are you intelligent?"

Officers Dave Portrey and Jeff Benkert of the Bainbridge Island Police Department (BIPD) were dispatched. Arriving in separate cars, they asked Bill Ostling if he'd called the police. He told them no, but perhaps his son had. The three men walked inside the garage, looked up a flight of stairs to Doug's apartment. The officers had asked Mr. Ostling no questions about how best to approach his son. Worse, according to Bill, they shunned his offer to help them understand Doug, his condition, what he might be going through.

Benkert and Portrey led the way up the stairs. One of them tried the door. It was locked. They sent Bill down to get a key.

From this point on, accounts of what happened next differ, the cops telling one story, Bill and Joyce another.

When Officer Benkert put the key in the lock and opened the door, Doug shut it and said, "I'm okay. Go away." Benkert pushed open the door. The officers saw Doug holding a double-bit ax "over his head" (according to Portrey) or "against his chest" (according to Bill). Officer Portrey discharged his Taser and hit Doug. Benkert then shouted, "Stop or I'll shoot." Which he did. Three times—as Doug was shutting the door. One shot struck a lampshade and ricocheted off the ceiling, the other two hit Doug in the legs. No account has Doug Ostling attacking either officer with the ax, which he had on hand for chopping kindling for his woodstove.

The officers put out a "shots fired" call and within an hour at least seventeen police units from three agencies showed up. But in the seventy-seven minutes following the shooting, no one entered the room where Doug Ostling was bleeding out. This, despite the fact that Bill begged the officers to let him into Doug's room. No, they replied. They would, following a dated and discredited protocol, wait for SWAT.

The Ostlings' son was dead by the time emergency personnel finally entered the room. Paramedics had actually arrived at the scene in about nine minutes but were kept waiting the whole time: a classic case of cops putting "officer safety" above the needs of those they were hired to protect and serve. According to experts, quick action likely would have saved Doug Ostling.

The Kitsap County prosecutor elected to file no charges against the officers, even though, incredibly, at the time of his decision the shooter had still not been interviewed. However, during a civil trial brought by the Ostlings, Officer Benkert went on to testify that it was "possible" Doug approached the officers not to attack them but to shut the door. Benkert also testified that he did not see Doug raise the ax over his head.

There were many failings of the police and justice systems in the handling of this case, from the 911 call to the (then) police chief's defensive, dramatic, and inaccurate statements in the aftermath—statements that, when shown to be false, went deliberately uncorrected by a chief who felt he had no "ethical" obligation to correct the public record. One glaring "oversight" was that Benkert was not interviewed by his own department until two and a half months after the death of Doug Ostling. Why not? Because, Benkert said, "Nobody asked me."[2]

Perhaps of greatest concern were the qualifications of each officer.

THE SHOOTER, DAVE PORTREY, had failed police tests in other jurisdictions of the state. In fact, according to Kimberly Hendrickson, civil service secretary for the city at that time, he had originally failed the Bainbridge Island test. Yet the department put him to work first as a reserve officer, and years later as a "paid, provisional" cop. Hendrickson, who went on to lead a citizens' effort to reform the BIPD, and who has since become a national expert on citizen oversight of police policies and practices, told me that "no questions were asked about [Portrey's] training or certification" before he was placed on the department's payroll.

Portrey's fellow officer, Jeff Benkert, had been on the verge of being fired by the Los Angeles Police Department for neglect of duty and lying when he applied for and got the Bainbridge job. After the shooting a former colleague in the LAPD wrote to Benkert on Facebook, "Hey man how you doing? Heard you did some combat qual???!!!" Binkert's response? "No sweat here . . . bad guy should have listened a little better."

In 2012, a federal jury in the Ostlings' civil trial awarded the family $1 million (plus over $300,000 in legal fees) for the wrongful death of their son. Through it all, one conclusion stood out: the city and its police department had failed to train their officers in the empathetic and skillful handling of people with mental illness.

The BIPD General Orders Manual called for officers confronting mentally disturbed persons to move slowly, minimize noise, take time to assess, gather information from the family, avoid physical contact or threatening or agitating behavior—all very basic, all very important—but the two officers largely ignored the written order. In fact, Portrey admitted he was unfamiliar with that section of the agency's manual. Further, although the dispatcher informed the responding officers that the caller could be in a state of "excited delirium," Officer Portrey had no idea what that meant. (How the dispatcher came to that conclusion in the first place is anybody's guess.) Excited delirium, or "ExDS" is usually associated with drug abuse, most often cocaine, and, according to the FBI, is a "serious and potentially deadly medical condition involving psychotic behavior, elevated temperature, and an extreme fight-or-flight response by the nervous system."[3]

Still, when asked to define the condition, Portrey testified that it's "where a person was, I believe, attracted to a shiny objects [sic]."[4]

IS IT ANY WONDER that police officers (and Americans in general) are so ill-informed about mental illness? Unless we are afflicted personally or have mentally ill family members or close friends, we're likely to experience the illness from afar, with disinterest or fear.

In 1955, when the United States had a population of 164 million, there were 558,239 patients in state and county psychiatric hospitals. In 1996, the population stood at 265 million and psychiatric hospitals were treating a mere 61,722. How did this come to pass?

A year after I became a cop, California governor Ronald Reagan essentially ended state housing and treatment of the mentally ill. In signing the 1967 Lanterman-Petris-Short Act, he made it all but impossible for a peace officer to obtain involuntary hospitalization for those in need. Other states quickly followed suit. It got to be a joke, a cruel one to be sure: If you came across an at-risk mentally ill person, you simply locked them up. Or, often against your better judgment, cut them loose.

In 1980, President Jimmy Carter signed the Mental Health Systems Act, intending to reorganize and rejuvenate community-based mental-health centers and improve life for the chronically mentally ill. But a year later, newly elected president Ronald Reagan engineered congressional repeal of Carter's program, replacing it with block grants to the states (a notoriously underfunded, bureaucratic, largely ineffectual move favored by Republicans), thereby ending the federal government's direct role in services to the mentally ill.

So, Ronald Reagan, leader of the free world, presiding over a nation of enormous wealth, found a way to extricate the government, at both the state and federal levels, from any true responsibility for mental-health services, including screening and treatment for those who posed an immediate danger to themselves or others. Combined with his decision to jail those addicted to drugs, Reagan exhibited a callous disregard for millions of Americans whose only crime was their illness.

(Ironically, the nation's law enforcers, despite their jobs having become tougher and less safe, just couldn't get enough of The Gipper. I recall watching my cops—members of the Intelligence detail, motorcycle cops, patrol officers—fall all over themselves to be photographed with the governor-cum-president each time he came to San Diego. He was a charmer, that one.)

It's true, institutionalization can be, and historically has been, abused. Not every mentally ill person belongs in an institution (the great majority do not), whether a state hospital or a community-based mental-health facility. But the numbers reinforce what emergency services personnel—police officers, firefighters, paramedics—and families of many of the nation's mentally ill people have been saying for decades. When your only option for an individual in crisis is jail or nothing, then that spells failure. This failure of political will, wisdom, and courage has made cops and corrections officers the ill-suited, de facto source of protection of and service to the nation's mentally ill.

I WAS A BEAT cop when Governor Reagan signed the state's new "mental health" act.

Pulling reliefs one Sunday afternoon, I was dispatched to a home in San Carlos, a quiet suburban neighborhood near San Diego's eastern border with La Mesa. It was a dreaded "check the welfare" call: a neighbor calls the police, says the man across the street has been "acting strange," or has been shouting profanities at an invisible foe, or hasn't been seen for a week, or. . . . You never knew what you'd find, though a ripe body was always a possibility.

I was, in fact, met with a strong odor as I rang the doorbell, repeatedly. But it wasn't the scent of rotting flesh. It was more like perfume.

An unusually thin thirty-something woman with short, brittle salt-and-pepper hair and a vacant stare finally answered the door. I felt like I'd stepped into a shower of a cheap, cloying women's fragrance. Tinged with what could be described as essence of body odor, urine, and feces.

Dressed in a white sleeveless blouse, heavily stained with sweat, she was barefoot. A filthy beige skirt hung limply from her stick-like hips. She rocked back and forth, something she continued to do most of the time I was with her.

"I'm here to see if everything's okay. May I come in?"

She stared beyond me. I asked again, waited a few moments and then walked in. And was almost overcome by a wave of nausea as the smells intensified in the enclosed space.

There were no paintings or photos on the walls, and not a single item of furniture in the living room. No TV, no radio that I could see. The kitchen, visible through the space between the counter and a ceiling-mounted cup-board, was empty of small appliances: no toaster, no coffeepot, no teakettle on the stove. A small stack of mail sat on a butcher-block island in the mid-dle of the kitchen. As did a flashlight and an industrial-size bottle of some off-brand yellow-tinted perfume or cologne.

"Are you okay?"

She stared at me.

"Do you live here?"

She said nothing.

"Do you mind if I have a look around?"

Her deep brown eyes were lifeless but, in my imagination, they granted permission. I motioned for her to follow, then began a survey of what I hoped was her home, though I suspected she might be a squatter. The three-bedroom, two-bath ranch house appeared to have been completely cleaned out. A handful of clothes in the closets, a single towel in the bathrooms. The toilets were filled to the rim with human waste, their lids down, which did little to mask the smell.

"Your room?" I asked, as we came to the master bedroom.

She shrugged, almost imperceptibly, but said nothing.

The room held one bed, no sheets, no bedding at all. Not even a pillow. It was apparent from the indentation that a human form had claimed one side of the double bed, over some period of time. Like all other rooms in the place, the drapes (or blinds) were drawn against the late-summer sun, and, I speculated, the prying eyes of neighbors. "Do you sleep here?" She did not reply. I placed my two hands together, on the diagonal, bent my head to them and closed my eyes. Then opened them, looked at her. "Sleep here?"

A slight nod, desultory, disengaged. Finally, we were "communicating."

In the kitchen, I turned on the tap in the sink. As with the bathrooms, there was no running water. The electricity had been turned off as well. I opened the cupboards. Nothing. No food. No dishes, plates, pots, pans, utensils. How did she survive? The refrigerator was empty but for numerous cans of warm Coca-Cola. I walked over to the sliding door and looked out on a concrete patio. A trash can overflowed with Coke empties. The grass, as in the front yard, was dead. No flowers or shrubs, one gangly tree in the middle of what had once been a lawn. As expected, the attached garage, off the kitchen, was completely empty, down to the studs.

I walked back over to the island and reached for the stack of mail. "You mind if I look through these?"

Again, the shrug.

"So, tell me again, what's your name?"

She didn't answer, but the name on the correspondence, mostly bills and flyers, seemed to fit. None of the envelopes had been opened.

"I'll be right back, okay?"

Her neighbors to the south were not home, but an elderly man answered the door to the freshly painted, nicely landscaped house to the north.

"We were hoping you'd swing by here, officer."

"Did you call us?"

"Sure did. Sorry I didn't give them my address when I called. We didn't know quite what to do. My wife's been threatening to disown me if I didn't call *somebody*."

"What's your neighbor's story?"

He proceeded to tell me that the woman was a "mail order bride," brought here, "underground," from "Poland or Czechoslovakia, one of those Eastern bloc countries" by a man who a few weeks later abandoned her:

> We thought they'd moved, but it was just him. Took everything, by the looks of it. Put it all in a rental truck and just took off. My wife and I, we pretty much keep to ourselves, but something's not right over there. You can't really see inside but early this morning, we heard some cans being tossed around. Thought it was cats or coons at first, but, anyway, my wife turned on our backyard floodlight and saw the lady, putting a bunch of cans into the trash. We didn't want to be nosy but the missus insisted I go over there, see if she needed anything. I waited till midmorning, went over and knocked. And knocked and knocked. She's in there, all right, but she didn't come to the door. We think maybe she needs some help. I don't know if you noticed the smell, but. . . .

"I'd like for you to take a ride with me," I said when I went back to the woman's house. She came along without protest, and I drove her to County Mental Health in Hillcrest.

I spoke to the receptionist through the hole in the Plexiglas wall that fronted her desk. "Who's her family doctor?" she asked.

"I'm pretty sure she doesn't have one." I explained everything I'd found in response to the check-the-welfare call.

"Well, I'll call the duty doc but you know he's not going to want to admit her."

I knew it was a long shot. CMH had sent memo after memo to all the county's law enforcement agencies, explaining that because of changes in the law and resulting budgetary reductions, the honoring of requests for "72-hour holds" would be few and far between. They offered no help to the beat cop, these memoranda. Several of my requests for holds had already been rejected. Although we'd been assured that "life-threatening" situations had top priority, the docs were turning us away left and right, even when we brought in individuals threatening suicide or homicide.

Or who were slowly starving to death.

It was ridiculous.

I knew the San Carlos woman was not an immediate threat, that she was not at the moment in "acute crisis." But what the hell? She needed help. I didn't have to ask, nor would she have answered: she knew no one in San Diego, or the whole of the country, I'm sure, with the exception of her "husband."

I checked with my sergeant, who checked with the watch commander. There was nothing we could do for her. As instructed, I drove her back out to San Carlos, scribbled my name and badge number on a piece of my notebook paper, along with the PD's pre-911 phone number, and left it on her kitchen counter.

I tapped the note with my finger. "Call the police department if you need help, okay?"

Still rocking, she looked at me and, I think, shrugged.

THE NUMBER OF MENTALLY ill people jailed in the year following passage of Reagan's California strategy doubled. Had my "mail-order bride" picked up a knife and, breaking through her lassitude, come at me with it, or had she been homeless and working the streets as a drug dealer or prostitute, I would have had the option of putting her in a less-than-pleasant but generally clean environment with a promise of "three hots and a cot." In other words, behind bars. Hardly a solution for those suffering chronic mental illness, especially in a country with the vast riches of the United States.

According to the National Alliance on Mental Illness (NAMI), 3.5 million Americans are afflicted with severe mental illness and 250,000 of them are in prison. Incarceration has replaced treatment. And, as those numbers grow, we can't keep blaming Reagan.

Given that fully half of all people killed by the police are mentally ill, and that mental illness is a sorely, nay, criminally neglected area of social policy and government services, the least we can do is demand and present the finest possible training for our police officers.

But what kind of training?

Most conversations about police mental-health training begin and end with the "Memphis Model," and for good reason. But well before events in Memphis, Tennessee, prompted development of the model there was an important antecedent, born of the movement to reduce family violence.

In the 1960s, psychologists Morton Bard and Bernard Berkowitz conducted early research into the "proper" police response to family crises (and by extension any situation involving humans in crisis, including mental-health emergencies). At that time (and, too often, now) "crisis intervention" was taught in the academy by police instructors who themselves typically had no specialized training. Their message was simple: people in crisis pose a major safety risk, to themselves, their loved ones, their neighbors, and the police. Therefore, "be careful out there."

Not overly helpful.

In 1967, Bard, a "community psychologist" and former police officer, taught an experimental class for the NYPD. Nine black cops, nine white cops, all volunteers, spent a month in the classroom learning about the psychology of family and "cross-racial" conflict, and how to reduce tensions and prevent violence and injuries—to family members and police alike. The goal was to achieve these reductions in violence without having to make an arrest, an idea that has been largely discredited by subsequent studies and research: physical custody arrests and enforced protection orders, while not foolproof, are critical tools in the campaign to end domestic violence.

Six desired outcomes of the New York program were monitored over a two-year period: (1) a decrease in family disturbance calls; (2) a drop in repeat calls to the same families; (3) a reduction of homicides within the precinct; (4) a decline among family-member homicides; (5) a reduction in assaults within the precinct; and (6) a decrease in injuries to police officers.

At project's end, only two of the desired outcomes had been achieved: a reduction in precinct-wide assaults and a decrease in police officer injuries (none among the "experimental" group, three within the "control" group). But there had been some good learning.

BARD AND BERKOWITZ TRAVELED across the country to the San Francisco Police Department to test out lessons they'd learned in New York. They rented a spacious, multistory house high atop a hill in one of the city's tonier neighborhoods.

On-duty patrol officers, knowing only generally what was in store, were summoned to the house, two at a time, via routine dispatch—a "family disturbance" call. There, they encountered actors (along with researcher-trainers and video technicians) who had been prepped and rehearsed to enact a realistic family crisis. Whatever cards they were dealt, the patrol officers were to handle the call just as they would a regular dispatch. Their performance was monitored and taped, as I recall, from the moment they pulled up to the curb line.

As SDPD's academy director at the time, I flew up to San Francisco to observe this innovative police training in action.

The researchers sat me on a stool in front of a monitor and I watched as a succession of patrol officers made their way to the front door of the house, gained entry, separated (or not) the "disputants," defused (or not) the conflict, and tried their best to calm and manage an escalating situation.

Some of the officers performed quite well. They were calm, polite, and well informed about the law and, more important, human dynamics. With others, "mistakes were made," some minor, some major, the latter of a nature that might well have led to injury or death had they happened in the real world.

I returned to San Diego with some important lessons, the most significant of which was the most obvious: If we want to help police officers become more adept at handling interpersonal crises, of whatever description, we must turn to experts to provide both the esoteric body of knowledge and the highly specialized skill sets essential to safe and successful intervention.

I began this chapter with the claim that most cities and counties have played host to the death of at least one mentally ill person at the hands of the police. One such killing in the city of Memphis triggered a movement with considerable life-saving potential. Because the Memphis Model has become the benchmark for police mental-health training and practices, it begs for an in-depth look.

IN 1986, ANN DINO and Helen Adamo had a lot in common. Each had a son with severe mental illness, each had become a member of the National Alliance on Mental Illness (NAMI Memphis), and each was outraged when Dino's son, Bubba, had to be driven to the hospital in a police car because the city's ambulance crew refused to transport a mentally ill person.

The two women met with the mayor and Adamo asked, "How would you like to read the headline tomorrow, 'Mentally ill man bleeds out in the back of a squad car?'"[5] The mayor and several other officials were sympathetic, and Adamo wrote a proposal to help police respond to "MI" cases with greater safety and efficacy. But the plan languished in the bureaucracy for a year and a half. Not until an incident in the fall of 1987 did a catalyzed community force both the police and the politicians to act.

As Sam Cochran, a Memphis police officer at the time, recently told Amy Goodman on *Democracy Now!*, "Our officers responded to a call . . . that [a twenty-seven-year-old mentally ill man] was armed with a very large knife. He was cutting himself. He was threatening family members . . . and neighbors that were also arriving on the scene."[6]

The subject of the call was Joseph Robinson. His mother had called the cops because she was afraid and needed their assistance. She had asked the officers to protect her son from further injury, to help him.

"Our officers arrived," as Cochran recalled it, and "after a very brief encounter with this individual, he was shot multiple times and died as a result."

After a very brief encounter. That phrase or variations of it appear with disturbing frequency in police and media reports. A police officer encounters a dangerous situation involving a mentally ill person, like the one on Bainbridge Island, for example, and hasn't the foggiest idea how to handle it—other than with force, a level of force almost always determined subsequently to have been legally justified, even though in most cases officers could have slowed things down and helped bring about a de-escalation of fear and tension. On Bainbridge Island, the fatal shots were fired less than five minutes after the officers arrived.

CITIZEN ANGER WAS RUNNING high in Memphis after the Robinson shooting. Protesters demanded the ouster of the police chief and the mayor, which Dino and Adamo rejected in favor of a different tactic.

They updated and presented anew their proposal for police mental-health training. This time, no doubt because of greater political urgency, the plan received an across-the-board enthusiastic response by official Memphis.

The police chief appointed Lieutenant Walter Crews to lead a community task force, to include Dino and Adamo, directors of public mental-health agencies, and "The Med," the Regional Medical Center located in Memphis. Private mental-health providers also sought a place at the table. The task force, under Crews's diplomatic leadership, soon built an entirely new, comprehensive, multidisciplinary approach to those experiencing mental-health crises. (Sam Cochran, who went on to retire as a major with the Memphis Police Department and who now consults with similar crisis-intervention programs throughout the world, took over from Crews in 1988.)

At the core of the program was a working collaboration among police officers, people with mental illness, their families, and mental-health professionals—in other words, the key stakeholders. The name for their partnership: the Memphis Crisis Intervention Team, or Memphis CIT. The team's officers, 225-strong, are volunteers, representing each precinct and providing 24/7 coverage for the entire city.

In addition to a comprehensive, forty-hour training program, taught by mental-health professionals—who also rode with the cops and responded to their requests for on-site professional assistance—the officers participated in drop-in sessions with those afflicted with mental illness. These informal sessions, convened under non-exigent conditions, helped all participants connect with and learn from one another on a human level.

Another key feature? Thanks to the commitment and common sense of Dr. Randy Dupont, clinical director of emergency psychiatric services at the University of Tennessee Medical Center and a founding member of the Memphis CIT, if the cops brought someone to the center for an assessment, they were not turned away with some bureaucratic excuse.

"Most crisis facilities' failings," Dupont said, "happen because they are underfunded, so they tend to restrict the doorway. Pretty soon there are facilities that will not take the handicapped, will not take the blind, the mentally ill, or those under the influence of alcohol and drugs. If I were [the] police, I would be asking, 'Well what *do* you take?' We are going to take all comers, and will sort it out. If it turns out to be a complicated medical problem which needs surgery, we can take that too. I think our ability to take care of the range of needs is what is impressive."[7]

Impressive, indeed. Evaluations of the Memphis CIT program reveal improvements in community safety, reduced officer call time on mental illness (MI) dispatches, and reduced response times. Injuries to officers dropped from over five per thousand events to under one per thousand. And, most impressive: prior to the introduction of the program, officers were jailing 20 percent of the mentally ill people they encountered; today it's 2 percent.[8]

INDISPENSABLE TO THE SUCCESS of crisis intervention teams is instruction, *by mental-health experts*, on what to do and not do as a police officer at the scene of a mental or behavioral health crisis. As noted previously, much of the learning is counterintuitive and in sharp contrast to what cops have been taught from the first day in the academy.

Training in de-escalation techniques is at the heart of such instruction. And, when you think about it, of all the skills a police officer needs—pursuit driving; traffic enforcement; responding to crimes in progress; crime scene protection; interviewing witnesses; interrogating suspects; the identification, collection and preservation of evidence; use of force, including lethal force; defensive tactics; arrest and control, and more—the mastery of de-escalation techniques is arguably the most valuable tool in a police officer's tradecraft kit. At any given moment, in any given situation, the person a cop is dealing with—in crisis or not—can "escalate," that is, become a danger to self or others.

De-escalation is a literal lifesaver. And, today, it is the talk of the nation.

Some of the talk, coming from street cops, can be a bit unsettling. In Seattle, in June 2015, an instructor stood before a class of antagonistic officers, "educating" them on the value and techniques of de-escalation. A reporter and a videographer from the *New York Times* were present, capturing every word, every action. One officer, obviously frustrated with what he was hearing, spoke up and shared an account of a man he'd stopped. "I pulled my gun out and stuck it right in his nose and I go, 'Show me your hands now.' He showed me his hands. I just de-escalated him from doing something." Apparently the only way he knew how.[9]

With other cops in the classroom grumbling and grousing right along with him, the sympathetic instructor responded, "I agree. I agree. Don't shoot the messenger. This is what the DOJ is saying, not me."

Both the student and the instructor are under investigation—so much for freedom of speech. (So much, too, for the belief that cops won't speak up or "act natural" if they know they're being recorded.)

I do think those officers were entitled to their opinions. Especially in a classroom. But in their street practice, they are not entitled to defy their department's policy. In the meantime, police officials, as well as critics of the police, are asking a very reasonable question about why their cops all too often rush to judgment, initiating physical confrontations or firing their weapons, when far safer outcomes could be achieved by slowing things down, sizing up situations, and calming tensions.

ON AUGUST 30, 2010, Seattle officer Ian Birk shot and killed a seventh-generation Nuu-chah-nulth First Nations wood-carver who, on a downtown street, was "armed" with a three-inch knife in one hand, a block of wood in the other. John T. Williams was drunk, deaf in one ear, and not complying with Birk's order to drop the knife—whose blade, not incidentally, was closed. According to the officer, Mr. Williams had displayed a "confrontational posture."[10] And that's all it took.

As an ex-cop, I would ask: How many drunks do not assume a "confrontational posture"? Why didn't Birk just back off? De-escalate the situation? Because he and several generations of police officers were hardwired not to calm things down. Incredible as it may seem, our "peace" officers are trained to do precisely what they ought not to do if public safety is the goal.

The Police Executive Research Forum recently surveyed 281 police agencies and determined that the median time spent on police firearms training was fifty-eight hours. On defensive tactics, it's forty-nine hours. "De-escalation" and "crisis intervention"? Eight hours each, with many departments providing *no* training in one or the other of these disciplines.[11]

DE-ESCALATION IS NOT MERELY "remaining calm," important as that is. No, de-escalation requires police officers to learn an entirely new set of skills and techniques. NAMI has assembled a list of "escalating" behaviors, and suggestions on how both therapists and police officers can most effectively respond to them. "Escalated behaviors" include: raised and or high-pitched voice; rapid speech; pacing; excessive sweating; balled fists; excessive hand gestures; erratic movements; fidgeting; aggressive posture; and shaking.

Not surprisingly, police officers may exhibit these same behaviors in tense situations. Especially common, in my experience, are raised and or high-pitched voice, rapid speech, and aggressive posture. As will be discussed in the next chapter, fear very likely accounts for this behavior.

As crisis intervention training (CIT) makes clear, "We are intuitively driven into 'fight or flight' mode when scared. However, in de-escalation, we can do neither. We must appear centered and calm even when we are terrified."[12] And that means, here again, *practice, practice, practice.* Cops must rehearse slow, deep diaphragmatic breathing in order to "decrease [their] own level of arousal." (What they certainly cannot be expected to do, in the real world, is turn their backs as they practice "slow, deep diaphragmatic breathing"—a ludicrous, gratuitous piece of advice rumored to have been a part of the NYPD's suggested de-escalation regimen, a rumor blessedly debunked—before police officer anger and defensiveness escalated.)

CIT INTERNATIONAL OFFERS NINE techniques of nonverbal communication (for example, "Maintain limited eye contact . . . and . . . a neutral facial expression"; "Minimize body movements such as excessive gesturing, pacing, fidgeting or weight shifting"; "Place your hands in front of your body in an open and relaxed position") and fifteen for verbal de-escalation (for example, "Remember that there is no content except trying to calmly bring the level of arousal down to a safer place"; "Do not get loud or try to yell over a screaming person"; "Do not be defensive even if comments or insults are directed at you"; "Be very respectful even when firmly setting limits"; "Do not try to argue or convince"; "Explain limits and rules in an authoritative, firm, but respectful tone").

The long list of tips and techniques ends with this pearl: "There is nothing magical about talking someone down. You are simply transferring your own sense of calm and respectful, clear limit setting to the agitated person."[13]

BY 2015, FORTY-FIVE STATES and 2,800 communities, including the District of Columbia, had embraced the Memphis Model. New York City is not among them (although its police department, reeling from the fallout of the Eric Garner case and a failure to use de-escalation techniques, is in the process of implementing a promising program of its own design).

During my tenure, Seattle adopted a variation of the Memphis Model. Like so many other cities, ours was in response to a tragic police shooting.

On September 30, 1996, my SWAT officers were deployed to a public-housing residence after the occupant, eighty-four-year-old Bodegard Mitchell, confronted a Seattle Housing Authority electrician who had come to his home to do some repair work. Mitchell, known to be mentally ill, took a shot at the electrician, who then ran from the residence and called the cops. A five-hour standoff ensued. When, finally, tear gas was used to flush Mitchell from the residence, he emerged with gun blazing, striking a SWAT officer in the shoulder. Mr. Mitchell was killed in a hail of return fire. His pistol turned out to be a pellet gun, totally irrelevant to the officers who had witnessed their fellow officer struck by what looked for all the world like a lethal weapon.

Nonetheless, that's no way for the life of a mentally ill, eighty-four-year-old man to come to an end.

Thanks to critics who asked, indeed demanded (of a very willing police administration), that we develop our own CIT, we did just that, and began sending small groups of officers through a weeklong training program—modeled after Memphis and taught exclusively by mental-health experts.

I kicked off each session on a Monday morning, returning Friday afternoon for graduation ceremonies, at which we heard from the officers. What did they get out of the week? How would it affect their work? Would it help make them more effective? Would they, and those in crisis, be safer as a result of this education? The answers were uniformly positive, and encouraging. And there was an unexpected bonus, too.

My cops spoke of insights that would help them not only in the work world but on the home front. They were forthcoming about nascent breakthroughs in relations with their non-cop friends, their spouses, their teenage kids. They spoke unabashedly, often emotionally, about the humanizing effects of the training. I've forgotten what we budgeted for the CIT instruction (it ain't cheap; a statewide program of relatively modest scope, aimed at all Washington departments, carries a price tag of $1.6 million for two years), but I know one thing: it was worth every dime.

In Seattle, we adopted one important variation of the Memphis Model. As we began to see the same kind of positive results our Tennessee colleagues had experienced—increased efficacy in dealing with those caught up in behavioral crisis, reduced injuries, fewer mentally ill people being carted off to jail, even improved officer morale—we decided that, eventually, every officer, not just a relative handful of specialists, would undergo the training. That goal did not survive my tenure, although both the department and the state legislature are currently pursuing funding for expansion (and the mandating) of CIT programs throughout the state.

CRISIS INTERVENTION TEAMS ARE not a panacea. In the best of models, issues of human unpredictability, of the all-too-ready availability of firearms, of our inability no matter how motivated or well trained, to prevent all "suicides by cop." But the power of the training and the practical support for our cops and our citizens cannot be overestimated.

Every police officer in the country needs to know, understand, and be able to skillfully apply the learning of crisis intervention training. As plaintiff's attorney Nathan Roberts said during the civil trial of the Doug Ostling shooting, putting cops on the street without critical mental-health knowledge is like giving them a "car with no brakes, a radio with no batteries, a gun with no bullets."[14]

If it is established that a particular officer, especially one who's been trained in crisis intervention, isn't temperamentally suited to the task, it's time to bench or fire that officer.

With prejudice.

A SUBJECT RARELY IF ever discussed within police circles, or in the larger society, is the presence of mental illness within the ranks of police officers. A review of the literature, even an extensive online search for "police officers with mental illness" or "mentally ill police officers" produced page after page of "training the police to deal with distraught persons" or "helping the police help those with mental illness." The National Institute of Mental Health (NIMH) defines "any mental illness" (AMI) as:

- A mental, behavioral, or emotional disorder (excluding developmental and substance use disorders);
- Diagnosable currently or within the past year;
- Of sufficient duration to meet diagnostic criteria specified within [the latest edition of] the *Diagnostic and Statistical Manual of Mental Disorders*;
- [Ranging in impact from] no or mild impairment to significantly disabling impairment, such as individuals with *serious mental illness* (SMI) [original emphasis], defined as individuals with a mental disorder with serious functional impairment which substantially interferes with or limits one or more major life activities.[15]

NIMH estimates that in 2013, there were 43.8 million adults, eighteen or older, in the United States with AMI. That comes to 18.5 percent of the adult population,[16] which raises the question: How many of the nation's 1 million law enforcement officers suffer from a form of mental illness, with mild to serious impairment? Given the manifest pressures of the job, the vulnerabilities of all human beings, and especially what we know about the effects of posttraumatic stress disorder (PTSD), how could we possibly conclude that mental illness is not an issue for America's police? And therefore for American society?

The National Center for PTSD offers, in plain, accessible language, a clear picture of the scope and nature of the phenomenon:

> Posttraumatic stress disorder (PTSD) can occur after you have been through a trauma. A trauma is a shocking and scary event that you see or that happens to you. During this type of event, you think that your life or others' lives are in danger. You may feel afraid or think that you have no control over what is happening.
>
> Going through trauma is not rare. About 6 of every 10 (or 60%) of men and 5 of every 10 (or 50%) of women experience at least one trauma in their lives. Women are more likely to experience sexual assault and child sexual abuse. Men are more likely to experience accidents, physical assault, combat, disaster, or to witness death or injury. Going through a trauma does not mean you'll get PTSD, though. Even though over half of us go through some type of trauma, a much smaller percent develop PTSD.[17]

In fact, according to the center, only 7 or 8 percent of the population will develop PTSD at some point in their lives.[18] But with no solid research to draw upon, we're left to speculate about the extent to which police officers suffer posttraumatic stress or, for that matter, other forms of mental or emotional suffering.

We know, from both clinical and anecdotal evidence, that police officers experience at least average if not greater-than-average rates of divorce, domestic violence, alcohol and other substance abuse (including "roid rage," caused by steroid use), other stress-related illnesses, and suicide. We also know that the work is inherently stressful, periodically traumatic, and, not infrequently, boring. Shift work, overtime, court appearances, off-duty jobs, poor personal habits, and inadequate coping mechanisms cause many officers to suffer irregular sleep and eating patterns—the rate of clinically defined obesity (40.7 percent) is higher for cops than for the general adult population (35.7 percent).[19] (However, the life expectancy of police offi-cers, presumed for years to be a full ten years less than that of the general population,[20] as well as the suicide rate for police officers, presumed to be fourteen to seventeen per 100,000 officers versus eleven among the public at large,[21] have both been disputed by meta-analyses.) Family or intimate-other relationships can also add to the stress, especially when officers fail to recognize the value of work-life balance, and of meeting their obliga-tions to the people they purport to love. And, of course, police bosses can contribute to an unhealthy environment through arbitrary or oppressive, inattentive, or neglectful practices.

More research on police officers' mental health is critically needed. In the meantime, one encouraging trend, perhaps inspired by recent contro-versial police shootings and in-custody deaths, is an increased focus on "wellness" within the ranks.

ENLIGHTENED POLICE LEADERS, MENTAL (and physical) health pro-fessionals, and community advocates can do much to help create a safe, hospitable, and, yes, healthy workplace culture within the ranks. Given the hours police officers work, and the conditions under which they labor, such an effort is long overdue.

It starts, I believe, with a deep understanding of the work, and how both the streets and organizational realities affect police officers—and how the officers' attitudes and behavior, in turn, affect the work itself. Kevin Gilmartin, a clinical psychologist, trainer, consultant, and former Arizona police officer, literally wrote the book on this: *Emotional Survival for Law Enforcement: A Guide for Officers and Their Families.* Gilmartin spoke to an executive class I took at the FBI Academy during my time in Seattle. Cov-ering a wide range of topics, one of the most relevant was his observation that, in time, many cops come to view themselves as victims and take on "victim attributes." They believe everyone is against them: the community, the brass, the courts, sometimes even their fellow officers.

Most big-city police departments provide a range of psychological ser-vices, from entry-level screening to short-term therapy, wellness coun-seling, fitness-for-duty appraisals (following a shooting, for example), operational support, organizational training and consulting, and more. Yet, according to the American Psychological Association, the vast majority of the country's 18,000 law enforcement agencies lack the resources "to assist troubled officers, let alone run prevention programs."[22]

If we want to help police officers maintain their own physical and emotional fitness, if we want cops who can safely, competently, and compassionately handle the mentally ill among us, we have no choice but to support wellness and training programs in every law enforcement agency in the country.

REFLECTING ON HIS SON'S life, cut short by an impulsive, uninformed Bainbridge Island police officer, Bill Ostling told the local newspaper, "He liked all the same things everyone else does. He just saw the world differently, . . . I cannot comprehend why they ever pulled the trigger."[23]

5

A SCARED COP IS A
DANGEROUS COP

EVER WITNESS A POLICE officer "lose it"? I'm talking about a screaming, profanity-laced fit while directing traffic around an accident, or at the end of a high-speed pursuit, or while trying to control an unruly crowd. Or to show Sandra Bland who's in charge of Texas's highways. Many such cops are driven not by anger, though that's certainly the visible manifestation of what a witness perceives, but rather by another common human emotion: fear.

During his grand jury testimony, Ferguson police officer Darren Wilson spoke of Michael Brown's threat level. Citing Brown's size, strength, and facial expressions, Wilson characterized the teenager as a "demon," with the strength of Hulk Hogan.[1] The officer convinced the grand jury that had he not shot the young man, Brown would have killed him. In short, Wilson admitted he was scared.

You may ask: Who wouldn't be?

Well, how about a confident, well-trained police officer with sound tactical and de-escalation and communication skills? One who has mastered his fears, who refuses to let anxieties, or a lack of impulse control, warp his perceptions and cloud his judgment—an officer who declines to *demonize* the people he encounters.

Fear is normal, and necessary—a lifesaver, in fact. And, truth be told, the job of today's police officer is more dangerous, that is, objectively scarier, than it was just ten or twenty years ago. Today's cop encounters far more guns—often in the hands of individuals who should never be allowed near a firearm. There is more "rampage violence" today (witness mass shootings in Aurora, Newtown, Charleston, Roseburg, and on and on). In police work, the next threat is just around the corner.

Apprehensive if not outright scared, most new cops wonder: How will I handle my first traffic stop? Arrest? How will I behave during a robbery in progress? A car crash? If it comes to it, will I be able to pull my gun, and, if necessary, squeeze its trigger? How will I perform in a fistfight, or a knife attack? Or in response to a gun-toting madman out to kill children? Fear lurks in each of these and myriad other real-world scenarios.

As it should: The absence of fear suggests a mental imperfection, one that can get a cop, or an innocent citizen, killed.

Yet the discipline of recognizing and managing one's fears is not taught in the police academy. Perversely, recruits are taught the opposite. They're taught to be afraid, very afraid. In defensive tactics and other courses, they listen to true-life stories as told by those who have been there. And they are shown actual car cam, helmet cam, body cam, and YouTube footage of brother and sister officers who've been bludgeoned, stabbed, shot, run over by 4,000-pound automobiles.

It's not that new cops shouldn't know the truth about the job's dangers, it's that they should know the truth, the whole truth, and much more than the truth: they should learn the value of knowledge, and wisdom, and self-discipline. You see, not every situation is dangerous, much less life threatening.

In fact, fatal assaults on police officers are statistically rare. The FBI reports that in each year over the past decade, an average of fifty-one (of almost 1 million) officers were feloniously killed. True, 57,000 were assaulted in the line of duty, but only about 25 percent of those incidents resulted in injury. These figures are impressively low when one considers that the nation's cops interact with citizens some 63 million times a year. That means that officers are assaulted in roughly 0.09 percent of all interactions, injured in 0.02 percent, and killed in 0.00008 percent.[2]

Policing has always been a much safer occupation than most believe. Indeed, police work does not crack the top ten of the country's deadliest occupations. Here's the 2013 mortality list:

1. Loggers
2. Fishers and related fishing workers
3. Aircraft pilots and flight engineers
4. Roofers
5. Refuse and recyclable material collectors
6. Mining machine operators
7. Driver/sales workers and truck drivers
8. Farmers, ranchers, and other agricultural managers
9. Electrical power-line installers and repairers
10. Construction laborers[3]

Firefighters consistently rank higher on the list than police officers, typically owing to multiple fatalities at particular kinds of fire scenes such as large commercial, industrial, or apartment-complex fires, wild fires, and the like. During my first month on the job in Seattle, four city firefighters lost their lives in a warehouse fire when a floor collapsed beneath them (an insurance-motivated arson; the killer, jailed in 1995, is due to be released from prison in 2018). By contrast, only two Seattle police officers lost their lives during my six years there, and there has not been an SPD line-of-duty death since 2009. Responding to the 9/11 World Trade Center attacks, 343 firefighters and paramedics perished, and twenty-three NYPD and thirty-seven Port Authority officers lost their lives.[4]

None of this minimizes the risks that police officers take every day of their working lives. Like firefighters, they are paid to put their lives on the line in order to help make their communities safer. But unlike firefighting, injuries and deaths in police work often come as a result of violence. Not many are willing to enter a line of work where, literally, some people are out to get you.

Nevertheless, I have observed a disturbing trend in my old job, namely, the tendency of police officers to put their own well-being above the safety of those they have been hired to protect and serve.

It's understandable, not excusable.

Abraham Maslow's classic hierarchy of human needs puts "safety" (namely, protection from the elements, security, order, law, stability, freedom from fear) second only to biological and physiological needs (air, food, drink, shelter, warmth, sleep).[5] In short, everyone, except those with suicidal ideation, wants to survive. Fear of death, particularly at the hands of another, is a primal emotion.

But there is something wrong with a person entering the police service whose strongest motive is not to serve, not to protect, but to "make it home at the end of shift."

Ask police officers why they become cops. The answer, before they hired on, is to "help people," "to serve my community," "to give back," or some such other variation on the altruism theme. (Me? Newly married, at twenty, I needed a job. And SDPD was hiring.) Of course, some will tell you they became a cop for different, distinctive reasons: "My dad was a cop," "I like working outdoors," "I like the job security of civil service," "I like the promotional opportunities," "I want to earn a detective's shield and solve mysteries," "I want to become NYPD commissioner, just like Tom Selleck, and preside over a brood of colorful cops at lively, shop-talk Sunday dinners," and so forth. (Psychological screening is now largely successful at blocking those who lumber through the door wanting to "eat raw meat and hit people.")

But I've never heard a police officer say, "I became a cop so that I could get home safely at the end of my shift."

IRONICALLY, A POLICE OFFICER improves his or her chances of surviving—not just a night's work but an entire career—by investing in an idea larger than a designated stretch of work known as a "shift."

Here's the pared-down premise: If you're a cop invested in working, lawfully, to help make the streets safe; if you've established a trusting, mutually beneficial partnership with the people on your beat; if you're well trained, and in possession of sound, job-related knowledge and skills; and if you're an alert, confident, psychologically hardy, emotionally resilient soul, you are far more likely to make it home at the end of shift than the cowed, twitchy cop whose obsession is to survive.

The trick is to recognize and master our fears, not paint over them in fashionable shades of macho and bravado. To that end, it is essential to understand the physiology and the anatomy of fear, how it works in our brains and in our bodies, how it affects our perceptions and influences the decisions we make.

Wanting to understand more about the extent to which heavy-handed cops are scared cops, I came home from work one day as Seattle's police chief and asked Lisa, my then wife and a clinical psychologist who had worked with cops in San Diego, for a lecture on the subject. (I'd found myself shaking my head that yet another otherwise caring and competent cop had gone ballistic on a nonviolent arrestee.) Lisa consented, and I took a seat at her feet, legal pad in hand.

"Fear begins," she began, "with a stressful stimulus. Say, a rookie cop is working alone in a high-crime area. A woman flags her down, tells her there's a stranger in the neighborhood, a big man in his twenties who seems to be casing the area. The complainant last saw him two or three minutes ago. The officer gets a good description, puts it out over the air, and sets out to see if she can locate the guy.

"Around the corner and halfway down the block, she spots a guy matching the stranger's description. He's walking slowly down the sidewalk, glancing into parked cars. The officer calls it in, gets out of her car, and approaches the man. He's agitated, wants to know why the hell she stopped him. She tries to calm him down but it seems to make matters worse—he's getting angrier by the second. Suddenly, he goes for his waistband." Lisa stopped, like she was finished.

"Yeah?"

"Yeah, what?"

"What the hell's the rest of the story?"

"That's it."

"That's *it*? You can't leave me hanging. What happens next?"

"I don't know, make it up. You didn't ask for a tale, you asked how fear works in the body. Would you agree that the officer—let's make her a rookie, on her own for the first time, has never pulled her gun on duty— would you agree she might be frightened?"

I tell myself I wouldn't be scared—as an experienced cop I'd be alert, poised to act. But a brand new cop? Afraid? "Sure, of course."

"Okay, let's take it from there. She doesn't know whether the guy's going for a gun. If he is, and she doesn't act, she's toast. Scary, yes?"

"Yep."

"Okay. So let's inject a tracer into her brain, from the precise moment she experiences the stressful stimulus, that fight-or-flight moment." As my personal shrink went on to describe the "steps" in the process of how fear works, I began diagramming, furiously. "We start with the fact that there are two neural paths involved in triggering and tracing fear, and that although they process data simultaneously, one moves quicker (processing with less precision) than the other (more precise processing). These two paths are important because, in the case of our officer, she could be toes-up if she relies exclusively on the slower, more accurate path. Not that she gets to pick; the entire process of fear operates unconsciously." She explained the two paths. When she finished, my diagram looked something like page 73:

Whew! And to think, all of this is accomplished in less than a second. I thanked Lisa and, as payment, poured her a glass of lightly chilled Sauvignon blanc. I then set about cleaning up the diagram, correcting all the misspelled physiological and chemical terms, and studying the most important flowchart of my academic and professional career, not to mention my personal life.

Is it necessary for police officers to be informed about the neural pathways, the glands, the other structures, all those behavior-governing chemicals in their brains? Probably not. But officers who have a solid theoretical and practical foundation of how fear works in their bodies, and who are repeatedly, prudently exposed in their training to realistic, fear-inducing situations, will become increasingly adept at (1) recognizing when their bodies are telling them, Hey, I'm scared here!, and (2) developing personal mastery over how they respond to the fear.

The best way forward, I'm convinced, is through formal, disciplined, adult learning, both in the classroom and in the "lab"—mock scenes—using an experiential approach (hands-on, technology-boosted, role-playing simulations).

Triggering event (stressful stimulus)
A perceived threat is registered by one or more of the senses (sight, sound, touch, smell, taste) which . . .

Sends this sensory data to the **Thalamus** which forwards it to the . . .

Amygdala (located on the fast, less precise path) and, to the . . .

Sensory cortex (In the slow, more precise path) for interpretation (what do the data mean?) which passes the data along to the . . .

Hippocampus to establish context (Is this new? Have I seen, experienced this before? The **Hippocampus** essentially asks, "Is it safe?")

If yes, it tells the **Amygdala** to back off the fight-or-flight response.

If no, it tells the **Amygdala** to stay in the game, at which point . . .

The **Hypothalamus** activates two systems . . .

The **Sympathetic Nervous System** and the **Adrenal Cortical System,** which in turn activate another two systems, the: **Glands** and **Smooth Muscles,** and the **Adrenal Medulla,** which . . .

Releases **Norepinephrine** and **Epinephrine,** which . . .

Combine in the **Bloodstream**, along with the product of the second of the **Hypothalamus's** activation of that second system, namely, . . .

The **Adrenal-Cortical System,** which releases . . .

CRH (corticotropin-releasing hormone), which activates the . . .

Pituitary gland, causing it to secrete the hormone . . .

ACTH, which arrives at the . . .

Adrenal Cortex, where approximately thirty hormones are released, finally, combining in the bloodstream with the contents of the **Adrenal Medulla.**

Moreover, it's long been recognized that the most effective training is that which fully engages the student-officer in the three basic learning "domains": cognitive, affective, and psychomotor. What does the officer need to think, to know, for example, about the law, or his or her department's use-of-force policy? What does the officer need to feel, or appreciate about the Constitution, community policing, the protection and preservation of human life? Finally, what skills—technical and interpersonal—does the officer need in order to load and fire a 9 mm semiautomatic, or to safely de-escalate a tense, touch-and-go situation?

When it comes to mastering one's fears, and confronting the existential fear of death or injury on the job (thereby "abandoning" one's co-workers or loved ones, or both), there can be no substitute for sophisticated, well-designed simulations that trigger, in a safe environment, the actual fear one experiences in the face of real-world threats: a high-speed pursuit, a shoot/no-shoot situation, a suspect hell-bent on doing in a cop. It's one of the reasons military and commercial flight instructors put their students in a simulator.

No one who saw the footage will ever forget it.

It started with a March 3, 1991, early morning chase on the Foothill Freeway in the San Fernando Valley of Los Angeles, a California Highway Patrol (CHP) unit in hot pursuit of a high-speed Hyundai containing three occupants. Several minutes later, the driver left the freeway and ran a red light, nearly causing an accident before coming to a stop at Osborne Street and Foothill Boulevard, near the entrance to Hansen Dam Park. Seconds later, three LAPD cars converged on the scene as a police chopper hovered overhead.

The two CHP officers, husband and wife team Melanie and Tim Singer, approached the car first, guns drawn. They ordered the occupants from the car. The two passengers complied, then dropped face down on the ground, as directed. But the driver remained behind the wheel. Melanie Singer shouted at him a second time. He stepped out, smiling, and "dancing." He waved at the helicopter overhead and, according to Singer's subsequent testimony, "grabbed his right buttock with his right hand . . . and shook it at me." At last, he complied with her order to lie on the ground. As the officer approached, gun still drawn, to make the arrest, one of the LAPD officers, Sergeant Stacey Koon, shouted at her to, "Stand back, stand back! We'll handle this!"

Handle it they did, as witnessed by no fewer than twenty other officers now present. And by local resident George Holliday.

Mr. Holliday, awakened by the sirens, the shouting, the flashing reds and blues, and sensing the magnitude of the moment, stepped out onto his balcony and trained his new SONY Handycam on the scene, thereby capturing for eternity LAPD officers Sergeant Stacey C. Koon, Laurence Powell, Timothy Wind, and Theodore Briseno as they tased, beat, kicked, and stomped the driver into submission. There were fifty-six baton blows alone, the majority delivered by Powell.[6]

The Rodney King beating became a catalytic moment in the life of the institution, and of the nation.

Within hours of the acquittals of the officers in state court, Los Angeles was engulfed in a firestorm of protest. Sixty-three people died (as confirmed in later research by the *Los Angeles Times*), 2,383 were injured, over 12,000 were arrested, and 3,100 property owners suffered $1 billion in damages.[7]

Question: What if the cops who brutalized Rodney Glen King had received hours of behind-the-wheel training, both on the asphalt driving course and in a realistic simulator? Imagine their bodies hooked up to sensors that monitored and measured their heart rates, galvanic skin response, blood pressure, even the chemicals surging through their brains and bodies. Imagine if over and over in their training they were subjected to the stressors involved not only during a high-speed pursuit but at the conclusion of that pursuit. Imagine expert, multidisciplinary instructors evaluating the officers' knowledge: not only their skills, poise, and self-discipline, including particularly their ability to maintain, or reclaim, their composure, but also their methods of de-escalating the situation and their arrest procedures.

Critics, "realists," point to the costs of such state-of-the-art technology and training. They're right, of course. Such an investment doesn't come cheap. But those doubters should be directed to the previously noted financial burdens of a single high-profile, high-consequences incident. In addition to the deaths, injuries, and property damage stemming from the L.A. riots, Los Angeles taxpayers settled with Mr. King to the tune of $3.8 million and paid attorneys' fees of $1.7 million.[8] More recently, four separate cities settled with the families of Eric Garner ($5.9 million), who was choked to death by an NYPD officer attempting to arrest him for selling "loose" cigarettes; James Boyd ($5 million), an unarmed homeless man killed when he was shot six times by two Albuquerque officers; Freddie Gray ($6.4 million), who died as a result of a severed spine caused by the use of excessive force and intentional recklessness by the Baltimore Police Department (BPD); and the unarmed Ricardo Diaz Zeferino ($4.7 million), who was shot and killed by Gardena, California, police as he was looking for his brother's stolen bicycle. Best estimate of yearly city and county payouts for police misconduct, nationwide? In the neighborhood of $1 billion.[9]

That kind of money could buy a whole lot of top-quality equipment for advanced training. Which, I'm convinced, would dramatically curtail reckless police pursuits, rash decision-making, and excessive force by officers so juiced by the turbocharged chemicals coursing through their bodies that they can't see straight or think straight. Or, often enough, shoot straight.

BUT, WHAT IF THE behavior of reckless or abusive officers was not caused by fear but something less benign? What if, apart from or in addition to any fear they may have been experiencing, they were under the influence of another emotion? *Sadism*, for example. Or *racism*.

What if they beat Rodney King for the pure, bigoted joy of it?

With at least one of the officers, Laurence Powell, such a case could be argued. Powell made statements both before and after the beating that would come back to haunt him, hurt the defense of the officers, and taint the LAPD for many years to come.

Just before responding to the CHP chase, Powell had cleared from a domestic violence call involving African Americans. He typed on the mobile data terminal in his car that the scene was right out of *Gorillas in the Mist*.

He was equally forthcoming when after the King debacle, during which he delivered most of the fifty-six baton blows, he wrote on the car's computer, for all his fellow officers to see, "I haven't beaten anyone this bad in a long time."[10]

It doesn't sound like Powell was frightened, more like he took great delight in expounding racist views and crushing skulls. One would hope that Mr. Powell, now working in the computer industry and reportedly living in the San Diego area, spent his two years in federal prison in sober self-reflection, pondering the damage he'd done to a fellow human being, and to the people and treasury of Los Angeles. Not to mention the reputation of his department, his fellow officers, and the entire institution of American policing.

One would also hope the days of Rodney King–style beatings are over. Sadly, they are not. Queue up YouTube's "Top 10: Worst Police Beatings Caught on Tape," if you've got the constitution for it. A problem with the production is that it was released in 2013. Which means, theoretically, the entire list could well be replaced by ten new entries at any time.

How many of these beatings were triggered by fear? We'll never know.

Why? Because fear tends to be a socially unacceptable, indeed an inexpressible emotion within the cop culture. What you see is emphatically not what you get, much of the time. A scared cop overcompensates, which means he or she is likely to come across as loud, abrasive, arrogant. And mean—a bully.

And that leads to an inescapable conclusion: scared cops are a danger—to themselves, and to the people they've been hired to protect and serve.

One important, indeed vital means of reducing the fears our officers face is to make sure they are adequately armed and well equipped—for domestic peace keeping and community policing, not a military occupation. And that they are painstakingly trained and self-disciplined, in every respect, in the use of these weapons and tools.

6

THE RISE OF
POLICE MILITARISM

IT WAS 1967. MANY US cities were up in flames, and police officers were being targeted by sniper fire and Molotov cocktails. The Los Angeles Police Department responded with the creation of the nation's first official SWAT team. In the ensuing years, three high-profile SWAT missions would sear the imagery of this new police approach into the nation's consciousness.

On December 6, 1969, two days after Chicago police shot and killed the sleeping Black Panther Freddie Hampton on a drug raid, two Los Angeles patrol officers reported having observed Left Coast Panther Party members Paul Redd, "Duck" Smith, and Geronimo Pratt in possession of illegal firearms. The department obtained search warrants, and two hours before sunrise on December 9, SWAT hit Panther headquarters at Forty-first and Central in Compton. Five thousand shots were exchanged during the four-hour siege. Although accounts vary, three or four Panthers and three or four cops were wounded before the Panthers surrendered. Nobody died.[1]

Next up, the May 17, 1974, assault on a barricaded Symbionese Liberation Army house at East Fifty-fourth Street and Compton Avenue. It was a made-for-TV movie moment involving a kidnapping, a "brainwashed" heiress, a bank heist, a band of radical urban guerrillas, and armed fugitives on the run. The SLA shootout was captured, live, by multiple media sources and broadcast to millions. Following another prolonged gunfight, with LAPD SWAT employing six ten-man teams, each team packing a .243 bolt-action sniper rifle, two .223 semiautomatic rifles, and two shotguns, in addition to their duty-issued pistols, the battle came to an end when the house burned to the ground. No police officers were wounded, but all six SLA members perished. (The "reeducated" Patricia "Tanya" Hearst survived, as did two of her captors, Bill and Emily Harris, who were holed up in a hotel near Disneyland, watching the drama play out on TV.)[2]

Then came the February 28, 1997, North Hollywood Shootout, in which two heavily armed and armored bank robbers held LAPD officers at bay for forty-five minutes. The perpetrators were wielding illegally modified, fully automatic AK-47-type weapons and wearing body armor that protected them from the standard-issue sidearms of that era's first responders: .38-caliber revolvers or 9 mm semiautomatics, plus, in some patrol cars, a 12-gauge shotgun. The stickup men simply refused to go down, the cops' bullets pinging off their armor.

It was not until SWAT arrived, with specialized weaponry, and commandeered an armored truck to evacuate the wounded, that police were able to bring the incident to an end. Ultimately, the two robbers were killed, one by a self-inflicted gunshot. All other injured victims—eleven police officers and seven citizens—survived.[3] The bank job, the televised street gunfight, and the image of city police officers raiding private gun shops in search of bigger guns and replacement ammo, generated much soul-searching within law enforcement.

Were our street officers adequately armed and protected for this new level of urban threat? Were our fleets and armories sufficiently equipped and supplied with the latest armored vehicles and munitions?

And then there was Columbine, that awful day in 1999 on a Colorado high school campus—twelve students and one teacher dead, twenty-four wounded.[4] The incident raised similar questions, but not just about the adequacy of law enforcement's guns and ammo. Columbine forced police to examine a profound tactical question: Should first responders, that is, regular patrol officers, be trained, equipped, and instructed to go in after active shooters? If you're a parent of a threatened child you wouldn't hesitate: of course the first cops on the scene must take swift action, not merely stand by in a secure location and await the arrival of SWAT. Yet until Columbine, that's precisely what first responders were taught to do: stand by, even as bullets pierce young bodies and casualties mount.

So, following the Hollywood bank shootout, and particularly as a result of the Columbine massacre, police departments changed course. They understood that there are more guns than there are people in the United States, that any disaffected, angry, or emotionally disturbed person could stockpile all kinds of weapons and bring them, with murderous intent, to a workplace, a movie theater, an elementary school. By the early 2000s, departments began selecting, training, and equipping at least a portion of their regular patrol officers to move in as quickly as possible. Typically, the trunks of their patrol cars contained special weapons, personal protective gear, and breaching equipment: bolt cutters, battering rams, sledgehammers, pry bars, window punches.

These beat officers, often acting alone or in pairs, are now taught to move *toward* gunfire. As many citizens have told me, "You couldn't pay me enough." Yet, this is precisely one of the critical duties we do pay our police officers to carry out.

HOSTAGE-TAKING, BARRICADED INCIDENTS are not as common as the TV cop shows might suggest. In their report "War Comes Home: The Excessive Militarization of American Policing," the ACLU noted that of eight hundred selected SWAT deployments in 2011–2012 a mere 7 percent of the raids were for "hostage, barricade, or active shooter scenarios." Given that those very situations define the original raison d'être of SWAT, it is particularly troubling to note that "just under 80 percent [of SWAT missions] were to serve a search warrant, meaning eight in 10 SWAT raids were not initiated to apprehend a school shooter, hostage taker, or escaped felon . . . but to investigate someone still only suspected of committing a crime."[5]

Can you say "mission creep"?

Further, because of these predawn drug-warrant raids, the overall number of SWAT missions has been steadily increasing. According to Eastern

Kentucky University professor Peter Kraska, an expert on police militarization, there were only a few hundred SWAT incidents in the 1970s. By the early 1980s, the number had grown to 3,000 a year. And by 2005 (the last year of collected data), there were approximately 50,000. Surely that number is higher today? Kraska affirms it, actually. He told me that because of public criticism and political pressure, there has been some slackening in the growth of SWAT teams, and in the number of missions. Yet he believes that as a result of random sampling work conducted in 2010, a 60,000-mission estimate is an accurate reflection of today's reality.[6] Certainly, there were plenty of SWAT members among the ranks of Ferguson PD, St. Louis County, and Missouri Highway Patrol officers policing the protests in the aftermath of the Michael Brown shooting.

IN 1990, THE 101ST Congress enacted the National Defense Authorization Act, Section 1028, which empowered the secretary of defense to "transfer to Federal and State agencies personal property of the Department of Defense, including small arms and ammunition, that the Secretary determines is . . . suitable for use by such agencies in counter-drug activities and [is in] excess to the needs of the Department of Defense." In 1996, Congress tinkered with the act, and it became Section 1033.

Since the original bill, DOD has provided approximately $5 billion in military surplus to local law enforcement.[7]

To many observers, the rationale seems defensible, if not elegant: When the military no longer needs certain expensive instruments of war—night-viewing goggles, grenade launchers, bayonets, assault rifles, armored land vehicles, watercraft, planes, helicopters—why not hand them over to local law enforcement? City and county cops are, to repeat, the nation's foot soldiers in the War on Drugs. They are engaged in combat against armed enemy forces. No one expects front-line officers to take knives to a gunfight. And given the protection offered by an MRAP or the offensive firepower provided by an AK-47, the granting of such military surplus to state, county, and local law enforcement seems to make some sense in this crazy world.

Or does it?

Although there is a time and a place for military-like tactics, weaponry, and equipment, it's indisputable that the nation's police have often misused and abused the "military approach." In many jurisdictions there seems to be a "boys with toys" mentality: if you have these "toys" on hand, you want to use them, "play" with them. And where personal and organizational discipline is lacking, people get hurt, cops and citizens alike.

Unfortunately, the federal government's generosity has not helped.

In my home state alone, according to a blog piece by *Seattle Times* reporter Jonathan Martin—in which he poses the question, "How Did America's Police Become an Army?"—police forces in three small jurisdictions now possess eighteen-ton MRAPs, one for each force, at a value of $733,000 per vehicle. Seventeen local departments have enough "combat-quality" rifles to outfit virtually every officer. And at least one agency, with only seven cops in a county of 4,000, received eighteen combat rifles, six .45 automatics, and six 12-gauge shotguns.[8]

I find myself disagreeing with Martin about one implied criticism: "The Thurston County Sheriff, the Forest Service office in Clarkston and the U.S. Customs and Border Protection all tricked out their gyms, getting tens of thousands of dollars of weights, treadmills, elliptical machines, 'steppers' and recreational equipment." The number of significantly overweight, out-of-shape cops in this country is alarming: 80 percent, according to the FBI.[9] The importance of health, physical conditioning, and self-confidence in a high-stress job like police work cannot be overemphasized. It can spell the difference between life and death, and I certainly do not begrudge these agencies that fitness equipment.

I am inclined, however, to agree with Martin when it comes to other federal surplus items sought and delivered: "outdoor grills, TVs, fax machines, underwear, snowshoes, portable generators, scooters, a lawn mower."

And that's not the worst of it.

In Morven, Georgia, according to the Associated Press (AP), "the police chief [of a three-officer department, serving seven hundred residents] has grabbed three boats, scuba gear, rescue rafts and a couple of dozen life preservers . . . in [a town whose] deepest body of water [is] an ankle-deep creek."[10] Can't be too careful.

And in Rising Star, Texas, population 835, the police chief, the town's only full-time cop, scored $3.2 million worth of military surplus in just fourteen months. The AP obtained an inventory of the hundreds of items. A partial list: "nine televisions, 11 computers, three deep-fat fryers, two meat slicers, 22 large space heaters valued at $55,000 (when new), a pool table, 25 sleeping bags and playground equipment."[11]

The Rising Star police chief's own star was evidently not in ascendancy: he was fired, though not for abuses of the Section 1033 program (like the twelve pairs of binoculars gone missing).

DESPITE THE ALARM HAVING been sounded by Radley Balko in his groundbreaking 2013 book, *Rise of the Warrior Cop: The Militarization of America's Police Forces*, in which he provides numerous examples of the misuse of SWAT, and the resulting heartaches, the country did not fully awaken to the militarization issue until Ferguson.

The wall-to-wall coverage of city and county cops decked out in military combat uniforms, packing military weapons, sitting high atop MRAPs and other military vehicles, launching flashbang grenades or tear gas, and pointing sniper rifles at unarmed citizens seems finally to have gotten the attention of Congress. And some changes are afoot.

On May 18, 2015, President Obama flew to Camden, New Jersey, to announce changes in the federal giveaway.[12] Those bayonets and grenade launchers? Off the table. And don't even think about ordering a tracked armored personnel carrier, a.k.a. a tank. Given what we've seen our police departments use since then, the president's action is not nearly enough, of course.

We must urge additional changes: a further tightening of regulations, assurances of training for agencies receiving 1033 equipment, establishment of a schedule of inspections by the feds, at a minimum. This is all decades overdue. Although law enforcement officials and most politicians are wary about curtailing the government giveaway (Congress voted overwhelmingly in June 2015 against Representative Alan Grayson's legislation that would have ended Section 1033), some experts, such as Peter Kraska, believe the program should be jettisoned entirely. If a local political jurisdiction wants and can afford its own military-grade battlefield vehicles and wartime weaponry, let the local taxpayers weigh in on the propriety of such equipment—and foot the bill.

However, even with the efforts of congressional members Tom Coburn, Claire McCaskill, Rand Paul, and, particularly, Hank Johnson (who well before Ferguson was promoting his Stop Militarizing Law Enforcement Act),[13] I see little chance for sustained, meaningful reform as Congress bends in the direction of not offending law-and-order constituencies, especially the nation's police.

Armed violence, including mass shootings, can erupt anywhere: an elementary school in Newtown, Connecticut, a movie theater in Aurora, Colorado, a McDonald's in San Ysidro, a Jewish Federation Center in Seattle, the campus of Virginia Tech. The list goes on and on. There is a legitimate need for American communities, large and small (with smaller jurisdictions taking a vigilantly regulated regional versus city-centric approach), to have a SWAT capability to respond to these incidents.

But the sooner we recognize the need to end predawn military raids on the residences of low-level, nonviolent offenders—or suspected offenders—the safer our communities, and our officers, will be.

THE AMERICAN PEOPLE CAN help reduce gun deaths—and the resulting internal pressure for increased militarization of our police forces.

The United States has the distinction of being one of the most violent industrialized nations on earth. And our gun deaths (homicides, suicides, accidents), exceeding 30,000 a year, are steadily increasing. It won't be long before they surpass motor vehicle fatalities, which have been steadily declining (from a high of 51,093 in 1979 to 33,561 in 2012).[14] What part of this picture do we not understand? Motor vehicles are registered, their drivers licensed. Seatbelts are required. Automobile safety features are frequently updated, and traffic safety laws enforced. Thanks to new laws (and to the influence of Mothers Against Drunk Driving), driving while under the influence is a far less common occurrence today than in years past. Regulation has worked.

Firearms, on the other hand, are the only consumer product not regulated by the federal government. As Kristen Rand of the Violence Policy Center told a reporter, "Teddy bears get tested to make sure they can withstand use and abuse by kids, but guns don't get tested to make sure they don't go off when accidentally dropped."[15]

As I argued in my previous book, *Breaking Rank*, registering all firearms and licensing their owners (contingent on passing a certified gun-safety course) would go a long way toward making America a much safer country. Yes, I know the argument: criminals don't obey the law; only the law-abiding comply with regulations. What this argument does not take into account is that a cop who runs across an unregistered firearm in the possession of an unlicensed individual—you may be sure it'll happen, often—can arrest that individual. And quite likely make a case on other unsolved crimes.

And, yes, I understand that millions of Americans own guns for protection—against criminals, against the ostensible threat of some future totalitarian government determined to gut our civil liberties and, in the process, erase the Second Amendment's right to bear arms. (Sorry, I just don't believe President Obama is out to grab guns; fear that he might do just that turned out to be the best thing to have happened to gun manufacturers and retailers, and the National Rifle Association.) But think about it. Scarcely a day goes by when we don't hear about a five-year-old pointing daddy's .357 magnum at his little sister and pulling the trigger. For all the success of the NRA in zealously protecting gun rights—and steamrolling faint-hearted politicians—the United States continues to lead the world not only in mass murders but in unintentional firearm deaths. For that reason alone, it's unimaginable that anyone would recommend a semiautomatic in the book bag or top right-hand drawer of a schoolteacher's desk. Even cops, who carry guns every day of their lives, have been known to put a slug into a computer in the squad room, the roof of their patrol car, or a fellow officer ... accidentally.

The problem is not too few guns; the problem is too many guns, where they don't belong. Implementing mandatory gun-safety courses (a fitting, traditional role of the NRA), registration, licensing, and, yes, better enforcement of current firearms laws—along with vastly improved mental-health services—will go a long way toward reducing gun tragedies.

SUCH IMPLEMENTATION WILL ALSO go a long way toward helping our cities look and feel less like a battlefield, which certainly contributes to the occupational mentality of too many of our police forces. Working together, police and communities can transform neighborhoods. Think Fort Apache in the Bronx half a century ago: vacant fields, burned-out abandoned buildings, crushing poverty. All that is now replaced by new apartment buildings and single-family homes—a diverse, healthy American neighborhood.

Not a war zone.

7

TOOLS OF THE TRADE: USE AND ABUSE

In order to reduce police officers' on-the-job risks (they'll never be eliminated) and to help them get the job done safely, lawfully, and humanely, the people they serve must support the proper use of state-of-the-art tools and tactics. In my experience both in San Diego and in Seattle, and from what I see around the country, it is almost always a violation of policy, poor training, misguided tactics, or a bias toward bigotry or brutality—in other words, the misuse of tools, not the tools themselves—that gets people killed, and cops in trouble.

This chapter may be difficult for some readers to reconcile, ideologically, with previous and forthcoming chapters on police work. But its message, which is utilitarian and "boots on the ground" (if you'll excuse the paramilitarism), is critical both to understanding and to fixing the real-world problems of America's police.

Just exactly what are those mysterious items arrayed around a cop's midsection? What's sitting in the passenger compartments and in the trunks of police cruisers? In the armory back at headquarters? What's their purpose? How and when are they employed?

If the police belong to the people, the people should know the answers to these questions. In their proper application, these tools are designed to help keep police officers *and* the community safe. And the more the community understands and supports its officers' legitimate, proper, and prudent use of these tools, the likelier that will happen.

OCCASIONALLY, A POLICE OFFICER will find himself or herself in a life-or-death situation, an unanticipated battle for survival in which "rules" give way to raw instinct. Before we embark on our inventory of police equipment, I ask you to picture yourself as that cop, in that moment:

> You've pulled up to the scene of a domestic-violence call at 3:00 a.m. You're on the front porch, talking with a woman who's been severely beaten. Her face is swollen, bruised, and bloodied. "He said if he can't have me, no one can," she says, through her terror and tears. "He ran out of the house after I called 911."
>
> "Who's 'he'?" you ask.
>
> "My boyfriend, *ex*-boyfriend. He—" Glancing over your shoulder, she screams and darts back into the house, the door slamming behind her.
>
> Bolting out of the darkness, the ex-boyfriend grabs you from behind, throws you to the ground, and sucker punches you. Then goes for your gun and screams into the night, "I'm gonna fucking kill you both!"
>
> Woozy, unfocused, your jaw broken and throbbing, you nevertheless realize what's in store if he is successful in snatching your gun. You're unable to reach your Taser, baton, pepper spray . . .

Let's leave it there, pondering possible outcomes, and return to the conclusion of this story at chapter's end.

The Los Angeles Police Department has done a fine public service by including on its official website (www.lapdonline.org/lapd_equipment) a very comprehensive list of its vehicles, uniforms, equipment, and weapons, accompanied by color photos of each item. I highly recommend taking a look at the site if you'd like to picture any of the following:

Duty belt. All law enforcement agencies mandate the carrying of certain equipment for uniformed personnel. I don't know of any, however, that deny their officers at least a certain degree of flexibility when it comes to type, brand, or placement on the belt. The duty belt? A 2.25-inch heavy leather or nylon belt, strapped by leather or nylon "keepers" to one's regular trousers belt. If leather, it can come in high gloss, low gloss, or basketweave. Attached to it, in ever-increasing numbers, are a variety of tools and weapons—whose utility, types, and brands are a source of endless locker-room debates among cops.

In 1966, when I became a patrolman, there wasn't much to argue about. We were equipped with a plain black duty belt (known in those days as a "gunbelt"), a six-inch .38 Smith and Wesson revolver, handcuffs and a handcuff case, a baton and its ring holder. We paid, out of pocket, for everything but the gun and the baton; today, there's almost always a reasonable if not generous uniform allowance as part of the officer's compensation package.

Let's start with the one personal-carry item, above all others, most identified with cops: the sidearm. And the discussion should begin with the tactical context.

Most chiefs have heard it, usually in the aftermath of a controversial "officer-involved" shooting, often at an emotionally charged community meeting. "Couldn't you have fired a warning shot?" or "Why didn't you just shoot him in the leg?" or "Why not shoot the gun out of his hand?" To a layperson unfamiliar with safety tactics (and bullets and ballistics), these questions are reasonable. I've heard them all. To a street cop, they're irrational, the stuff of bad TV.

A *warning shot?* Might work, but it's more likely to trigger an armed person's own trigger-pull. *Shoot the opponent in the leg?* Not if you have a gun pointed at you. Cops are instructed to fire at "center mass"—the heart, the lungs, the vagus nerve (some are told: two to the chest, one to the head). In short, they are taught to *shoot to stop the threat.* (Not "shoot to kill," as my fellow recruits and I were instructed.) In theory, a shot to the legs could stop a threat, and it has been done. In practice, however, very few police officers are skilled enough or lucky enough to actually strike a thigh or a kneecap—at any distance. Even then, the threat of return fire is very real. *Shoot the gun out of his hands?* Please. That's a tactic best reserved for Saturday morning cartoons, or the dusty Westerns of yesteryear.

Semiautomatic pistols. The type of sidearm most common today is a 9 mm or .40-caliber "semiauto" (Glock, Smith and Wesson, Sig Sauer, Beretta, Ruger, Walther, H&K, and a few other less common brands). Semiautos feature magazines or "clips" that hold from ten to fifteen rounds (bullets), depending on the type, size of the weapon, and the caliber. By "racking" the slide, pulling back on the mechanism and releasing it, the first round is loaded into the chamber. The first shot requires a greater "trigger-pull," or pounds of pressure, than second and subsequent shots. It's the recoil of the weapon on initial firing that produces energy to advance the next and each new round "semiautomatically" into the chamber (with spent rounds ejected out of the weapon)—and with less need for trigger-pull strength (an issue for some cops). A semiauto requires the shooter to pull the trigger for each shot, unlike a fully automatic weapon that fires for as long as one keeps the trigger depressed.

In the 1970s and 1980s, most local law enforcement officers were still carrying "wheel guns," six-shot revolvers, essentially the same personal weapon carried by cops since the 1800s. However, by the mid-1980s, city and county police were being outgunned by heavily armed drug dealers and gangbangers intent on expanding markets, protecting profits, exacting revenge. These individuals, some in their early or preteens, were more than willing to engage police officers in running gun battles. When I arrived in Seattle in 1994, most patrol officers were still packing six-shooters. In one of my first actions, we converted to semiautomatics, preceded by an intensive, must-pass, two-day training program.

The NYPD, under Commissioner Ray Kelly, began phasing in 9 mm semiautos in the fall of 1993. The *New York Times* commented: "Mr. Kelly said the change should not be seen as a sign that the department is determined to keep pace in a kind of urban arms race."[1]

How else to interpret the commissioner's motive? In fact, making sure my cops were not outgunned was precisely my motive for adopting the new weapons. Police officers were dropping like flies, relatively speaking, as they attempted to do battle with better-armed criminals. The *Times* article went on to note that "Mr. Kelly is moving the country's largest police force into step with hundreds of other cities, including Houston, Miami and Washington, and also with the New York State police and the transit police. The Miami force uses ammunition clips that hold 15 rounds."[2]

Kelly conditioned adoption of the new weapons with two restrictions, reflecting the concern he'd held for years that semiautomatic pistols were simply too dangerous in an urban environment. First, he limited the rounds of each magazine to ten and, second, he ordered the trigger mechanisms tightened so that they would be more difficult to fire.

I would judge both of Kelly's preconditions as problematic. The virtue of a semiautomatic pistol is that it provides greater firepower for the officer. Limiting the number of rounds held in a magazine to ten unnecessarily jeopardizes officer safety and the safety of those our cops are sworn to protect. Imagine a first responder in a gun battle with a barricaded and active school shooter. Asking a cop to call "King's X," a time-out, in order to reload, because she's been authorized only four rounds more than she would have had in an old-fashioned revolver defeats the purpose of issuing a thirteen-, fourteen-, or fifteen-round semiautomatic weapon. Tightening the trigger pull? Same objection, plus another: some police recruits, mostly but not exclusively women, have struggled with a firearm that demands twelve to fifteen pounds of pressure in order to pull the trigger on the first shot (second and subsequent shots typically come in at around four pounds).

The Los Angeles County Sheriff's Department, successfully sued by a woman deputy who'd failed her firearms class, ostensibly because she was unable to muster the extra force needed to squeeze off that first round (with sufficient speed and accuracy), decided a few years ago to switch to a firearm with a lighter trigger pull (and three different grip sizes to fit different hand sizes). There have been problems, to be sure. In 2012, there were twelve accidental discharges, though none involved the new firearm. In 2013, there were eighteen, eight involving the new firearm. In 2014, there were a total of thirty accidental discharges, twenty-two involving the new gun.[3]

On a positive note, women recruits, whose firearms failure rate in the academy had been 6.4 percent, saw that rate drop to less than 1 percent. And firearms scores across the board went up dramatically.[4]

I side with firearms experts (I can shoot straight, but I'm most definitely not an expert) who contend that extensive, repetitive training is necessary to (1) learn to "index" one's trigger finger (that is, keep it off the trigger, out of the trigger guard, and parallel to the slide) unless ready to fire, (2) develop keen "muscle memory," (3) become intimately familiar with the features of one's personal sidearm, and (4) understand, at a visceral and cognitive level, when one is justified in pulling the trigger.

Hideaways. In May 1990, San Diego police officer Steve Staton stopped a motorist for a traffic violation on Interstate 805. As Exhibit A in the ongoing campaign to convince cops that there is no such thing as a "routine traffic stop," the driver, twenty-nine-year-old Mario Merino, immediately got out of his car, pulled a gun, and fired at the officer. Staton was struck multiple times in the back, but his vest stopped the rounds (leaving him with hideous bruises but no holes). Staton leaped over the guardrail and attempted to use it for cover in order to return fire. But Merino also jumped the railing and landed on the officer. He grabbed onto Staton's duty 9 mm and the fight was on. Staton tried wresting the gun away but was unable to do so. Knowing the gun wouldn't fire without its magazine in place, he tried to hit the release, but Merino's grip kept that from happening. In a fight for his life, his own gun pointed intermittently at his face, Staton muscled his way onto the suspect's back and pulled his hideaway pistol from inside his vest pocket. He fired eight times, ending the threat. And Merino's life.[5]

I never carried a hideaway, partly because the job simply wasn't as dangerous as it is today and partly because in those pre-bulletproof-vest days, the only logical place to hide it on a warm, jacketless day was in an ankle holster, and that rubbed me the wrong way. (I did carry an ankle-holstered .38 snub-nose as a chief and can attest that a gun on your ankle slows you down in a foot chase.)

Statistically, the chances that a patrol cop would need a hideaway gun are quite small (not to mention impossible to calculate because of gaping deficiencies in national reporting practices). But tell that to Steve Staton.

There is, of course, a distinction between a "hideaway" and a "throw-down" gun, which has had the serial number filed off. The former refers to a legitimate safety practice, the latter to covering one's ass in a bad shooting. Cops who carry throw-downs are betting they'll be involved in a bad shooting, and therefore in need of a Big Lie.

Holsters. Yes, holsters. This is a significant safety issue for police officers. Any jurisdiction that skimps on providing the very finest holster—namely, one that provides maximum weapon retention while allowing for a smooth and speedy draw—is compromising the safety of its police officers.

Tasers. Developed over five years (1969–1971) by Jack Cover, a NASA researcher, the Taser, in its several forms, has made a dramatic addition to a police officer's "less-lethal" options.[6] There is no such thing as a purely "nonlethal" weapon, for any device carries potential for a fatal outcome, caused by misuse, dumb luck, or medical misfortune. (By the fall of 2015, forty-seven officer-involved deaths following use of the Taser had been recorded for that year. Medical examiners had produced findings in nineteen of them: seven homicides, five "undetermined," six "accidental," and one "natural causes.")[7] When fired, the pistol-like, compressed-nitrogen weapon propels two electrodes, dart-like and barbed, which produce "neuromuscular incapacitation" via electric shock. Those manufactured for police use have a range of up to thirty-five feet.

Alternatively, the weapon can be used in "drive-stun" mode, essentially a "pain compliance" technique (along with "come-along" holds and other interventions)—based on the assumption that enough pain will put an end to an assailant's aggression, or at least provide time to apply the cuffs. Drive-stun, which does not incapacitate, per se, is accomplished by placing the weapon against the individual's body (preferred locations: collarbone area, forearms, outer thighs) and activating the charge. TASER International makes four models, with varying levels of voltage and wattage. Most police agencies opt for the most powerful, the TASER®Advanced M26c or the TASER® X26c, each of which discharges 50,000 volts at twenty-six watts.

There are other companies out there but, at the moment, TASER has pretty much cornered the conducted electrical weapons (CEWs) market.

(They're making big inroads into the burgeoning police "body-cam" market, as well, which prompted a colleague to ask whether the company is "spreading disease," electrical shocks, then offering to sell "medicine" in the form of devices that capture evidence of the practice.)

What is the effect on a person who's been shocked? In a word, incapacitation. In two words: incapacitation and *pain*. The electrical signal overrides the central nervous system and causes muscle tissues to contract uncontrollably. These spasms, accompanied by a sensation of vertigo, are sufficient to cause even the healthiest physical specimen to collapse into the fetal position. The person will be in a dazed condition for several minutes, plenty of time to take the offender into custody and end a threat. Most cops, reporters, and critics who have requested or have been required in their training to experience the Taser report that it "hurt like a sonofabitch" and that they remained conscious and cognizant the whole time.

The TASER company maintains that use of the weapon "does not cause permanent damage or long-term aftereffects to muscles, nerves or other body functions," including cardio functions—even if the person shocked is equipped with a pacemaker or an internal defibrillator. The company cites several medical studies (particularly one by Wake Forest in 2007, and another in 2012) to support this claim. Dr. James Jauchem, former senior research physiologist with the US Air Force's Directed Energy Division and an expert in CEWs, agrees with others whose research concludes that though Taser-related deaths are rare they do occur, and almost always in people with preexisting cardiovascular disease or who are sufficiently under the influence of certain drugs that the actual cause of death is an overdose. Skepticism and continuing research are very much in order,[8] even as "success stories" are worth noting.

Security-camera footage from August 8, 2015, of an apartment complex parking lot in Port Clinton, Ohio, captures a bare-shirted young man menacing people with a large knife and refusing police orders to drop it. As the officers approach him from behind, he turns and advances on them, again refusing their orders to drop the knife. They tase him and he falls face forward, completely unable to move. The uniformed officers rush him, and one kicks the knife away. They lift him to his feet and handcuff him.[9]

From what I see in the footage, the cops would have been legally justified in shooting the man. This is a good example of how and when a Taser should be used.

But there are too many examples of how and when a Taser should not be used—enough to raise the fundamental question, among prominent critics, of whether there is a place for the CEWs in modern police work.

For starters, a police officer should never use a CEW against a person whose passive resistance to arrest or lawful command poses no physical threat to the officer, or anyone else. A handcuffed prisoner who is merely mouthing off does not constitute justification for use of a CEW. Use under these and similar circumstances is tantamount to torture and, with few exceptions, should be grounds for dismissal.

CEWs should not be used on pregnant women. The severe muscle contractions caused by the shock of the weapon can abort the pregnancy or cause serious injury to the unborn. Given that virtually any female from, say, eleven to sixty, or older, could be pregnant, wouldn't it be prudent to just ban the use of CEWs against girls and women? No. Keep in mind that a Taser is an alternative to lethal force, and that females of virtually any age are capable of life-threatening attacks. Police officers cannot be expected to stop in the middle of such a dangerous situation to try to ascertain whether a subject is pregnant. But, where they know of a woman's pregnancy, they must use alternative means to overcome the threat.

Because virtually every standing, running, skateboarding, rollerblading, bicycling, or motorcycling person incapacitated by a CEW is going to fall, officers have an obligation to consider the physics and topography of anticipated use. Bridges and freeway overpasses, for example, are extremely dangerous locations. The literature is replete with examples of individuals who survived the neuromuscular incapacitation of a CEW, only to die from injuries suffered from a resulting fall.

The weapon should not be used around any flammable material, including gasoline and gasoline vapors, butane, meth labs, and so on.

Nor should CEWs be used on the mentally ill, which, naturally, begs the question of how a police officer knows in advance of a person's mental illness. The best in-service training in the world will not equip police officers to render expert diagnoses of bipolarity, schizophrenia, paranoia, or any other form of mental illness. But that doesn't stop people from "acting crazy" or citizens from calling in to report a "mentally ill" or "emotionally disturbed" individual. Research does confirm the need for officers to be aware that some mentally ill people, including those threatening suicide, have died as a result of being tased. There are reports, for example, of a woman stabbing herself after being shocked and of a man putting a gun to his own head, then pulling the trigger after he'd been tased.

In 2014, the *Miami New Times* conducted a yearlong investigation into "Taser abuse" by the area's three largest police agencies. The results paint a disturbing picture:

> The previously unreported event [the tasing of a "dirty and disheveled" homeless man, cowering defenseless in a market, an incident that did not lead to an arrest, or even produce a report] is just one of dozens of troubling taserings . . .
>
> In less than eight years, Miami Police, Miami-Dade Police, and Miami Beach Police officers have used their Tasers more than 3,000 times. At least 11 men have died after being tasered by cops during that same period, including five in the past 16 months. On average, at least one person per day is tasered by police.
>
> Some of those tasered were violent criminals. But most were unarmed, many posed no threat to police, and some were suspected of minor infractions such as loitering or skateboarding.[10]

Amnesty International, which for years has campaigned against the misuse of Tasers, examined hundreds of US cases resulting in the deaths of people shocked by CEWs.[11] Its 2008 report analyzed autopsy reports in ninety-eight cases. In 2012, the organization cited two particularly troubling death cases, the first involving a forty-three-year-old unarmed motorist in San Bernardino County who died after three officers tased him as many as sixteen times (repeat applications, or even one shock used on those with heart conditions or who are under the influence of certain drugs, raise dramatically the risk of a fatal outcome).

The second case involved Roger Anthony, of Scotland Neck, North Carolina. The sixty-one-year-old Anthony was disabled, prone to seizures, and hard of hearing, and lived alone in an independent-living community. John Turner, a cop for only a month, responded to a call that Anthony had perhaps fallen from his bicycle and might have injured himself. After spotting him pedaling down the street, Turner flipped on his emergency lights and activated his siren, but Anthony did not respond. Turner got out of his car, yelled at him, then shot him with his Taser. Anthony fell off the bike. He was transported to the hospital but arrived brain-dead. He was taken off life support the next day.

"The best we've been able to determine is that he offered no threat," Scotland Neck mayor James Mills told WRAL.com.

Given these and many other deaths and injuries directly or indirectly related to CEWs, we should question whether Tasers even belong in the tool kits of today's police officers.

I believe they do. For two reasons.

First, even if TASER claims are exaggerated (the company maintains its CEWs have saved over 152,000 lives), there is no question that many deaths and injuries, to officers and suspects alike, have been prevented.

Second, although the TASER company has been undeniably persuasive in its corporate marketing and successful in its worldwide sales, citizen critics have also helped to make CEWs a growth industry. (Only a handful of departments in the 1970s and 1980s equipped their officers with Tasers; today only a few do not.) Early support for the tool came particularly from community groups angry over the killing of unarmed black men by white cops. At or near the top of their lists of demands: "adoption of 'nonlethal' weapons."

It is worth noting that Ferguson officer Darren Wilson said in his grand jury testimony that he chose not to be equipped with a Taser. He stated that the tool "is not the most comfortable thing. They are very large, I don't have a lot of room in the front for it to be positioned."

Wilson is a big man, six-feet four inches, 210 pounds. It's not hard to understand why, with everything else on his duty belt—mace or pepper spray, retractable baton, handcuffs, his handgun, spare ammo—he wouldn't want to add yet another item to the mix. Yet it's hard not to speculate on the possibility of an entirely different outcome had he "elected" to carry—and use—a Taser against Michael Brown on that August afternoon in 2014.

I have no problem with the concept of all police officers—large, small, strong, not-so-strong, big-handed, small-handed—generally being allowed to choose from a menu of options besides their own less-lethal, agency-authorized weapons. But at some point the agency must take a stand: if Tasers save lives, everyone carries one, "comfort" be damned. Besides, wouldn't Darren Wilson have more room around his midsection than, say, a 160-pound co-worker?

We don't need to eliminate the Taser, a demonstrably valuable tool, but we do need to continue research, development, and refinement of this less-lethal technology, along with rigorous training and strict, well-regulated, well-supervised policies and procedures for use.

At a minimum, every law enforcement agency should have in place a policy mandating, in every possible instance, the issuance of a loud, verbal warning—"TASER! TASER! TASER!"—before pulling the trigger. As with the racking of a shotgun, the warning itself might cause a threatening or resisting person to see the value of surrendering.

Emphatically not recommended is the cowardly, disgraceful vernacular language that Texas trooper Brian Encina used with a nonthreatening Sandra Bland: "I will light you up!"

An officer too lazy or unskilled in the application of a CEW—and other less-lethal tools and techniques, including de-escalation tactics—needs to correct those deficiencies, or find another occupation.

Finally, there is only one form of discipline for an officer who uses a CEW as a means of torture: termination and prosecution, to the fullest extent of the law.

WORKING OUR WAY AROUND the duty belt of a patrol officer, past the handgun, past the Taser, we come to a chemical agent: a holstered canister of Mace or, more likely, pepper spray.

Mace. The original Mace, invented by Allan Lee Litman in 1965, after a colleague of his wife had been mugged on a Pittsburgh street, is essentially a small container of CN tear gas (phenacyl chloride).[12] Dissolved in hydrocarbon solvents, packaged in an aerosol can, and sold as "Chemical Mace," the product is a "lachrymatory" agent, meaning it produces tears, pain, a runny nose, and temporary blindness.

Pepper spray. The gold standard for personal chemical agents, OC (oleoresin capsicum), or pepper spray, is the top choice of police departments in the twenty-first century. Replacing standard Mace (CN gas) in the 1990s, for the most part, its active ingredient is capsaicin, a chemical found in chili peppers. Like the original mace, it irritates the eyes, causing tears and pain, along with temporary but convincing blindness—which incapacitates most combative people: generally, if you can't see, you can't fight. Pepper spray is mail carriers' first defense against aggressive dogs and, as I learned on a recent hike with a friend in Glacier Park, what bear-savvy hikers pack when on trails shared by grizzlies or black bears.

It is uncommon that a person sprayed with OC will put up much of a fight or attempt to escape. It is also uncommon for OC to cause death, although, as with Tasers, the chemical can be a contributing factor in deaths.

Triple-action pepper spray. Some pepper sprays also contain CN gas and a UV marking dye that can be helpful in both identification and subsequent prosecution.

Studies have shown that the effects of pepper spray, including the triple-action variety, can be far more severe than those of CN gas.[13] Those sprayed with OC have reported, for example, that they felt their eyelids, indeed their eyeballs, were boiling, blistering, literally "on fire." Blindness can last from fifteen to thirty minutes, and the burning sensation on the skin can last from forty-five to sixty minutes. Spasms, capable of producing uncontrolled coughing and difficulty breathing, are known to last up to fifteen minutes. All of this makes it essential that police officers who carry pepper spray be trained, skilled, and motivated in the art of "talking down" someone they've sprayed, encouraging them to breathe normally, for example. A water flush is of limited or no value, though some experts recommend baby shampoo to cut the oil resin. It is also marginally helpful to advise rapid blinking to produce more tears. Ultimately, time delivers the only real relief. Finally, those with asthma or other preexisting respiratory problems are at particularly high risk for complications.

Baton. Also carried on the duty belt is a police baton, a.k.a. billy club, nightstick, cudgel, stick, bat, truncheon, and so on. There are three types— straight stick, straight stick with side handle, and collapsible. Batons are made of wood, metal, rubber, or plastic and are put to essentially three purposes: crowd control; close-quarter hand-to-hand striking (offensive) or protection (defensive) moves; or rescue operations, for example, smashing a window to get to a trapped and or injured person. When not in use, the straight stick, averaging about two feet in length, rests in a ring attached to the duty belt. (I used to do what most other cops do when getting into the car, namely, slipped it out of its ring and nestled it onto the floorboard, hoping to remember it upon exiting.) The collapsible, expandable, or retractable baton (activated by a flick of the wrist) is roughly the same size as a straight stick when telescoped out, and about eight inches when collapsed. It rides in its own holster on the duty belt.

It was not until the 1960s that most police departments began issuing directives not to "brain" people with the standard-issue straight baton (wood when I signed on, high-impact, hardened plastic a year or two later). The SDPD and most other departments had made it clear by then that the baton, of whatever type, was to be used only in a jabbing or whipping motion, no full-force, overhanded blows to the skull—of the variety seen in Alabama in Selma, Montgomery, Birmingham. Or on prominent display during the 1968 Chicago "police riot" at the Democratic National Convention.

Numerous, more recent examples of the misuse of the police baton, many caught on cell-phone cameras, are instructive. From Puerto Rico to Stockton, California, from the NYPD to tribal police in North Dakota, we find evidence of cops beating nonresisting people with their batons.[14] Some footage shows officers holding people down as their fellow cops administer stick beatings, often about the head.

For years, strikes to the head or face (with the exception of *life-threatening* situations) have been outlawed by responsible agencies. Likewise for blows to the spine, groin, sternum. The striking motion—against preferred targets such as thighs, quads, and biceps—is a whiplike blow designed to produce pain, maybe even temporary paralysis. But not traumatic brain injury or bone fractures.

Flashlights. When you need light, you need light. Nighttime comes to mind. But so too does daytime: searching a drainpipe for an armed fugitive; scoping out carpeting on the oblique for a critical piece of trace evidence; looking for a lost child in a dark, abandoned building; even temporarily blinding and disorienting a dangerous suspect (if the officer happens to be carrying a high-powered LED flashlight). This latter technique was described by a Navy SEAL as the best way, short of a firearm, to stop someone on a rampage. If you've ever caught yourself in the extremely intense beam of a focused LED flashlight, you know what I'm talking about. In fact, I highly recommend that individuals concerned for their personal safety carry a small LED flashlight (of at least 100 lumens) at all times when they're out and about. Even during daylight hours.

There is a continuing debate within police circles over the carrying of long, heavy, batonlike flashlights, such as the Maglite or the Kel-Lite (nicknamed "Kill Light" by a number of officers back in the day). In fact, in 2007, the Los Angeles Police Department, under then chief Bill Bratton, who, disturbed by news video of his officers beating an auto theft suspect with two-pound flashlights, banned Maglites and other flashlights that can be used as a baton.

Bratton replaced these with the Pelican 7060, developed in a rare partnership between LAPD and the private company. The critically acclaimed LED flashlight retails for over $130—and, at under nine inches in length, is essentially incapable of being used as a baton. The new light was a response to criticism—and helicopter news footage—of a severe beating of an auto theft suspect in 2004 by an L.A. cop using a Maglite. The old policy allowed for use of the industrial-strength flashlight as a baton but only under "exigent circumstances." That's a sound policy: you don't go around smacking a person in the head with a two-pound, footlong flashlight. (Unless, and I can't say it too often, that person is a heartbeat from wresting your sidearm from its holster and turning it on you, or another person.)

Walkie-talkies. It's no exaggeration to call the walkie-talkie on an officer's duty belt a lifeline. Two-way portable radio communication (in base-
station to mobile-units form) was pioneered in 1923 by Senior Constable
Frederick Downie of the Victoria, Australia, police.[15] Today, car radios link
officers to one another as well as to a centralized communications center,
and steady improvements have made the modern portable UHF (versus
VHF) walkie-talkie much lighter and more reliable.

Yet, as recently as 9/11, emergency operations were severely hampered
by poor (or in some cases nonexistent) wireless communications. Officers
of the NYPD, for example, reported receiving ample notice on their walkie-
talkies to evacuate the North Tower, but the surviving firefighters in that
building said they received no such notice on their portables. There was
more than enough valor to go around that terrible day, as we all know. But
according to oral histories of surviving firefighters, most of the dead perished in the North Tower because they were unable to hear the frantic ra-
dioed pleas of their commanders on the ground (or the amplified warnings
of a circling police helicopter) that the North Tower would soon experience
the fate of its demolished sister to the south.

Walkie-talkies allow officers to get out of their cars and spend time in-
teracting informally with the citizens on their beats. They also make police
work a thousand times safer. With the mic cord threaded through a cop's
uniform epaulet, wireless communication can, with some models, become
a hands-free, voice-activated proposition, adding immeasurably to both
safety and efficiency.

Whether it's radio "dead spots" in certain geographical areas (a common
problem in many cities and rural areas) or a failure to purchase and maintain
the best possible wireless radio communication systems and equipment,
every political jurisdiction has a fundamental duty to provide a fail-safe,
personal-carry lifeline to police and other emergency-services personnel.

Handcuffs. One of the safest, smartest things a cop can do in a tense, physically threatening situation, and in all instances of an arrest, is to reach
for her handcuffs—law and logistics permitting. (The courts frown on

unlawful detentions but generally smile on reasonable actions where officer or citizen safety is objectively at risk.)

All law enforcement officers are instructed to "double lock" the cuffs, meaning the bracelets can no longer be ratcheted tighter, thereby biting into the wrists of the person in custody. (Double-locking is accomplished by placing the "non-business" narrowed tip of the handcuff key into a small hole in the cuffs.) One of the most common citizen complaints I investigated as a sergeant (or oversaw as a chief) was that an officer had applied the cuffs "too tight." Seated in the back seat of a police car, a prisoner, hands cuffed behind his back, is in an inherently uncomfortable if not painful position. A conscious decision not to double lock the cuffs (no officer who's been around for more than five minutes "forgets" this procedure) demands a conscious decision from the brass to discipline the officer.

OPN—Orcutt Police Nunchaku. Mention of this tool conjures visions of a bare-chested Bruce Lee whipping "nunchucks" back and forth and over his head at lightning speed before lashing them around the neck of an enemy or crushing his opponent's skull with one of the "sticks." As carried and used by police, nunchaku are tools of leverage and pain compliance. Slip one of the twelve-inch hard plastic sticks under a leg or an arm, leverage the other, connected by a three-inch nylon cord, toward the first stick, exert force, and (optionally) twist. The pain can be excruciating, and those subjected to it are likely to comply immediately. As a less lethal tool, officers who use nunchaku swear by them. Critics, including anti-abortion protesters who sued the San Diego Police Department for using the tool against them in the early 1990s (an unsuccessful $5 million action),[16] have a different take on them, contending they are offensive as opposed to defensive weapons and have no place in police work.

My own take? Nunchaku have a role. But, as with all other highly specialized tools, officers who choose to carry them should be highly trained, certified, and recertified regularly. And their use, again as with all other such tools, must be carefully regulated by policy and supervised by diligent bosses.

Knives. Many patrol cops will at some point in their careers need a folding-blade knife, a sharp one. No, not to attack potential assailants—wielded in a fight, a knife is an unambiguously (and lousy) deadly force option—but rather as a cutting tool: seatbelts at traffic collisions, tied-up victims, any number of more mundane applications. For those who carry them, either on the duty belt or in the trauma plate pocket of the ballistic vest, a three- to four-inch high-quality, serrated-blade rescue knife is the tool of choice.

ALREADY WE'VE SEEN A number of weapons and tools affixed to an officer's duty belt. In addition to an authorized sidearm, a Taser (or other CEW), a canister of mace or pepper spray, a walkie-talkie, a pair of handcuffs, a baton or nunchaku, a flashlight on a belt ring (or if a smaller type, in its own pouch), and possibly a knife, it's not unusual to find one to three extra ammo magazines, an extra set of cuffs, a key ring or "silent key keeper," and a pouch for disposable gloves.

In fact, as I was working on this section of the book, sitting in The Penguin, my favorite coffee shop in Anacortes and waiting for the ferry to take me back to my cabin in the San Juan Islands, a couple of uniformed city cops wandered in for a cup. I counted the tools and weapons on their gun belts: twenty-three between them!

What I didn't see and what you likely won't find on any police officer today is a **sap** or a **blackjack**. These weapons, along with the **iron claw**, a "come-along" device, faded from view decades ago in almost all law enforcement agencies. It's my view that however sinister-looking a tool (saps and blackjacks are leaded, leather-covered striking weapons, roughly eight to eleven inches long, weighing from ten to fourteen ounces), if it offers a legitimate alternative to lethal force it is worth a second look. If officers are thoroughly trained, comfortable with and capable of using the weapon proficiently and prudently—and if the organization is vigilant in its supervision—why not allow individual officers the choice? Especially for those working alone, or in rural areas where backup might be long minutes if not hours away.

Sometimes it's a good thing when the old becomes new again—especially when lives are at stake.

Next, we move on to other equipment, too large to fit on a duty belt.

Shotguns. Recall the discussion in Chapter 6 of the 1997 North Hollywood bank robbery, after which law enforcement agencies across the country introduced the "patrol rifle," a weapon seemingly tailor-made for just such an incident. Unfortunately, a good number of those agencies also eliminated shotguns in favor of a rifle capable of firing .223 cartridges. These rifles occupy a vital place in police work but so, too, do shotguns.

Throughout the 1960s and 1970s, many police departments refused to allow patrol cops to carry shotguns in their cars. That was an image thing, for the most part. San Diego was one of those agencies that had for years rejected the weapon. The department was all about "softening" its image: white cars; tan, nondescript uniforms; no canines; and, of course, no shotguns. But the shotgun has always offered great versatility—apart from the psychological value of the unmistakable "acoustics" of the weapon being racked, conveying to an armed, holed-up suspect that the cops are on scene and mean business. It can fire buckshot or slugs (essentially converting it to a patrol rifle) and serve as a delivery system for "less lethal" munitions such as stun bags and chemical agents. It can even, through simple modification, function as a breaching weapon, which is to say it can blow a hole through a fortified door where the lock used to be (some call it the "Avon" round).

But its greatest value is its stopping power in a close-quarters gun battle, as San Diegans, who witnessed just such a firefight on their TVs on April 8, 1965, would attest. I recall working at the National City Pet Hospital, just south of San Diego, and taking a break to watch the drama unfold.

Shortly after ten in the morning on that dark, rainy day, twenty-eight-year-old Robert Paige Anderson strolled into the Hub Loan Company at Fifth Avenue and F Street in downtown San Diego and asked the manager if he could see a 30.06 rifle. The manager, Louis Richards, sixty-one, brought out a rifle and handed it to the man. Anderson asked for ammunition, Richards obliged. Anderson loaded the weapon, pointed it at Richards and said, "This is a robbery. Hand over the money." Richards attempted to flee, but

Anderson shot him in the back. As the victim lay dying in the doorway of the shop, his terrified employee, sixty-three-year-old Theodore Sweinty, fled up the stairs to the second story, where he hid in a storeroom.

Uniformed patrol officers and plainclothes detectives were on the scene in no time. They surrounded the two-story building and a pitched gunfight ensued. Hub Loan being in actuality a pawnshop, Anderson had access to numerous weapons and a stockpile of ammunition. The drama had all the makings of a long standoff.

A few blocks away, at police headquarters at 801 West Market Street, Patrol Sergeant A. D. Brown had just gotten off work. He heard over the police radio that his fellow cops were being shot at, which pissed him off. He grabbed a shotgun and some shells and rushed to the scene.

Under the direction of an inspector and lord knows how many lesser superiors, the cops exchanged shots with Anderson for hours. Off-duty cops showed up, fired all the bullets they had on them, then left. Tear gas was used, to no avail. A US Navy shore patrolman, Frank Morales, showed up with a load of concussion grenades. The cops stood back as the gunner's mate tossed one inside the shop. It blew the windows out and doused the lights. But Anderson remained inside, continuing to crank off rounds. Outside, the fifty-two-year-old editor of the *San Diego Independent,* Robert Crandall, dropped dead of a heart attack.

Sergeant Brown, who had strapped a steel plate to his chest only to remove it because of its weight, crept up to the entrance and, taking fire, was able to pull the manager out of the doorway. Richards's body was placed on a gurney and carted off.

Finally, someone decided that the only way to get the shooter out of there was to send someone in after him. Brown, of course, volunteered. As did Lieutenant Hugh French. No shots were fired as the two cops entered. In fact, the place was quiet. And dark. Tear gas stung their eyes and clouded their vision, but they successfully cleared the first floor. French (apparently not knowing of the presence of the hiding employee) fired several rounds through the ceiling before Brown started up the narrow staircase, his shotgun pointed straight ahead. Reaching the top, he entered a hallway with doors on either side. The silence was broken by the sounds of a trigger being pulled. *Click. Click. Click.* Anderson had jumped out of hiding and, pistol in hand, attempted to shoot Brown. But he'd loaded the gun with the wrong ammunition. Anderson turned and bolted down the hallway, Brown in hot pursuit. The suspect darted into one of the rooms, and the sergeant followed, only to come face to face with the shooter. Not waiting to see if Anderson had fixed his ammo problem, Brown fired three times, his first round tearing into the suspect's left arm, to devastating effect. The second slammed into the shooter's right arm, to similar effect. The third, a round to the gut, ended the longest police gunfight in US history, to that date: four hours, eight hundred rounds exchanged.[17]

Any cop and probably most lay people can point to dozens of tactical mistakes made by the SDPD that day (who suggested firing blindly into the ceiling?). But remember, this was before the advent of "special weapons and tactics," before specialized training, and drilling. Before cops were being shot at with any regularity.

In a life-threatening situation, apart from an officer's sidearm, the most valuable tool at his or her disposal is the old-fashioned 12-gauge shotgun. The weapon belongs in every police car in the country.

Patrol rifle. But what if lives threatened are a distance away, say, fifty or a hundred yards or more? What if those threatened are students at Columbine High School? Or toddlers and parents at a day care in Memphis, or Granada Hills, or Salina? Diners at a McDonald's in San Ysidro? Rifles, providing greater accuracy and stopping power at greater distances, are an essential weapon in modern policing.

Police Chief magazine offers a definitive discussion of the advantages and disadvantages of the "patrol rifle."[18] Its conclusion comes down on the side of equipping selected, highly qualified first responders (a.k.a. beat cops) with a patrol rifle. Handled properly, a rifle program saves lives. And there's no more important mission for America's cops.

Arming "motor officers" (meaning motorcycle officers) with these weapons also makes sense, as they can typically get to a critical incident, say an armed hostage situation, faster than patrol cars—but only if several key variables are controlled. One of those variables is the weapon itself: can it be safely and securely stored, protected from the elements, easily accessed by the officer?

The other variable, of course, is the officer, who should be properly trained for such weapons use. In 2013, a motor officer, giving an anti-drug presentation at Newman Elementary School in Chino, California, was shocked to learn that a school child had walked up to his unattended motorcycle and pulled the trigger of its mounted AR-15. One kid described an "explosion" as a round struck the steel plate at the bottom of the mount, sending sharp metal fragments in every direction. Two children were treated for shrapnel injuries, including one who required eye surgery. Whether an equipment malfunction or "operator error," the officer had a duty to secure that weapon before he left his motorcycle unattended.

Canines. As a "dog person," I can't bring myself to label a police dog a tool, a weapon, or a piece of equipment. Indeed, to their own police officer handlers, K-9s are partners. And family members: the dogs live with their handlers, bonding with the officer's spouse, partner, children.

K-9s perform a wide variety of legitimate tasks, but one utterly illegitimate duty is riot control.

The TV footage of a snarling, lunging German shepherd menacing protesters on the streets of Ferguson in 2014 was painful to watch. Painful because it evoked memories of Theophilus Eugene "Bull" Connor's use of attack dogs on nonviolent civil rights demonstrators in Birmingham, Alabama, in 1963. Painful because the Ferguson officer, totally responsible for that animal's behavior, appeared to be egging the dog on, contributing to an image of today's police as insensitive, brutal, and racist. That picture alone was enough to set back years of efforts to strengthen relations with communities that have historically been abused, neglected, and oppressed by the very people there to serve and to protect them.

Legitimate tasks for K-9s? As with their human counterparts, some dogs work patrol while others specialize.

Patrol. Most patrol K-9s are German shepherds, though many are Belgian Malinois (leaner, faster than shepherds), and almost all are unneutered males—yes, testosterone is a factor, but if they're especially good at their work they may also be used for breeding.

Patrol K-9s are indispensable for building searches, tracking dangerous criminals, finding lost kids, locating evidence at crime scenes, and protecting their partners, other officers, and innocent victims.

In San Diego, back in the late 1980s or early1990s, we decided to increase our K-9 corps from a dozen or so dogs to forty-four, an unprecedented all-at-once increase. Why? Because we were shooting too many people who were coming at our cops with knives, baseball bats, even masonry trowels and garden stakes—"edged" weapons. The shootings were legally justified, according to the district attorney (DA). But we were convinced we could cut that number and had an obligation to do so.

Like racking a shotgun or flipping a retractable baton, a big, toothy police dog—preferably one that growls on cue—can have a desirable psychological, de-escalation effect on an edged-weapon-wielding assailant. So we assigned the additional dog units around the clock (though mostly at night) and all over the city. And we instructed our regular patrol officers to specify a K-9 unit when calling for backup in tense situations involving a developing armed standoff or an assault. Result? Officer-involved shootings dropped dramatically.

Some departments call their patrol K-9s "attack" dogs, an unfortunate choice of terms—an observation I offer not in service to political correctness but to the cause of accuracy. Make no mistake: if someone decides to attack his handler, the dog will spring into action, playing both offense and defense—aggressively. In fact, on command, a police dog will, depending on the agency, either "bark and hold" or "bark and bite." Beware the agency that embraces the latter policy. Either way, you probably don't want to find your wrist or ankle in the grip of an animal with a bite force of 240–800 pounds and blind loyalty to his handler.

With their keen sense of smell, patrol K-9s search with far greater speed, safety, and success than their two-legged partners. I recall riding with a dog named "Axel" and his human partner in Seattle one night. (Axel was a drooler and spent most of the shift with his massive jaw parked on my right shoulder.) It was a slow night and the only call of note was a request for

Axel to search a darkened crawl space of an abandoned house. He found no suspect, but we all left feeling confident he'd done a better job of scouring that forbidding space, with its pitch-black nooks and crannies, than all us bipeds together.

Search-and-rescue dogs. Although most patrol dogs do a fine job of tracking suspects (Seattle's K-9s never failed to amaze: it seemed they "always got their man"), search-and-rescue dogs are highly specialized. Of course, the stereotype is of bloodhounds on the scent. And for good reason. A human's olfactory membrane contains 5 million receptors (or "scent cells"), a German shepherd's has 225 million (as does a beagle's), but the bloodhound's has 300 million, more than any other dog.[19] Whether hopelessly lost in the woods or buried under tons of snow in an avalanche, your best hope of rescue just might rest on "human's best friend," and his or her nose.

Detection dogs. Trained to detect drugs, explosives, electronics, and more, these animals are often featured in human-interest stories—like "Bear," a playful black lab used in the arrest of former Subway pitchman and child-porn offender Jared Fogle; the dog was recently sold to the Seattle Police Department to help investigate Internet crimes.[20] For my money, of course, I'd transfer all the drug dogs to the bomb squad.

Arson dogs. A notoriously difficult crime to investigate, arson probes have benefited tremendously from these specialists. Arson dogs are capable of picking up the scent of tiny traces of accelerants at suspected arson scenes.

Cadaver dogs. They've probed the debris at the World Trade Center towers, combed the aftermath of earthquakes, tornadoes, and other natural disasters around the world, and scoured possible dump sites of suspected serial killers. Cadaver dogs, trained to detect the slightest odor of decomposing bodies, are phenomenally successful at this most gruesome (to us) assignment. Their noses are so sensitive, they can detect bodies under running water. Debra Komar of the University of Alberta is recognized internationally as the pioneer of this important work. Partnering with the Royal Canadian Mounted Police Civilian Search Dog Association, Dr. Komar developed training techniques that have resulted in almost 100 percent accuracy. If a trained cadaver dog does not alert on a body, there is little likelihood there's a body to be found.[21]

A final, sad and maddening note on police K-9s: over the past seven years at least twenty-nine police dogs have baked to death inside their handlers' vehicles.[22]

With an outside temperature of 75°F, the inside of a closed car will reach 118°F within an hour and at 85°F it will hit 128°F.[23] Some cops have left their animals for several hours; one, in Warwick, Georgia, left his charge, Sasha, for three days—not knowing how she'd found her way into the car. These incidents are difficult for anyone with a heart to contemplate. But a photograph in an investigative report is one I'll never forget. No, it's not of Sasha's "bloated and decomposing body."[24] Rather, it is a photo of the interior of a New Orleans police SUV.

In May 2009, handler Jason Lewis of the NOPD left his partner, Primo, a six-year-old Belgian Malinois, inside a specially equipped vehicle, its air conditioner running, while he went inside to take a shower. By the time he returned, the air conditioner wasn't functioning and the car's inside temperature had risen to just under 130°F. Primo's body temperature had spiked to 110°F. According to a vet, a dog's cells begin dying at 105°F degrees, and seizures and organ failures occur soon after.[25] In a desperate, futile attempt to escape and save his own life, Primo had ripped the sturdy interior of the car to shreds.[26] (Then-superintendent Ronal Serpas fired Lewis, who had pled guilty to a misdemeanor charge of animal cruelty. Three years after Primo's death, a state appellate court reinstated the officer after having found no evidence of negligence.)[27]

Because of a lack of reporting standards, no one knows for sure how many of the nation's 20,000 police dogs die each year from such jaw-dropping neglect (the most common excuse: "I forgot he was there").

Technology holds part of the answer. A system, with the all-too-cute but memorable name "Hot Dog," will, as the temperature rises, automatically roll down the windows, activate a cooling system or fan, and set off the car's siren. The cost? From $500 to $1,000 per vehicle. That's a small sum to pay even if framed purely as an investment: police dogs cost up to $50,000, and that's without annual training, vet bills, and food.

Here's the other part of the answer: human vigilance. A cop who "forgets" and leaves his dog in a veritable oven while (1) getting ready for work, (2) catching some Zs, or (3) stopping off for a nooner needs to be fired and prosecuted.

Vests and other ballistic gear. As I've written previously, there are some aspects of officer safety gear (and tactics) I've chosen not to disclose publicly. Specs on so-called bulletproof vests and other ballistic gear fall into this category. Suffice it to say that both the community and police administrators owe it to their cops to equip them with the finest possible protective gear—and to ensure systematic maintenance and replacement: there's nothing like strapping on a reeking ballistic vest on a sweltering day, especially knowing its protective properties have been compromised by time and sweat. We have the science to help us determine relevant actuarial tables and replacement schedules. We must use that science.

Tear gas. "The first thing you hear is the bang. Then the clatter of something metallic hitting and rolling across the pavement. Then, out of the black of night, come the screams." Thus did Terrence McCoy open his August 14, 2014, *Washington Post* article[28] on the battle in Ferguson, Missouri, between police and protesters. The police had used tear gas to quell what they determined to be an increasingly violent crowd.

The use of chemical agents on nonviolent people is inexcusable. As McCoy points out, the use of tear gas is banned by the Chemical Weapons Convention of 1993, signed by almost every nation in the world, including ours. Incredibly, it is not banned for domestic purposes, including riot control.

CN, the active agent in the personal-carry product Chemical Mace, serves the same purpose when used against a combative, projectile-tossing crowd or in an effort to flush from a building an armed and barricaded suspect.

CS gas is stronger than CN, but its effects dissipate quicker. Both types of tear gas are typically delivered in "grenade" form through a modified shotgun or a specialized grenade launcher. As has been seen, from Ferguson to Cairo, Egypt, demonstrators have often lobbed the gas canisters back at police.

In a recently settled suit, Ferguson protesters and the three St. Louis County police forces involved agreed to conditions that will curtail future use of tear gas during demonstrations. Under the agreement, the cops will be required to issue "clear and unambiguous warnings" and give people sufficient time to leave the area, before employing the chemical agents. They must also take steps to minimize the impact on those who are complying with their orders, ensure a safe escape route, and, most significant, not use tear gas against lawful protesters.

Impact rounds. In Oakland, California, during an Occupy Movement protest in October 2011, twenty-four-year-old Scott Olsen, an Iraq War vet, was hospitalized in critical condition with a skull fracture, broken neck vertebrae, and swelling of the brain. He'd been struck in the head by a police projectile. The City of Oakland settled with the two-tour former marine in 2014 for $4.5 million.[29]

Most lay people refer to them as "rubber bullets." During 1999's "Battle in Seattle," in TV footage repeated almost as often as the Rodney King beating, a uniformed cop from the Tukwila Police Department is seen kicking a protester in the groin, then firing a "rubber bullet" into his chest as the young, unarmed man attempts to back away from the officer. Another report described the projectile as a "beanbag from a high velocity rifle."[30] This suggests a basic lack of information about the variety of less-lethal weapons and ammunition available to law enforcement.

In fact, "impact rounds"—basically ammo other than lead bullets—come in many sizes and shapes, and of varying composition, delivery systems, and tactical applications. What they have in common is their utility as less-lethal ammunition. They're fired at low-to-moderate velocity, their rounds large enough, in surface area, to prevent skin penetration and severe injury. In other words, they are designed to inflict pain and to immobilize, though not to injure (permanently) or to kill.

Impact rounds are divided into "direct-fire rounds" and indirect, or "skip-fire" rounds, the former intended to be fired directly at a target, the latter onto the ground, dissipating energy and rebounding up into the target.

Following is a list of common (and not-so-common) impact rounds that might be found in a law enforcement agency's arsenal:

Baton rounds. These cylinders consist of rubber, foam, plastic, or wood and, depending on their density, can be used for either direct or skip fire.

Beanbag rounds. Consisting of birdshot encased in a fabric bag, beanbag rounds are designed for direct fire.

Pepperballs. These rounds are direct-fire capsules that, as the name suggests, disperse pepper spray. Fired from high-velocity weapons, to help ensure breakage on contact, they can sting. If they don't burst open upon impact and release their pepper spray load, their efficacy is considerably lessened.

Stinger rounds. Also known as rubber buckshot, this ammunition consists of rubber balls (.32 to .60 inches) contained within a buckshot shell. They are used for direct fire and are less powerful than baton rounds.

Rubber slugs. Launched by a 12-gauge shotgun, these projectiles (some of them fin-stabilized) are used against targets between twenty and forty yards away (others are designed to be used at shorter range, still others at longer ranges). The potential for ruinous outcomes, from nasty hematomas to broken bones, even death, is very real. But in the hands of a well-trained, proficient shooter, using rifle sights and targeting only large muscle groups and soft tissue, and never targeting the head, neck, spine, kidney, and groin areas, rubber slugs belong in the arsenal of less-lethal weapons.

12-Gauge drag stabilized® rounds. The manufacturer of this ammunition states that it has "secured its place as the Law Enforcement Communities' number one choice for a specialty impact munition to be used as a dynamic, high-energy, single target round for incapacitation or the distraction of a non-compliant, aggressive subject. It has been successfully used against a broad range of individuals from fleeing subjects to 'suicide by cop' situations." The round is a tear-shaped bag filled with #9 shot and outfitted with "tails" that trail the shot and stabilize it. Recommended range is twenty to fifty feet.

Flashbangs. Many have seen accounts of the May 2014 predawn "drug raid" on a home in Habersham County, Georgia. Those with the stomach for it have examined photos or videos of the face of nineteen-month-old Bounkham "Bou Bou" Phonesavanh. The baby was nearly killed in the raid when sheriff's deputies breached the door to the home and "inserted a device," according to Sheriff Joey Terrell.[31] The device they "inserted"? A stun grenade, commonly known as a "flashbang."

Flashbangs have extraordinary shock value, producing a blinding flash of light and an explosion that registers over 170 decibels. Vision is impossible for about five seconds after the blast, and so is hearing, caused by a disturbance of fluid in the ear.[32] The intention is obvious: catch people by surprise, completely shock and disorient them so they can't even think about firing a weapon or otherwise attacking you.

Flashbangs are considered less-lethal weapons, though they can cause concussions, other traumatic brain injuries, and severe burns—in fact, they have been responsible for fires that have burned buildings to the ground, and they have taken lives.

It was amazing that baby "Bou Bou" survived his ordeal, even more amazing that many law enforcement agencies continue to conduct these raids without knowing what's on the other side of the door.

Empty-hand combat. I believe the most critical "tool" at the disposal of a police officer is his or her body—and the mind that goes with it. However confident, however alert a cop might be, there is always the possibility of a situation that doesn't allow for the use of *any* of the tools or weapons listed here. A cop who's blindsided and finds herself in the clutches of a bigger, stronger opponent must rely on "empty-hand" techniques, not only to extricate herself but to take into custody her assailant. It's a cliché for a reason, and the cop culture has spoken: a police officer is not allowed to lose a fight. That explains why so many cops plunge into dangerous or ambiguous situations rather than waiting for backup or taking evasive action. Or thinking.

The martial arts, in their many forms—aikido, judo, jujitsu, karate, and others—offer useful options. But each requires extensive, ongoing training and personal discipline, and very few law enforcement agencies provide sufficient entry-level much less continuing education and training—in any form of empty-hand combat. Given the rapidly growing popularity of the mixed martial arts within the general population, including those who have no use for cops, this failure greatly undermines officer safety.

Smart cops will pick a form of empty-hand combat from an agency-approved list (which should include boxing), keep themselves in top physical condition, go to the gym and practice, practice, practice. Contrary to popular opinion, police officers who are mentally conditioned and superbly skilled in empty-hand discipline are much more confident and much less likely to resort to excessive force.

The LVNR, or lateral vascular neck restraint. What you saw in that video of the choking of Eric Garner was not, as many cops in New York and throughout the country were quick to point out, a "choke hold," per se. In truth, it was worse.

Under the circumstances that existed at the time (and not based on what we know to have been the grim outcome), it was not an acceptable method of restraint. The video clearly shows that Officer Daniel Pantaleo had Mr. Garner in a "bar hold," which is to say his forearm was placed under Garner's chin and across his trachea. Forensic medical experts understand that an injured or collapsed trachea, especially when combined with "positional pressure"—like a bunch of cops jumping on your chest—can easily, through asphyxiation, kill a person. And that was, in fact, the medical examiner's ruling in the Garner case.

The finding also cited as contributing factors the deceased's acute and chronic bronchial asthma, and his obesity and hypertension.

Had Pantaleo been trained and certified in LVNR, or the "Kansas City method," and had he used that method on that summer day on Staten Island, there's every reason to believe Garner would be alive today. (Of course, had the officers been more persuasive verbally and had they employed sound de-escalation techniques, a physical confrontation very likely could have been avoided altogether.)

To understand how the LVNR method works, look at the Garner video again. Notice how Pantaleo's forearm is positioned. Now imagine that arm extending further up, around Garner's ear instead of under his chin. Imagine the officer's bicep and forearm forming a "neck brace" and "cradling" Garner's carotid arteries. Such a position affects the circulatory system but protects the airway, leaving it unobstructed during the confrontation.

The LVNR looks like hell when it's being applied, but it works. And it's safe. And, most valuable, it's a great equalizer when smaller, weaker cops find themselves in a physical confrontation with a bigger, stronger adversary. The Kansas City Police Department reports that it has used the method for over forty-two years, without a single incident of death or serious injury. Nor, remarkably, have they ever been sued over its use.[33]

The LVNR is a valuable tool. It's a shame so many chiefs and sheriffs have outlawed it—the result of several controversial deaths resulting from a combination of the misuse of the hold and "positional asphyxiation," caused by cops wrestling a man to the ground and then sitting on his chest, or forcing him to lie on his stomach between the front and rear seats of a police car, cuffed behind his back. Punching, kicking, spitting prisoners are problematic, to be sure. But the measures I've described can kill a person, especially if that person has a preexisting medical condition (obesity, heart disease, asthma, or other respiratory problems) or is under the influence of certain drugs, especially cocaine. If in taking such people into custody, every officer at the scene knows this information, applies the LVNR correctly, and does not keep such prisoners on their stomachs except very briefly (and, then, only when it is absolutely necessary), lives will be saved.

I was by turns heartened, then disappointed when my esteemed colleague Sheriff John Urquhart of King County, Washington, announced he would reintroduce the previously banned method into his department. A short time later he made a second announcement: he would not be authorizing his deputies to use the LVNR, after all. Why not? Community opposition.

John Urquhart is an honorable man, and a fine law enforcement leader. His commitment to listen to the citizens he serves is real, and laudable. But this episode strikes me as a situation where an informed citizenry can help its law enforcement agency turn good policy into better policy. Like bringing back a valuable tool that, owing to an uninformed citizenry—and police abuses, to be sure—has been lost.

Vehicles. Great variation exists in the "rolling stock" (and airborne and water-based apparatus) of America's law enforcement agencies, from sedans to SUVs, motorcycles to motor scooters, dirt bikes to ATVs (all-terrain vehicles), dune buggies, marked cars, unmarked cars, undercover cars, K-9 cars, MRAPs, fixed-wing aircraft, helicopters, horses, jet skis, patrol boats, and so on.

From the public's point of view, one of the most important questions boils down to whether those blue and red lights in the rearview mirror belong to a real cop. Occasionally some jerk purchases the makings of a "police" uniform, paints his car in "official" colors, installs a light or two, straps on a gun, and pins on a tin badge. Impersonation of a police officer is either a felony or a misdemeanor in every state. It's a serious crime—often committed in the furtherance of other crimes, from extortion to sexual assault to murder. No one knows for sure how often this happens, but in Detroit, for example, where the number of police impersonators is on the rise—and where, in 2013, a thirty-five-year-old woman was shot and killed and her twelve-year-old sister wounded by early morning non-cop invaders shouting, "Police!"—officers have cautioned residents not to open the door or pull over on the roadway until they are satisfied they're being approached by someone in full uniform and with proper credentials.[34] When in doubt, it's smart to call 911. Briefly, cops should look like cops and drive identifiable police vehicles.

My bias in purchasing police vehicles is that they provide maximum comfort for those who drive or ride in them all day, shift after shift: strengthened seats; top-quality shocks and suspension; enough leg- and headroom; and, though I'm death on reckless high-speed pursuits, sufficient power to get the job done.

Rolling stock is a high-ticket item for the taxpayers, but failure to purchase and maintain the right vehicles, for the right purposes, is both fiscally and operationally shortsighted.

That said, one of the things this country needs right now is cops getting out of those vehicles, walking a beat, talking with people, spending as much time as possible working to build positive relations, and trust, with the citizens they protect and serve.

Body-worn cameras. "Against," I told a West Seattle resident when he gave me a "for or against" choice at a community meeting in the late 1990s. It was a hypothetical question, to be sure. The very idea of a "body-worn camera" was years from becoming a topic of serious conversation. When he first mentioned it, I pictured a bulky "handycam" on every cop's shoulder. How would that work?

"You know it's coming, Chief. Why are you opposed?"

Cops "wearing" cameras? Some use of video technology made sense (crime scene reenactments, field sobriety tests, etc.), but cops "filming" *all* their daily interactions on video?

The guy was well-intentioned but a bit of a technogeek. I explained my position. "Several reasons I'm opposed," I told him. "First, it's just not right, morally or ethically, for us to be recording citizens without their consent." I envisioned victims of car crashes, home burglaries, sexual assaults, domestic violence, even motorists stopped for minor violations—emotional, in trouble, with cameras rolling. No. Cameras would compromise the dignity, and the privacy, of our citizens.

And, what of the cops? Sure, if they knew their every move was being captured for posterity, there's a chance they'd up their game, be on their best behavior. But at what cost? Would video scrutiny make them "pose"? Would it dampen their enthusiasm for innovation and imagination? Say a cop wanted to go to bat for an in-custody suspect, help the young offender move onto a better path? That's not illegal, but what would the officer's traditional law-and-order peers have to say on the subject? And those less than ideal officers? Wouldn't they, under the influence of cameras, become even more officious, or legalistic?

Further, as an administrator, recognizing the huge everyday costs of staffing, equipping, and running a police department, how in the world would we be able to afford a high-priced camera for every cop on the beat? Beyond the substantial capital outlay, what about the costs of maintenance and repairs, and storage, and retrieval? How would the rules of evidence be affected? What would the local prosecutor—and the defense bar—have to say about such a fundamental change in the handling of criminal (and traffic) cases?

Even with inexorable progress in camera technology—miniaturization, video quality, battery life, durability—wouldn't the wear and tear of 24/7 patrol work result in numerous damaged or destroyed devices? How would it play if a department had an established "camera program," thereby raising everyone's expectations that the devices would be available—and turned on, recording everything—but there weren't enough cameras to go around? How would a defense attorney handle the news that, no, we don't seem to have a video of your client's arrest for resisting that officer back on June 17?

So, all things considered, no: cameras on cops made no sense.

Gradually, though, my thinking changed. Those strong reservations about body-worn cameras weakened over the years. Cameras are coming, I told myself, and they're here to stay (today over 25 percent of all law enforcement agencies employ them, and over 80 percent are evaluating their use). And that's a good thing.

The ACLU agrees. After expressing serious reservations early in the conversation, the nation's premier civil liberties organization published a report in 2013 (updated in March 2015) headlined: "Police Body-Mounted Cameras: With Right Policies in Place, a Win for All." The following, excerpted from the report, is noteworthy:

Although we at the ACLU generally take a dim view of the prolif-eration of surveillance cameras in American life, police on-body cameras are different because of their potential to serve as a check against the abuse of power by police officers. Historically, there was no documentary evidence of most encounters between police officers and the public, and due to the volatile nature of those en-counters, this often resulted in radically divergent accounts of inci-dents. Cameras have the potential to be a win-win, helping protect the public against police misconduct, and at the same time helping protect police against false accusations of abuse.

We're against pervasive government surveillance, but when cameras primarily serve the function of allowing public monitor-ing of the government instead of the other way around, we gener-ally support their use. While we have opposed government video surveillance of public places, for example, we have supported the installation of video cameras on police car dashboards, in prisons, and during interrogations.[35]

The ACLU, noting that cops "enter people's homes and encounter by-standers, suspects, and victims in a wide variety of sometimes stressful and extreme situations," warns against the potential to invade people's privacy and urges strong, rigorously enforced policies that would not allow the police to "'edit on the fly'—i.e., choose which encounters to record with limitless discretion. If police are free to turn the cameras on and off as they please, the cameras' role in providing a check and balance against police power will shrink and they will no longer become a net benefit."[36]

Fortunately, a large number of police executives agree with the ACLU and other civil libertarians. In 2014, the Police Executive Research Forum, supported by the Office of Community Oriented Services of the Depart-ment of Justice, published a landmark document, "Implementing a Body-Worn Camera Program: Recommendations and Lessons Learned." Based on surveys, interviews, a 2013 daylong national conference of police offi-cers and executives, federal officials, scholars, and experts, and additional extensive research, the two agencies have made the case that cameras can be (indeed, have been) instrumental in improving the policies and practices of police, and the community-police relationship. They identify the following specific benefits: increased accountability and transparency; reduced complaints and improved resolution of officer-involved incidents; identification and correction of internal agency problems; and enhanced evidence documentation.[37]

In November 2014, the Rialto, California, police chief, Tony Farrar, and his colleagues at Cambridge University (United Kingdom), published the results of a scientific experiment on the effects of body-worn cameras on police practices.[38] The study showed that use of force by Rialto officers wearing the cameras fell by 59 percent and that complaints against them fell by 87 percent, compared to the previous year. Similar positive results have been reported in Arizona in Mesa and Phoenix, as well as other jurisdictions.

For these and other reasons, as part of the overall $263 million criminal justice reform package, President Obama is moving forward with a proposed "Body-Worn Camera Partnership Program" to fund $20 million (part of the sum in matching grants to local law enforcement) for cameras, storage, and community policing training.[39] Applications are rolling in, especially now that we find citizen activists and police union officials singing off the same sheet of music.

But, lest we get too excited about the future "civilizing" effects of the cameras (on both police and citizen behavior), we should heed the cautions and advice presented in an excellent *Harvard Law Review* article:

> This widespread galvanization over body cameras exemplifies the human tendency, in times of tragedy, to latch on to the most readily available solution to a complex problem. But as the outcome of [Eric] Garner's case demonstrates, even when high-quality, graphic footage is available, officers may still not be indicted, let alone convicted.
>
> . . . Moreover, body cameras are a powerful—and indiscriminate—technology. Their proliferation over the next decade will inevitably change the nature of policing in unexpected ways, quite possibly to the detriment of the citizens the cameras are intended to protect.

. . . Citizens should also remain vigilant—observing and recording the conduct of police within their communities rather than complacently allowing themselves to be surveilled by the state. And finally, *wider systemic changes must be undertaken in conjunction with the deployment of body cameras to ensure that our legal process truly provides justice for all, rather than simply justice for some* [emphasis added].[40]

Drones. In the fall of 2012, the Seattle Police Department held a public hearing to show off its two 3.5 pound Draganflyer X6 Helicopter Tech drones. They were purchased in 2010 for $82,000, through a regional Homeland Security grant, and approved by the Federal Aviation Administration. The devices, outfitted with still, video, and infrared cameras (the latter for live-viewing applications) were to be used in emergency circumstances: hostage situations, search-and-rescue operations, pursuit of armed felons, bomb threats, detection of hot spots in fires. Or in the collection and analysis of traffic data on the city's notoriously clogged streets.[41] At least that's what Assistant Chief Paul McDonagh was trying to tell the one hundred people in attendance before he got shouted down.

"We don't trust you with the weapons you do have," yelled a man who identified himself as General Malaise. Much of the opposition to the drone program came from community critics, left and right, who were fearful of privacy invasions. Doug Honig of the ACLU of Washington told the *Seattle Times* that there was "tremendous, widespread concern among the general public."[42]

Fears of compromised privacy were, and remain, very real. But much of the concern voiced that night was based on an underlying mistrust of the department following several highly controversial incidents, most notable of which was the indefensible killing of the Native wood-carver, John T. Williams. "Murderer!" was one of the shouts that echoed off the walls of the Garfield High School meeting room.

"We expected a large turnout and a passionate discourse," police spokesperson Sean Whitcomb said. "We want to hear the concerns and shape our policy to reflect that."[43] Although there was evidently little "discourse," Whitcomb and the rest of the city heard those concerns: the mayor and the police chief decided that SPD should ground the drones and return them to the vendor.

When a return turned out to be more difficult than expected, the little birds were packed up and shipped to the Los Angeles Police Department in 2014. If anything, the citizens' reaction there was even fiercer. By year's end, Chief Charlie Beck was assuring protesters that their new aircraft were "still in the box."

There were, of course, citizen advocates, in both cities, pushing for adoption of a drone program. They cited all the tactical benefits pushed by the cops and added one more argument: the possibility that the diminutive aircraft would one day replace noisy, far more expensive manned helicopters. Dennis Brandow of Bellevue, who'd come to the public meeting at Garfield High from across Lake Washington, told Christine Clarridge of the *Seattle Times*, "I think it's crazy. They're all [his fellow citizens] bitching about technology that's already here. It's really ignorant. In five to seven years, you're not even going to see TV helicopters in the air anymore. It's like the Internet. Some people might not like it, but it's going to happen."[44]

He's right, of course. When have we ever witnessed advancing technology put on the brakes and make a U-turn?

I'm with the ACLU on this one. We can take note of the "many beneficial uses, including search-and-rescue missions, scientific research, mapping, and more," but drones, "without proper regulation" and "equipped with facial recognition software, infrared technology, and speakers capable of monitoring personal conversations would cause unprecedented invasions of our privacy rights." An even greater fear is of "interconnected drones [that] could enable mass tracking of vehicles and people in wide areas. Tiny drones could go completely unnoticed while peering into the window of a home or place of worship."[45]

To guard against these intrusions into the private lives of Americans, the ACLU is fighting for enactment of "uniform rules . . . to ensure that we can enjoy the benefits of this new technology without bring us closer to a 'surveillance society' in which our every move is monitored, tracked, recorded, and scrutinized by the government."[46]

The civil liberties organization has urged adoption of the following safeguards:

Usage Limits: A drone should be deployed by law enforcement only with a warrant, in an emergency, or when there are specific and articulable grounds to believe that the drone will collect evidence relating to a specific criminal act.

Data Retention: Images should be retained only when there is reasonable suspicion that they contain evidence of a crime or are relevant to an ongoing investigation or trial.

Policy: Usage policy on drones should be decided by the public's representatives, not by police departments, and the policies should be clear, written, and open to the public.

Abuse Prevention and Accountability: Use of domestic drones should be subject to open audits and proper oversight to prevent misuse.

Weapons: Domestic drones should not be equipped with lethal or non-lethal weapons.[47]

Before the program was shelved, the Seattle City Council considered an ordinance that would have banned use of drones for "general surveillance" and "flights over open-air assemblies." It would also have required issuance of a warrant for any non-emergency applications.

I believe it is both inevitable and desirable for law enforcement to employ drones, but only under the circumscribed conditions outlined by the ACLU. There may come a time—we're not there yet—when growing levels of community-police trust would permit adoption of a policy allowing the use of airborne less-lethal weapons.

Again, the challenge is not the tool, not the technology. The challenge is trust. If the police earn it, everyone reaps the benefits.

NOW, LET'S RETURN TO the story we interrupted all those many pages ago. Recall that you're a patrol officer; that you've been dispatched to the scene of a domestic violence call; that a violent ex-boyfriend has jumped you, wrested your gun out of its holster, and is keeping you from reaching any of the other tools or weapons on your duty belt. You're in a life-or-death struggle to reclaim your firearm, both hands locked around your assailant's hands, when:

> out of the corner of your eye, you spot a four-pound decorative river rock. You're losing the battle anyway, so in a daring decision you suddenly release one hand, grab the rock, and, mustering all your strength, raise it high over your head and bring it down as hard as you can. A direct blow to the head. Your attacker goes limp, releasing his grip on the gun.

You're shaken, but okay. The victim is safe. The ex-boyfriend, on the other hand, is dead on arrival at the emergency room.

What do you think your community is going to say? The mayor? The media? Your precinct commander? Your chief? I would hope their reaction would be unanimous. You did what you had to do to stay alive, and to save the life of a citizen you'd been hired to protect and serve.

That some might disagree, we call life.

THERE YOU HAVE IT, a police officer's "tool kit," and a sampling of how most of its devices are put to use, or misuse. I hope my bias is apparent: we have an obligation to send our cops onto the streets of US cities with the tools they need to get the job done safely, and properly.

I don't believe we "fix" American policing by stripping its cops of these valuable if not essential tools. We fix the police by insisting that every officer honor human life, above all else, and that he or she treat the citizenry with dignity and respect—and by providing the finest equipment, training, and continuous retraining to ensure that all officers know when and how to employ these tools.

Cops are human, they make mistakes. Some willfully abuse their authority or misuse the equipment they've been issued. In the final analysis, there is no substitute for sound judgment on the part of individual officers. Or for a chief willing to fire cops who are unwilling to live by the rules.

THE CITIZENS OF EVERY town, city, and county must make their voices heard in support of (1) adequately and properly equipping their local police, and (2) insisting on thorough training and rational supervision in the use of each of these tools of the trade. It's also critical, in the larger context of citizen oversight, that means and methods of community monitoring of all of it be developed and supported.

Finally, as noted throughout this book, both police leaders and community activists must work to ensure that every police officer is physically, emotionally, and ethically fit to meet the demands of reasoned and responsible police work.

It does little good to put a lethal or—often as important—less-lethal weapon in the hands of a racist or a bully.

8

THE TALK

YEARS AFTER MICHAEL BROWN'S death in Ferguson, Missouri, large numbers of the nation's cops continue to argue that race had nothing to do with the killing. Indeed, the Columbia (Missouri) Police Officers' Association declared the one-year anniversary of Brown's death "Darren Wilson Day," contending that "he [Wilson] was thoroughly investigated . . . and [that he] did NOTHING wrong."[1] The union felt that Wilson had been persecuted, that he was the "victim in all this." I'm convinced, on the other hand, that the teenager's race had much if not everything to do with his death.

The conventional wisdom among cops is that race is categorically not a factor in their decisions to stop and frisk, detain and arrest, draw and fire their weapons. The only consideration, they say, is the situation—and the legal authorization and moral justification to take action. Most police officers would have us believe they are officially colorblind (as if observing racial and cultural differences is a bad thing), and that they make their decisions based strictly on the "facts." Context doesn't matter. History doesn't matter. The preexisting relationship between cops and communities doesn't matter. White cops' inordinate fear of black men doesn't matter. As Darren Wilson told Jake Halpern of the *New Yorker*, "I am really simple in the way that I look at life. What happened to my great-grandfather is not happening to me. I can't base my actions off what happened to him."[2]

To be clear, some white cops know better. They are able to see beyond the blue wall and recognize the effects of deeply embedded racism, of systematic discrimination. These cops understand that racism operates, and has done so historically, at multiple levels: structural, institutional, individual (or "personally mediated," as defined in Camara Jones's "A Gardener's Tale"—in which she also speaks of the "internalized racism" that afflicts victims of the sickness of racism).[3] These officers may also have read Michelle Alexander's *The New Jim Crow* and may have come to understand how, intentional or not, police collude with, indeed *supply*, a system that imprisons disproportionate numbers of blacks and Latinos.[4]

And they may have learned why so many in communities of color harbor such abiding distrust of the police.

DIRUL-ISLAM SHAMSID-DEEN IS A thirty-eight-year-old chef. A fine one, I can attest, having enjoyed many a delicious meal where he works his magic at an upscale restaurant here in the San Juan Islands of Washington state. He came out of the kitchen one night and, knowing I was at work on this book, struck up a conversation. One thing led to another, and I asked him if he'd be willing to sit down with me over a coffee, expand on what, as a young child, his black father had told him about the police. He agreed, and one morning, a week or so later, we sat down to talk. About "The Talk."[5]

Born in Watts, raised by a single dad who moved his son into West Los Angeles when the boy was four, Shamsid-Deen spent his formative years "living the ghetto life," he told me. His father had, "from the time I was old enough to understand" delivered not just The Talk, but an "endless lecture series" that continued into the young man's teen years and beyond.

Many cops recoil at the mere mention of The Talk. As if they have been cast, automatically, unjustly, in the role of the villain. As if young black kids are taught, groundlessly, to fear and loathe the police. Indeed, Patrick Lynch, the NYPD's union leader, reacted angrily—so sincerely angry that it surprised me—when Mayor de Blasio commented on having had The Talk with his own biracial teenage son, Dante. Lynch, it would seem, might benefit from a conversation with his boss. "Every black I've ever dealt with tells me that they tell their kids the same thing," Bill Bratton told a journalist.[6] And pretty much every police executive I've ever dealt with will tell you the same thing. They hear it all the time in the black community. "My biggest fear is not that my son gets jumped into a gang," two young African American mothers told me, one in San Diego, the other a few years later in Seattle. "No, sir, my biggest fear is that he gets stopped by [one of my officers] and the next thing I know I'm getting a call from the morgue." I don't mean this in a cruel way, but sometimes I think cops like Lynch are suffering from learned cluelessness.

It would be beneficial, I believe, for cops everywhere to learn how one black male child, Shamsid-Deen, was taught to behave in the presence of police officers. And how that instruction, from his primary role model and male authority figure, affected his early life. And his lifelong perceptions of the police.

From South Central Los Angeles to West L.A. is a thirty-minute drive. Culturally, the two neighborhoods occupy two different worlds. When Shamsid-Deen's father made the move in the mid-1970s, he did so to make life better, safer for his son. His greatest fear for his child was not the gangs of South Central, the random violence of the streets, the gunshots ringing out at all hours of the day and night. It was the behavior of the LAPD cops.

Shamsid-Deen's early childhood "lecture series" was a product of paternal love—and, yes, fear. "According to my father, it was never a matter of *if*. It was always a question of *when* I would get pulled over." *When* he would face abuse, or worse, at the hands of the police.

From what the young man would go on to hear, witness, and personally experience in life, he came to understand both the necessity and the wisdom of his father's admonitions, the nonstop grilling of his son. What do you wear? How do you drive? What do you do when you get pulled over? How do you comport yourself, talk to a police officer?

Shamsid-Deen learned to dress neatly, "always neat," in order "not to bring attention to myself." He came to think of clothing as a "costume," designed to reduce his chances of getting stopped. Or, if stopped, to increase the odds of surviving the encounter. He wore clean trousers, his shirt always tucked in. He learned that a pressed white shirt usually meant he would not be ordered to the ground, and spread-eagled. And, as his father mandated: there would be no bulges in any item of clothing, ever. To this day, it's automatic: Shamsid-Deen refuses to get into a car without putting his wallet and cell phone in plain sight.

Isn't this all just a bit over the top? A bit dramatic? I asked, "If you can separate, even for a moment, the fears instilled by your father, what did you think of the police, what were your independent perceptions of them?"

"Absolutely terrified," he said, a look on his face that suggested he was reliving for those few seconds the "near panic attacks" he would get each time he was pulled over. And as a teenager in Westside—University of California–Los Angeles, Brentwood, Beverly Hills—that happened "a few times a year." Especially when he was driving his father's black BMW, a car he gave up because of the frequency of police stops.

A LITTLE ADDITIONAL SHAMSID-DEAN family background: The young boy's father "did not cook." Consequently, the two ate out often, "almost every day." Breakfast and dinner, a different restaurant or café all the time. The young boy told his father he wanted to be a waiter, to which his father replied, "Nope. You're going to be an engineer." Naturally, Dad was an engineer. So, in his late teens and early twenties Shamsid-Deen spent three years studying engineering in Boulder, Colorado. Then, "at the tail end of Kuwait," he joined the US Navy, where he was quickly tapped as a specialist in electronics, traveling the world making repairs to expensive, sophisticated electronics equipment.

Out of the navy and back in the States, his early interest in waiting tables had shifted to preparing the food to put on those tables. "I was struck by the power of the chef," he said. "Running the kitchen, barking orders—*Do this! Do that!* Finishing up a shift, bellying up to the bar and tossing back a drink." The lifestyle appealed. And he soon realized he had an aptitude for it, so he enrolled in culinary school. And went on to cook in New York and Chicago, and later in Portland, Oregon, where he ran his own small eatery in the then "sketchy," now gentrifying neighborhood of Burnside. The area's beat cop was a regular customer.

The chef and the cop talked often about a controversial police shooting of a young, unarmed black man in the neighborhood. Possibly under the influence, possibly suffering from mental illness, the man had been reported hanging around a car, acting suspiciously. Shamsid-Deen was struck by the white officer's thoughtfulness, his lack of defensiveness. He "genuinely wanted to understand how the black community was reacting to the shooting." The two men found themselves in agreement: the involved officer should have waited for his backup, which, in all likelihood, would have spared the disturbed man's life.

WAS SHAMSID-DEEN EVER IN trouble with the cops? Yes, he confessed. Once when he found himself "in the back seat of a stolen car," a joyriding case. And another time for driving on a suspended license (for unpaid parking tickets). Not unusual offenses for teenagers of any color or social status. Did he feel discriminated against on those two occasions?

"No, I didn't." Although . . . "You know, poor white kids don't get The Talk. They don't need it. But even if you're a middle-class black kid from an intact family? You need it. Guaranteed." He said it with an urgency that made clear his conviction that black parents would be guilty of child neglect if they failed to have The Talk.

We chatted for a long time, almost two hours. I asked him about current events, about Michael Brown, Eric Garner, Tamir Rice, Akai Gurley, Tony Robinson, Walter Scott, Freddie Gray, others. He told me, "It boggles the collective mind of black Americans that a grand jury doesn't indict in these cases. There are never any repercussions. It's a slap in the face to the black community. [It's] very rare that we hear about justice being served."

He believes police officers are overly aggressive toward blacks because of three things. "One, ingrained racism. Two, fear. And, three, because of the tactics they've been taught."

Shamsid-Deen believes the American people, black and white, are "waking from a coma" and are starting to see what's wrong with policing. "People are saying race relations in this country have never been worse. They're looking at Ferguson, Baltimore, New York. . . . There's truth to that, of course, but let's understand a couple of things: what you're seeing has always been going on. But that's just the point, now you're seeing it, because of these." He picked up the iPhone I'd been using as a recorder, tapped its screen.

"Now, because it's happening all the time, and because everyone knows it, more and more young black men are saying to the cops, 'No! You are not going to beat me.'"

This kind of talk infuriates cops, especially their union leaders, who feel duty bound to try to talk many in the black community out of what they believe, what they perceive, what they feel. What they have experienced.

What the nation needs, said Shamsid-Deen, is more cops like the one he met in Portland. Professional police officers whose personal default setting is to treat all people with dignity and respect.

IMAGINE MY SURPRISE WHEN in February 2015, I opened *Slog*, a crime and news blog by Ansel Herz, and saw a big, color photograph of a former colleague, Ron Smith, newly elected president of the Seattle Police Officers Guild. The photo accompanied a most unusual interview.[7] Unusual, in my experience, for several reasons.

First, Smith was smiling, sort of—something I rarely saw when we crossed swords, which was often during my tenure at the Seattle Police Department (1994–2000). He was also sporting major tattooage on both arms, along with a stylin' grunge-era goatee. Not exactly the image most folks associate with the city's cops.

Second, Herz blogs for the *Stranger*, a weekly newspaper co-founded by the cartoonist James Sturm and Tim Keck, who had previously co-founded the *Onion*, and home to Dan Savage's savagely funny, unabashedly irreverent sex and politics columns. The *Stranger* has been a vehicle for a steady stream of "anti-police" commentary. Generally, it is alternately shunned or slammed by Seattle's rank and file.

And, third, Ron Smith's answers were, to say the least, unexpected. Coming as they did from a police union boss.

Herz asked Smith to elaborate on what he'd written a week before on the Seattle Police Guild's Facebook page, to wit: "Times have changed and we must also change to adapt to societal expectations." Herz asked him what that really meant, "particularly in light of incidents over the past year in which officers have taken to social media to use racially inflammatory rhetoric, defend the militarization of police, and rant about gay people."

Smith's answer to such cops? "You applied here. And you have to treat people all the same. You have to serve the community. If you don't like the politics here, then leave and go to a place that serves your worldview."[8]

My reaction was pretty much the same as Herz's: "It was exciting language from the head of a union that in the past, in its monthly *Guardian* newsletter, has described efforts to combat racial profiling as 'socialist policies' from 'the enemy' and argued that officers should be able to call citizens 'bitch' and 'nigga.' Smith said all Seattle police officers need to 'check their bias at the door' when they walk into work. Bias-free policing training, which officers [recently] underwent in four-hour sessions was the best training he'd experienced throughout all of last year." And, as he told his interviewer, he wanted more of it.

Herz challenged Smith on whether a cop who has "internalized derogatory stereotypes about blacks or gays, for example, could realistically remove those biases from an interaction with someone on the street."

Smith replied, "That's an overt attitude. There's no room for that. I don't know how you check that at the door. That's like playing dress up. . . . We need to treat everyone the same. Regardless of race, gender identity, economic class—all the same. . . . I stand firm on the fact that if you don't like . . . the political environment of the city, then go someplace else. . . . You gotta change with the times. You gotta embrace what we have here."

I read the whole piece, twice. Looking for evidence of what they did with the real Ron Smith.

"The man's for real," Seattle's new police chief, Kathleen O'Toole, told me at a conference early in 2015.[9] "We're working well together."

Although that may be "sleeping with the enemy" language for many police union members, this kind of relationship between the top cop and the union prez bodes well not just for the department but for the citizens of Seattle.

And though it's both reasonable and necessary for unions to work hard and smart on behalf of their members—protecting and advancing traditional bargaining aims: hours, wages, terms and conditions of employment—many police unions either shy away from supporting essential reforms or they oppose them outright, often with a great, heaping glass of vitriol.

That aptly describes the beverage of choice of the Patrolmen's Benevolent Association (PBA) of the NYPD.

THE NYPD'S PATROL COP union, under the leadership of Patrick Lynch, has fought to improve police officers' working conditions. It has championed improvements in hours, wages, and other bread-and-butter issues, has fought for legitimate due process rights for its members, and, according to its website, has contributed to a host of charities and other worthy causes. All well and good, high-minded efforts.

But Mr. Lynch has also called on his membership to "split New York into [the union's] friends and [its] enemies."[10]

Why would the leader of 24,000 of NYPD's cops issue such a provocative, indeed inflammatory statement?

It all goes back to de Blasio's campaign for mayor, during which the candidate expressed withering criticism of community-police relations under his predecessor, Michael Bloomberg. De Blasio was especially critical of the police department's stop-and-frisk policies, and of the staunch defense of those policies mounted by Bloomberg and his commissioner, Ray Kelly. The campaign strategy worked, and De Blasio took 72 percent of the vote in 2013.

As mayor, he continued to express his dissatisfaction with heavy-handed policing, only now with the power to do something about it. He appointed Bratton, and the two men went to work—more or less—on the stop-and-frisk problem.

Then came the Eric Garner in-custody choking death. After a grand jury failed to indict Officer Daniel Pantaleo, and the streets of New York seemed ripe for the kind of social upheaval witnessed in Ferguson following a St. Louis County grand jury's decision not to indict Darren Wilson, de Blasio took to the microphone at a news conference, invoking his own family—his wife, Chirlane, who is black, and his mixed-race son, Dante:

> Chirlane and I have had to talk to Dante for years about the dangers he may face. A good young man, a law-abiding young man, who would never think to do anything wrong, and yet, because of

a history that still hangs over us, the dangers he may face—we've had to literally train him, as families have all over this city for decades, in how to take special care in any encounter he has with police officers who are there to protect him.[11]

The mayor also invoked Martin Luther King Jr.'s statement that an "injustice anywhere is a threat to justice everywhere."

Given the union head's rousing (and totally expected) defense of Pantaleo, it should come as no surprise that Lynch quickly denounced de Blasio's statements. The following morning, he held a press conference of his own, informing the public that "police officers felt . . . they were thrown under the bus" by the mayor. More revealing, and disturbing, was his statement in response to a reporter's question:

> He [the mayor] spoke about, we have to teach our children, that their interaction with the police, [*sic*] and that they should be afraid of New York City police officers. That's not true. We have to teach our children, our sons and our daughters, no matter who they look like to respect New York City police officers. Teach them to comply with police officers, even if they feel it's unjust.[12]

The mayor, he concluded, "needs to support New York City police officers."

I do wonder: if Mr. Lynch had a young black son, knowing what he knows about good officers and bad, self-disciplined and rash or racist cops, would he not have the same conversation with his own son? If his answer is no, I call him out here and now. He's either not being honest with himself, or with us. No responsible parent of a black male—or female—child would fail to have The Talk.

LYNCH THEN TOOK TO the stump and encouraged his members to trash the mayor, announcing a reaction strategy: "Our friends, we're courteous to them. Our enemies, extreme discretion."[13]

Confusing language, Mr. Lynch. Did you actually say, out loud, that your cops should take sides? That they should make nice with their pals but employ less-than-professional practices against their "enemies"? We need Lynch's help in parsing, specifically, the term "extreme discretion." What, exactly, did he mean when he uttered those words during a profanity-laced, surreptitiously taped, closed-door session with his delegates on December 12, 2014? The most benign interpretation, I suppose, has him promoting a work slowdown (although his spokesperson denies that meaning). Or, was he advocating something entirely different, some more ominous job action against people who have the nerve to criticize police officers?

Either way, his statement (reminiscent of President Bush's post 9/11 comment, "Either you are with us or you are with the terrorists") adds considerable weight to critics' claims of biased policing.

Police have been disparaged throughout the history of the institution for taking sides. For siding with landlords over tenants, merchants over consumers, men over women, straights over gays, rich over poor, white over black, and, in a nod to irony, management over labor (check out the role of police violence in union busting, dating back to the late 1880s, then check out the role of police unions as they discover they are labor).

The last thing today's police officers need is a labor leader espousing anything less than an honoring of the guaranteed right of every citizen to fair and equal protection under the law.

THEN CAME THE SHOOTINGS, on December 20, 2014. Two New York City police officers, Rafael Ramos and Wenjian Liu, were sitting in their car in Brooklyn when twenty-eight-year-old Ismaaiyl Brinsley approached the passenger-side window, assumed a firing stance, and fired several rounds into the heads and upper bodies of Ramos and Liu. The officers did not have a chance to draw their firearms. Brinsley, who had traveled to New York from Baltimore to do precisely what he did, in avowed revenge for the deaths of Michael Brown in Ferguson and Eric Garner on Staten Island, had a long criminal record and had shot his ex-girlfriend in Baltimore before heading for New York.[14]

Brinsley fled after the shootings and, as officers closed in on him, used the murder weapon to kill himself.

Following the deaths of the officers, Lynch stated that "blood on the hands starts on the steps of City Hall, in the office of the mayor."[15] He then either choreographed or simply condoned the actions of some of his members as they turned their backs on the mayor. They did so at the hospital where Ramos and Liu had been taken. They did so at each of the officer's funerals. And they did so at an NYPD academy graduation.

LYNCH'S PATROLMEN'S BENEVOLENT ASSOCIATION began an ad campaign in the fall of 2014 in support of a pay raise for its members. It informed New Yorkers that their cops are: "Overworked. Understaffed. Underpaid. Unappreciated."[16] A bit whiny, perhaps. And, I'll guarantee you, not all of New York's finest are overworked (or universally "unappreciated," for that matter). But let's concede that a case can be made that the NYPD is understaffed (hard to establish, especially since Mayor de Blasio, after months of resistance, agreed in June 2015 to an extra 1,300 cops—the equivalent of adding an entire Seattle Police Department to its ranks) and that its members are underpaid (much easier to prove). How likely is it that by hurling ad hominem insults and threatening biased policing, the municipal money gods will look kindly upon higher salaries?

INTERESTINGLY, THE TWO UNION presidents, one in Seattle, the other in New York, appear to have switched roles of late: Smith claiming he was misquoted, his words taken out of context in the *Stranger* interview, Lynch telling reporters he now has a "respectful" relationship with hizzoner. Like politicians everywhere, these two cops, I suspect, are learning important lessons on how to read and lead: how to read the times, the politics, the personalities, the important battles; and how to lead their respective organizations to a better place. These are undeniably taxing times for everyone involved in local law enforcement. I would hope today's police leaders, whether in the union hall or in the top-floor, corner office at headquarters, find a way to work, with the community, to eradicate endemic racism in all its ugly forms and, in the process, build a much stronger, more trusting community-police relationship.

For that to happen, attitudes must change.

9

WE'RE THE COPS,
AND YOU'RE NOT

THE CALL CAME OUT as a late-night disturbance. A loud, raucous, back-yard wedding reception. It was off my beat but I was only a few blocks away, and I got there in less than a minute, guided as much by the thumping mariachi *corridos* as my internal GPS or the Brothers Thomas.

We rarely waited for backup in those days, especially on routine calls such as this. "We got a complaint!" I shouted at the woman who finally heard me banging on the door. Mother of the bride, dressed to the nines, shoes kicked off for the dancing.

"What?" she asked, cupping a hand to her ear.

"A complaint," I repeated. "You're going to have to tell the musicians to crank it down." I wasn't unfamiliar with such calls, having in my pre-cop days played in a rhythm-and-blues band at frat-house parties at San Diego State, bashes frequently crashed by the city's finest.

"Just a minute," she shouted. "Let me get my husband." She turned, headed through the living room toward the backyard. I didn't need this, and I certainly didn't have a "minute." I was busy, damn it, trying to collect my numbers for the night. The idea was, get your numbers out of the way early so you'd have time for real police work later in the shift: going after burglars, stickup men, other felons, not babysitting or mollifying disturbers of the peace.

A moment later, the woman's husband, three sheets to the wind, barreled up to the door. "What's the meaning of this?" he demanded as if he were somehow in charge. I would have to set him straight.

"Step outside, sir."

"I will do no such thing. I know my rights." Such as not allowing the cops into his home without reasonable suspicion of a crime or probable cause for an arrest? He stuck a finger in my face, the tip of which brushed my nose. (Though I suppose it could have been the wind.) "This is private prop—" He didn't finish the sentence, couldn't. Not with my right arm wrapped snugly around his neck. Moments later, this father of the bride, decked out in rented frilly, baby-blue tuxedo shirt, black trousers with a shiny stripe down the side, and patent leather shoes, was trussed and marinating in the back seat of my cage car.

"Get him out of here, Stamper," my boss, Sergeant Kenny Reson, said. He'd arrived just in time to see me lowering Father of the Bride to the ground and cuffing him.

Really? I was just getting started: the groom himself, and the bride and assorted other friends and kin had migrated to the front porch and were screaming insincere questions and heartfelt epithets. Just begging to be busted, they were. I had room for at least two more in my car. Three criminal arrests were always better than one.

"Now!" Reson said.

"Yes sir." I headed over to Highway 94 for the trip downtown, leaving my fellow officers to clean up my mess. Fortunately, being cops, they understood.

Throughout my first fourteen months on the job, I set the standard for Constitution-bruising, human-rights-abusing, *I'm-in-charge-here* police work. So I know whereof I speak. I carry with me to this day a cellular memory of what it means to be "above," and to mistreat the people I was there to protect and serve. And what it feels like when power goes to your head, when your badge grows heavy on your chest.

Earlier, I argued that sometimes it's fear, rather than ire, that causes cops to "go off" on citizens, do unjustified violence to them. I also raised the specter of cops gone wild because, well, they want to. Now, let's consider this: that abusive officers are doing exactly what they have been taught— not necessarily in the classroom, but in the locker room or in the front seat of a patrol car.

Many younger cops have been instructed by their seniors to act like they own the streets. They are in charge—of everything and everyone. (Often, unfortunately, including their spouses, their children, their former friends.) Run from these officers, they will chase you, whether on foot or in a vehicle—innocent citizens be damned. Ask these officers a naïve or impertinent question, offer a suggestion, or, worse, criticize them or challenge their authority, you will be made to understand, in words, demeanor, or both: *I am a cop, and you're not.* So shut the hell up and let me do my job.

Such officers become their role. They embody their authority. That is both tragic and dangerous. As Sandra Bland's family can attest.

This all-too-common mentality is a bastardization of an important, indeed an essential, quality in a police officer: the ability to take control of or de-escalate perilous or sensitive situations. There's nothing more comforting at a chaotic scene than the arrival of a calm, confident professional who takes charge: the cop who helps get injured victims off to the hospital, a rowdy barroom under control, a dangerous suspect into a pair of cuffs. All with an authoritative yet calming, deft touch.

It's been said that a weakness is often a strength carried to an extreme. If this is so, I suspect that many, many officers have taken to an extreme their personal authority and duty. Their attitude seems to be, what's the use of having power if I can't abuse it? They, like me in my rookie period, lack the discipline and the good manners to bring with them to a scene problem-solving rather than problem-causing behaviors.

Good cops learn they don't have to be assholes.

I'm convinced it's possible, through selective unlearning and new learning, to help transform at least some "assholes" back into well-respected police officers. Yes, back into appreciated officers—as noted previously, most new cops approach the job with enthusiasm and a positive attitude. I know I did: I would become a respectful cop, would never use the N-word, would help the people I'd been hired to protect and serve. But it's not long before the acculturation process works its mojo, and our attitudes and behaviors turn south.

What needs to be "unlearned"? Bigotry and bias, of course, and, as it grows on the job, cynicism, as well. And the habits that spring up from that fertile, toxic soil—all of which need to be unpacked, examined, and properly disposed of.

And what needs to be learned? The answer might very well come from a surprising source.

The Baltimore Police Department, home to a long tradition of strained community-police relations—and, in April 2015, home to the death of Freddie Gray—just might hold the answer to how we can "relearn" important lessons.

In January 2015, Jonathan Page began training new BPD recruits in a "repetitive mental exercise." A cognitive neuroscientist from Dickinson College in Carlisle, Pennsylvania, Dr. Page has demonstrated that cognitive training can help new recruits recognize their biases, make better decisions under stress, and improve relations with the citizenry.[1]

The idea is to get the recruits to "run through their minds both on the job and off, while out on patrol or cruising the grocery aisle" six words: "breathe, scan, cover, threat, distance, escape." Slow, deep breathing, of course, is intended to keep the officer's heart rate down—crucial to accuracy of perception, not to mention stress management. The deliberate scanning of one's surroundings allows the officer to avoid tunnel vision and observe things one might not otherwise see, such as a victim or an armed suspect. And, by helping officers recognize their biases and improving relations with the community, the method promises to help them understand the irrelevance of skin color to one's official decision-making—except in searching for a robber, or a missing five-year-old, where accurate descriptions of physical characteristics matter. *Cover, threat, distance,* and *escape* are single-word cues that, if conditioned into a disciplined approach, dramatically improve both officer and citizen safety.

As Page puts it, "The words . . . are just a way to kind of create an architecture in the brain to help you see and understand situations, take in information very rapidly. . . . Part of that is emotional training, emotional intelligence; part of it is looking at biases."[2]

One BPD recruit, Andrew Definbaugh, who, along with thirty-five other new officers graduated in August, told a reporter, "Police officers have to make split-second decisions, so this is kind of a good way to understand the situation enough to go ahead and do what you believe would be the best option at the time." Speaking of a person who seems "angry and agitated," Definbaugh said, "Now I'm not going with those preconceived notions of what I see immediately. I'm trying to understand the situation. And I owe it to the community to try to understand what they are going through before making my judgment on what it is."[3]

The "Cognitive Command" (C2) curriculum is new, but it has been piloted in clinical trials—with C2-trained officers apparently staying calmer during (and remembering more after) a simulated crime scene than their control counterparts. Page is on a leave of absence from Dickinson, preparing to implement the program nationally, including in Seattle. Time will tell whether it lives up to its promise.

Given the structure of policing, the strength of its workplace culture, and its well-established tendency to reject "outsiders'" efforts at internal change, skepticism is warranted. But if "rewiring" the neural architecture of a cop's brain—while at the same time enhancing his personal safety—is doable, by all means let's get on with it. It just might be a way to help encourage senior cops to reconnect with the good feelings they had when they came on the job.

REAL AMERICANS

COPS EITHER LOVED HIM or hated him. Movie-star handsome, Princeton-educated (in "rhetoric and persuasion"), eloquent, charismatic, full of himself, George Thompson, internationally renowned expert on "tactical communication," paced back and forth in front of the classroom, affectionately branding selected cops in the audience "brain-dead," labeling their ideas "no good," ordering them to "make a note!" He could be insufferable, to be sure. One member of the audience marched up to me at the first break of Dr.

Thompson's SDPD in-service class back in the 1980s on "Verbal Judo" and announced, "Get him out of here, Chief, or I'll...."

You'll what? Did I mention Thompson was an ex-cop who earned a 2nd Dan black belt in Judo, and that he was built like a lifeguard on Muscle Beach?

The class over, my staff and I studied the evaluations. I'd never seen such a division of opinion. Roughly half the students gave him a 5 (basically "walks on water"), the other half a 1 ("tar and feather the bastard"). Forget his outsized personality for a moment—what was it about George Thompson's message that so thoroughly enraptured or enraged twenty-five San Diego cops and their sergeants and lieutenants?

In brief, Thompson talked about "Real Americans." And how good cops knew how to talk to them. And bad ones didn't.

What's a "Real American"?

CONSIDER A SEATTLE COP who came face to face with just such a specimen on July 9, 2014. The officer may well have set a record for a cop repeating herself. Captured in living color on her patrol car's video and audio cam, she stops an African American man on a street corner in the Capitol Hill neighborhood. Minding his own business, the elderly veteran leans against a golf club, a putter, as he waits for the light to change. The officer gets out of her car, tells him to "drop the golf club!" To which William Wingate replies, in explanatory but firm fashion, "No. This is *my* golf club . . . I've had it for twenty years."[4] The response of a *Real American*, I can hear Thompson say. I can only imagine his reaction had he known what was about to happen next.

As the video rolls, Officer Cynthia Whitlatch *yells* at Wingate, repeatedly ordering him to drop the club. "I'm going to ask you for the, I don't know, *thirteenth* time" to put the club down. She even tells him, twice, that their interaction is being "audio- and video-recorded." By actual count, she tells Wingate *twenty-two times* to drop the golf club.

Oh my.

In my imagination, with each new order, Whitlatch shrinks a couple of inches. By the time she's bellowed the order almost two dozen times, to zero effect, she's the size of a munchkin. Speaking munchkinese, no less. While the object of her ire stands tall, a study in dignity and genuine puzzlement, his trusty putter at his side, asking her to "call someone."

Finally, she approaches Wingate, seizes the "evidence," handcuffs him behind his back, and escorts him to a prisoner van, which he has difficulty boarding, for transportation to jail. But with no "audio- and video-recorded" evidence to support her claim that the man took a swing at her, or otherwise threatened her, he's released. The charges are quickly dismissed, and his makeshift cane, used on his daily ten-mile walks, is returned to him.

William Wingate, seventy, is suing the city in federal court, seeking at least $750,000 in damages. Apart from the obvious complaint, against the officer and the City of Seattle, it is further alleged that Whitlatch personally lobbied the City Attorney's Office to have Wingate charged with obstructing a police officer. She claimed he was "one of the most obstinate, uncooperative and obstructive suspects" she had encountered during her seventeen years in patrol.[5]

LOOK, I'M NOT SAYING citizens should defy a police officer's order. On the contrary, my strongest advice to all citizens is to follow, explicitly, a cop's instructions—and, if wronged, file a complaint, and then sue, if so desired. It pays to remember the tools and weapons carried by police officers, and to recall, as well, that some cops are all about pushing their weight around and abusing their authority. Wingate, who knew he'd done absolutely nothing wrong, took a chance that sunny afternoon in Seattle. On any given day you can find fresh footage on the Internet of angry, shouting, sputtering cops insisting in no uncertain terms that their orders be followed, now!

Every time I see such a police officer, including those with the best of intentions, and with every right to make lawful demands on their fellow citizens, I wonder whether things would have been different had they learned a few simple lessons from Thompson.

In driving home his message on "verbal judo" for law enforcement officers, Thompson put together a list of "seven things cops should never say to anyone." They're all instructive:

1. **"HEY YOU! COME HERE!"** Thompson describes this oft-heard command as "loose, lazy, and ineffective language." His preferred

alternative? "May I chat with you?" The point? "Polite civility can be a weapon of immense power."

2. **"CALM DOWN!"** Thompson says, "This command never works, so why do we always use it? Because it flows naturally from our lips." As with many effective de-escalation techniques, a counterintuitive approach is best. Our resident professor suggests that officers "look the person in the eye and say, gently, 'It's going to be all right. Talk to me. What's the matter?' The phrase 'What's the matter?' softens the person up to talk and calm down; where 'Calm down' hardens the resistance."

3. **"I'M NOT GOING TO TELL YOU AGAIN!"** Have we beaten this one to death? One additional point, from Thompson: "The phrase is, of course, a threat, and voicing it leaves you only one viable option— action! If you are not prepared to act, or cannot at the time, you lose credibility, and with the loss of [credibility] comes the loss of power and safety. Like the rattlesnake you have made noise, and noise can get you hurt or killed. Better to be more like the cobra and strike when least expected." An example? "'Sir, is there anything I could say that would get you to do A, B and C?' I'd like to think so. If the answer is NO, we act while the subject is still talking! We do not telegraph our actions nor threaten people, but we do act when verbal persuasion fails." (And, he might have added, when we have the authority to do so.)

4. **"BE REASONABLE!"** The problem with this one, according to Thompson, is that it carries the same emotional baggage as "Calm down!" It raises hackles, and defenses. Instead, he counsels, "Use the language of reassurance—'Let me see if I understand your position. . . . '" At which point the officer would paraphrase, in language "more professional and less emotional," what the person has said, which "absorbs the other's tension and makes him feel your support. Now you can help them think more logically and less destructively, without making the insulting charge implied in your statement, 'Be more reasonable!'"

5. **"BECAUSE THOSE ARE THE RULES!"** (or **"THAT'S THE LAW!"**) "If ever there was a phrase that irritates people and makes you look weak, this is it!" Thompson says. "Note, a true sign of respect

is to tell people why, and telling people why generates voluntary compliance. Indeed, we know that at least 70 percent of resistant or difficult people will do what you want them to do if you will just tell them why!"

6. **"WHAT'S YOUR PROBLEM?"** I love Thompson's explanation: "This snotty, useless phrase turns the problem back on the person needing assistance. It signals this is a 'you-versus-me' battle rather than an 'us' discussion. The typical reaction is, 'It's not my problem. You are the problem!'" I wonder how many times, as a brash rookie, I heard that thrown back at me. Dozens, I'm sure. And, as Thompson puts it, "The problem with the word ['problem'] is that it makes people feel deficient or even helpless." (Had I been trying for that effect during my rookie days? Looking back, the answer is "probably." I know I lorded it over people, baited them, hoping they'd take a swing at me so I could show them what I'd learned in defensive tactics class.) "It can even transport people back to grade school," Thompson said, "where they felt misunderstood and underrated. . . . When asked, 'What's your problem?' the other already feels a failure. So the immediate natural reaction is, 'I don't have one, you do!' . . . Substitute tactical phrases designed to soften and open someone up, like, 'What's the matter?' 'How can I help?'"

7. **"WHAT DO YOU WANT ME TO DO ABOUT IT?"** Thompson calls this a "pseudo question," one that is "always accompanied by sarcasm," revealing the cop's "exasperation and lack of knowledge." It's the kind of question "heard from untrained sales clerks and young officers tasked with figuring out how to help someone when the rules are not clear. When you say, 'What do you want me to do about it?' you can count on two problems: the one you started with and the one you just created by appearing to duck responsibility."[6]

The Thompson alternative? "Offer to help sort out the problem and work toward a solution. If it truly is not in your area of responsibility, point the subject to the right department or persons that might be able to solve the problem. If you are unable or unqualified to assist and you haven't a clue as to how to help the person, apologize. Had the officer said to the complainant, for example, 'I'm sorry, I really do not know what to recommend, but I wish I did, I'd like to help you. Remember, insult strengthens resistance and shuts the eyes. Civility weakens resistance and opens the eyes."[7]

IN EXAMINING THE RECENT spate of controversial deaths at the hands of police—from Ferguson to Pasco, New York, to Albuquerque—it's crucial to ask whether the officers did, in fact, give voice to one or more of the "seven things cops should never say to anyone." I'd be willing to bet your salary that these cops resorted to at least one of these "brain-dead" statements.

Look at Thompson's list, study what was said by the officers, and *how* it was said. With two possible exceptions (the Cleveland shooting of Tamir Rice and the North Charleston shooting of Walter Scott, the first likely attributable to out-of-control fear, the second to a craven disregard of human life), I believe we can reasonably conclude that if these officers had used different language, had they presented themselves as caring, professional, perhaps less "emotional," they would have saved, not taken, lives.

THOMPSON'S "REAL AMERICAN"—ESSENTIALLY anyone willing to "question authority," as the bumper sticker succinctly puts it—is more than metaphor. Implicit in his definition, and in his classroom examples, is a fundamental question: for whom do the police work? It's rarely put elegantly when a motorist, angry at getting a ticket, screams at a cop, "You work for me! I pay your salary!" But the truth of the statement is self-evident. The officer *does* work for the motorist, and the taxpaying motorist *does* pay his salary. And that ought to count for something.

Bad cops might answer correctly if taking a civics test, but there is no way in hell they see themselves working for disgruntled motorists—or any other citizen. For them, every contact is a one-up/one-down proposition. And they are always in the one-up position. Early in their career, they may have come to justify that way of thinking and acting based on (deeply flawed) officer-safety concerns. But now they have come to believe in and, indeed, to embody their sense of superiority.

GEORGE THOMPSON PASSED AWAY, from throat cancer (I'll leave the symbolism to others) in 2011. During his lifetime, even as he exchanged his movie-star looks for that of a balding WWE wrestler, even as that compelling voice became tired and raspy, he taught over 1 million students, more than half of them cops and corrections officers.

It's a shame some of his students were more interested in shooting the messenger than in absorbing the message. In any case, comprehensive instruction in de-escalation and tactical communication, of the type Thompson taught, must be mandatory for every officer in the country.

In September 2015, Seattle police chief Kathleen O'Toole fired Cynthia Whitlatch. She's appealing.

THE THRILL OF THE CHASE

Another manifestation of the we're-the-cops-and-you're-not mentality rears up every time a motorist puts a foot on the gas and tries to outrun a cop. Your local PD is no place for action junkies, yet there can be no denying the rush that accompanies a pursuit, whether in a car or on foot.

The hardest thing in the world for most cops to do is back off. From the classroom to the locker room, the culture teaches them: you cannot back away, or back down, and you certainly cannot lose. Whether it's a fistfight or a car chase, you must come out on top. Allowing certain suspects, under certain circumstances, to evade arrest just might be the smartest thing a police officer could do in a given situation, but that doesn't seem to matter. Every fiber of a cop's being is dedicated to catching those who flee, especially those who have hurt other people. It's a noble aspiration, but one that demands strong policies, tactical smarts, close supervision, and steely self-discipline.

And that comes from both temperament and experience. Training simulations are great, essential in fact, but there's nothing like having to make decisions in the real world, in real time. And living with your choices, good or bad.

Summer 1967. I've been a cop for a year and a half. The five of us had been at it for almost two weeks. Each late afternoon we gathered in Burglary, decked out in our grubbies. We went over the pin map, gleaned details from the latest case reports, agreed on our tactics, then headed into the field. Our mission? Detect and apprehend the suspect(s) responsible for a residential burglary series dating back to the early 1960s. As the rookie of the team, I got to sit on a tall stool, night after night, in the back of the San Diego Police Department's one unique undercover vehicle: an old light-green pickup, with a camper shell. And a turret, into which I would stick my head and peer out through the louvers, praying to catch sight of the bad guy(s).

We were confident we'd figured it out. Our suspect(s) would slowly drive the broad, winding streets of Del Cerro, an upscale subdivision north of San Diego State University, looking for lights to come on at dusk. A residence that remained dark likely meant no one was home, making it a prime target. On the night in question, I was perched on my stool, swiveling this way and that, eyeing two houses, one to my left and the other to the right, whose interiors had stayed dark after the sun went down.

I watched a burgundy Pontiac GTO circle the block, twice. I keyed my walkie-talkie (the size and weight of a brick in those ancient times) and let the others know. "Two white males, twenties, clean-cut. Slow rate of speed, definitely on the prowl." It was hard to contain my excitement. "This could be it." Completing its second trip around the block, the GTO pulled up and parked a couple of car lengths right in front of the "vacant" pickup. The occupants got out and strolled nonchalantly to the north side of the darkened house on my right, disappearing from view. I whispered into the walkie-talkie and reported my observations. "Hollis," the senior cop on the detail, responded.

"On my way. Keep an eye on 'em," he said.

My heart skipped several beats as I saw light beams emanating from inside the residence. "They're inside!" I said. "With flashlights!"

"Don't spook 'em, for God's sake!" Hollis replied. "Stay put!"

Moments later, I watched as they returned to the car, each carrying a bulging cardboard commissary box. I breathlessly reported this development to Hollis, whose headlamps I saw at that very moment, coming up from behind.

The driver suspect opened the trunk of the GTO and the two men, glancing over their shoulders at the arriving car, hurriedly placed the boxes inside. Hollis pulled in behind them in his unmarked car (a "pastel" borrowed from Vice). He switched his radio to Public Address and said, with "command authority," "San Diego Police!" I darted out the back of the camper and rushed up to Hollis's vehicle just as the GTO sped off.

"Jump in!" Hollis shouted. I got in, slammed the door.

The chase was on. "Call it!" he said.

I grabbed the mic and informed the dispatcher of car and suspect descriptions and, with varying degrees of accuracy, a running account of our changes in streets, directions, and miles per hour. Hollis, who'd worked the area for several years, was most helpful.

Through the streets of Del Cerro we raced, the GTO staying well out in front. Traffic was blessedly light. Finally, after several minutes on surface streets, the GTO headed south to Interstate 8 and onto the westbound on-ramp.

That's when things turned serious. "Westbound I-8 from College," I told the dispatcher. "Seventy miles an hour . . . eighty . . . eighty-five . . . ninety. . . . "

Hollis backhanded my knee to get my attention. He shook his head. Message received. I pictured the dispatch sergeant in the "business office" at 801 West Market, a click away from keying *his* mic and ordering us to back off. Doing the bidding of the brass, the old farts who'd forgotten what it was like to be a cop.

"Slowing down," I said into the mic. "Approximately seventy now." Which had the benefit of being true, in that the GTO was starting to fishtail its way down the Fairmount Avenue ramp. How the driver made it, how *we* made it, was beyond me. Moments later, after a series of dangerous maneuvers through moderate traffic northbound on Fairmount, we found ourselves westbound on San Diego Mission Road. Today, at night, that road would be lit up with condos, tennis courts, strip malls, streetlights, gas stations, and the famous Mission San Diego de Alcala. On that night, however, the entire route from Fairmount west to what is now I-15 was pitch black. Which made it an act of singular insanity when the bad guys cut their lights—and maintained speeds of fifty or better.

The only thing crazier was the two of us continuing the pursuit.

Hollis did his best to keep up, our heads bobbing back and forth like boxers, peering through the windshield into the darkness, trying to keep the occasional brake lights of the GTO in sight. It was a losing proposition, and Hollis finally admitted defeat and backed off.

Other units, however, had screamed into the area, their sirens echoing all around us (the pastel had no siren, not even a single red spot). Up ahead we eyed a fellow cop, parked, waiting, at the I-15 junction. The getaway car barreled down on him, its daring driver able at the last moment to make the right turn to northbound I-15.

The patrol officer put it in gear and immediately lit him up. And the chase was done: inexplicably, the driver of the GTO simply pulled over and stopped. Hollis and I, who'd fallen in behind the marked unit, bailed out of our vehicle and rushed the car. The passenger put his hands on the dash, the driver kept his on the wheel. They'd given up. Just like that, after all those years of outsmarting cops all over Southern California.

We split them up, Hollis taking the driver. I escorted the passenger to the back seat of a cage car, one of several on the scene: a gaggle of cops had pulled up to gawk at the phenomenally successful burglars—whose luck had finally run out. I slid in beside my guy.

"How come you stopped?"

"We seen that red light come on, and we knew we was busted. I mean, a CHP [California Highway Patrol] car? No way we could outrun him." (Poor sap. The "highway car" was a beat-up '64 SDPD Ford with over 90,000 miles on it, the latest of its serially recapped tires as bald as a newborn's butt.)

Our two AWOL marines from El Toro copped to well over a hundred burglaries, dating back to 1961. In addition to items stolen from that evening's Del Cerro job—jewelry, cash, two checkbooks, other valuables—we recovered all kinds of additional stolen property, including an LAPD detective lieutenant's badge.

I hadn't been behind the wheel, but I had experienced the sheer joy of the chase, and the thrill of the bust.

When I got home in the early morning hours, after inventorying the loot, writing out one of the two arrest reports, and celebrating with the team until dawn, I crept into my infant son's room and stared down at him in his crib. And it hit me: the wisdom of a certain senior officer.

I was still in the academy at the time, spending half a shift in the classroom, the other half in the field.

I'd been dropped off, by a "transportation unit," next to another of those beat-up patrol cars, this one in the parking lot of a bowling alley in the Lomita Village neighborhood of Southeast San Diego.

"You drive," the ill-tempered old cuss said.

"Yes, sir."

"Humphries" got out of the car, ambled around to the passenger side, removed his helmet (a felony, if the sergeant or, God forbid, the lieutenant caught you). He settled in—and was snoring by the time I pulled out of the parking lot.

Fifteen minutes later I was in pursuit of a speeder, westbound on the curving one-lane Paradise Valley Road. Humphries came alive.

"Back off!"

"What?" I'd clocked the dark Impala at sixty-five, was gaining ground on it.

"I said back the fuck off!"

"He'll get away," I said.

"Pull over."

I slowed down, found a section of shoulder wide enough to accommodate us, and pulled off the road.

"Cut the engine."

I cut the engine.

"You mind telling me what the fuck you were doing?"

I wanted to say, *My job!* I'd been warned about Humphries. He refused to play the numbers game. Sergeants didn't scare him, nor did the rest of the brass. Or their rules.

"He was twenty or thirty over the limit," I said.

"'Twenty or thirty over.' Is that what you want them to put on your tombstone? 'He was twenty or thirty over'"?

Humphries proceeded to tell me about another San Diego cop who had worked nights, the same beat. November 25, 1963. Rookie Michael Bushman was due to get off work. He never showed up. The dispatcher tried to raise him, repeatedly. No answer. No other units had seen him since 2:00 a.m., when he'd pulled into a gas station on Imperial Avenue. At 4:30 a.m. an all-out search was launched. Three hours later a patrol cop found Bushman's car, upside down in a dirt gully off Paradise Valley Road. Dead at the scene, he'd been ejected from the car.

"You want to kill yourself, knock yourself out," Humphries said. "But not with me in the car." How would I have felt, he demanded to know, if, because I'd decided to drive like a maniac, I had wiped out an entire family?

It came back to me as I stroked my son's cheek: that one-sided conversation, months before, with Humphries. Whatever his faults, whatever his personal priorities (working an off-duty job during the day, snoozing half the night away in the front seat of a police car), Humphries had nailed at least one professional priority. And he'd gotten my attention, however belatedly.

All it took was staring down at Matthew in his crib and thinking back to Humphries's question about that hypothetical family. It finally got through to me, for good.

A DECISION TO ENGAGE in or continue a reckless chase is, by definition, stupid. Whether or not it ends in a collision, that kind of driving is subject to administrative review and discipline, not to mention the possibility of criminal charges and civil penalties. Officers and their agencies have been held liable, and rightly so, for property damage, injuries, and deaths caused by a decision to continue a pursuit in the face of multiplying risks.

When it comes to high-speed chases or other emergency driving, police officers—and their communities—must ask, "Is it worth it?" Might it be better—saner, smarter—to back off, get a plate number, and find another way, another time to get the job done? One that doesn't unnecessarily risk innocent lives?

You see, police pursuit crashes kill more than a person a day, and one-third of the victims are uninvolved in the chase, completely innocent. In fact, a recent comprehensive study by *USA Today* reveals that more than 15,000 people—5,000 of them innocent bystanders and passengers—have been killed, and tens of thousands injured, in police chases since 1979.[8] Moreover, every six weeks, a police officer is killed in a police pursuit. What does that say about cops who constantly talk about "making it home safely at the end of every shift"?

Almost all of these deaths can be prevented through sound, vigorously enforced policies and procedures; comprehensive, repetitive training; informed driving techniques; conscientious field supervision; and alert, self-disciplined police officers.

This would be a good place to talk about pursuit driving techniques (and new tools and technologies, for that matter, some of which are innovative and most promising). But I'm going to pass, on grounds presented earlier: the less certain people know about certain police tactics, the better. On the other hand, it can't be stressed enough: current scientific and technological research into mechanical means of safely stopping a fleeing motorist must continue posthaste. Lives are at stake, and the solutions are out there. From what I've read, it's just a matter of time before police will have the means to shut down the engine of an "evading" motorist.

We'll never know whether Michael Bushman was pursuing a speeder when he went airborne off Paradise Valley Road. We do know he left behind a loving family, a wife, and a two-year-old daughter.

And it was likely that he had committed at least one of the "ten deadly errors" of policing.

PIERCE BROOKS WAS A legendary LAPD homicide detective who led the investigation into the kidnapping and murder of a Los Angeles police officer over half a century ago (a case that formed the basis for Joseph Wambaugh's bestseller, *The Onion Field*). Brooks, who suffered in later years from Alzheimer's disease and who died in Springfield, Oregon, in 1998, was a pioneer in the field of serial killer profiling. According to his longtime partner, Dan Bowser, who spoke with a reporter following Brooks's death, "He was the closest thing I ever saw to Sherlock Holmes. With his precision and his dedication, there was nobody better at that type of work."[9]

Brooks was also deeply committed to another police specialty: keeping cops alive.

THE TEN DEADLY ERRORS OF POLICING: BACKGROUND

BROOKS'S INTEREST IN THE subject led to the compilation of an inventory of fatal behaviors that formed the spine of his classic 1976 book, "... *officer down, code 3,*"[10] which predates the far more expansive work of "officer survival" experts, such as Charles Remsberg, co-founder of Calibre Press and author or co-author of several popular textbooks on officer safety and survival. Remsberg, now editor in chief of the Force Science Institute's newsletter, more than any other individual, save perhaps his colleague, Bill Lewinski, of Minnesota State University (who has made a handsome living defending cops accused of lethal and excessive force), has wielded the greatest influence over police-officer safety policies, training, and tactics during the past thirty-five years.

It is irrefutable that the "officer-survival" mentality has played a significant role in the increased aggression and militarization of American law enforcement. I saw it in San Diego, saw it in Seattle, and have seen it throughout the nation. However, while critics who accuse Remsberg and Lewinski of "pseudo science" may well have a point—they are, after all, advocates—I believe most of the controversy surrounding the field has come to pass largely because of misunderstanding, misinterpretation, and misapplication of the officer-survival message. At its base, the message is this: too many cops are fatalistic. As Remsberg has pointed out, they've convinced themselves that if their number is up, it's up.

With the exception of pure ambushes, which are uncommon occurrences, cops can do much to enhance their own safety and, yes, make it home every shift, night after night, for an entire career. Without coming across as G.I. Joe.

As I learned from talking with him back in the 1990s, that was a fervent wish of Pierce Brooks: namely, that cops be both safe and "courteous." He put together his "Ten Deadly Errors," he told me, after having attended "one too many cop funerals." To this day, the list hangs in police lockers throughout the country:

1. Failure to maintain proficiency and care of weapon, vehicle, and equipment;
2. Improper search and use of handcuffs;
3. Sleepy or asleep;
4. Relaxing too soon;
5. Missing the danger signs;
6. Taking a bad position;
7. Failure to watch their hands;
8. Tombstone courage;
9. Preoccupation;
10. Apathy.

Although it's tempting to analyze the list in sequence, I prefer to break it down more or less by order of importance, starting with an issue that intersects directly with officer safety and a current source of widespread citizen dissatisfaction with America's police: No. 2, "Improper search and use of handcuffs."

We'll talk about handcuffs later. Police officers are taught to "pat down" or "frisk" an individual when they have a "reasonable suspicion" the person may be involved in a crime and may be a danger to the officer or others.

However controversial it may be, the legitimacy of "stop and frisk" is firmly established in law (*Terry v. Ohio*, 1968), and such stops have helped communities prevent crime, and their police departments to detect and apprehend those who commit it. (Read the *Terry* case for an example of some very fine police work by a sixty-two-year-old Cleveland detective, Martin McFadden, who on Halloween day, 1963, observed and then arrested three highly suspicious men who were casing a store with a probable motive of robbery, the kind of robbery that often turns into murder.

McFadden, acting on reasonable suspicion, found two guns in a pat-down of the three men.)[11]

Terry was a long time ago, and it's but a single case of a stop-and-frisk success. What has been the more recent experience? Well, in New York City, more than 4 million residents have been subjected to stop-and-frisk procedures over the past decade.[12] A weapon was found in less than 1 percent of the stops. More telling, a report from Bill de Blasio's office, while he still served as the city's public advocate, found that minority men were "overwhelmingly" targeted by the practice. Yet in 2012, the NYPD recovered a weapon in only one of every forty-nine stops of whites, one of every seventy-one stops of Latinos, and one of every ninety-three stops of African Americans.[13] Is there any wonder that young black men, in particular, believe they are victims of police discrimination?

Pat-downs are confined to outer clothing and, when conducted in good faith (that is, lawfully), are a legitimate and important public-and-officer-safety tool. But what of an actual search? Police officers are permitted by law—and required by their agencies—to search individuals taken into physical custody. The search is usually conducted at the site of the arrest, after the prisoner has been handcuffed but before being placed in a police vehicle. (Strip searches, on the other hand, are generally forbidden, at least until the prisoner is booked into jail, at which time custodial officials may require the prisoner to strip nude and submit to a body search, including cavities.)

Cops may also search vehicles if (1) they have a warrant, (2) the search is incidental to an arrest, or (3) they have probable cause to believe the arrestee is involved in criminal activity (minor traffic violations don't count).

I'M ACUTELY AWARE OF the rationale for a post-arrest field search, given that when I was a new cop, and riding with an officer of even less experience, I committed one of Brooks's "deadly errors." We'd just arrested two men for a commercial burglary on El Cajon Boulevard in East San Diego.

"You search them?" I asked when I'd finished nosing around inside their car (case law of the era allowed warrantless, incidental-to-arrest vehicle searches).

"Yes, sir. All set."

We put the two men in the back seat of our car and drove downtown.

Shortly after we cleared the sally port of the San Diego County Jail, I received a radio call to phone the watch commander. Imagine my surprise when Captain Bill Schenck informed me that the sheriff's jail crew had discovered a total of three knives on our two prisoners—not one, not two, but three knives. Not a time for excuses: I served my suspension and considered myself lucky. Those jail deputies are unarmed, and, as the senior officer on Unit 35-East, their blood would have been on my hands had our prisoners decided to attack.

MOST LAW ENFORCEMENT AGENCIES require all prisoners to be cuffed following an arrest and prior to being transported. The proper method, unless a prisoner's physical disability makes it impossible, is to apply the cuffs behind the back, thereby reducing opportunities for the arresting or transporting officer to be attacked, whether at the scene or from the backseat of a police car. (A favorite academy "sea story," probably an urban myth, has a shoplifter, a sweet little old woman, cuffed in front out of respect for her age, using a six-inch hatpin to stab the arresting officer in the neck as he drove her to jail.)

One of the most disturbing images in recent times is the practice of handcuffing an individual who has been shot by the police and who appears to be lifeless.

"Cuffing people after they've been shot, or when they're dead, or when they're dying," Ronald L. Kuby, a civil rights lawyer, told a reporter, "is one of the ugliest, most barbaric, unnecessarily horrifying things that the police do, and they do it as a matter of course."[14]

Mr. Kuby is right on both points. The optics are horrible, ghastly in fact—and often reflect an utter lack of human decency and compassion. But, yes, handcuffing individuals shot by the police is done "as a matter of course." It's policy.

What gives sound policies their soundness is that though intended to govern, standardize, and legitimize individual officer actions, they do leave room for exceptions. The kind of exception, for example, that was made for

Michael Brown, whose dead body was, in fact, left uncuffed. (Leaving his remains in the street, however, for almost four hours, was both unmerciful and indefensible, as well as inflammatory.) The cuffing of Walter Scott, on the other hand, shot at eight times and struck in the back five times, while fleeing from North Charleston, South Carolina, police officer Michael Slager, strikes many, including this ex-cop, as unwarranted. In the extreme.

Why handcuff a downed suspect in the first place? Simple. Some individuals who have been shot by the police, sometimes multiple times, sometimes in the head, sometimes with high-powered rifles . . . survive. The International Association of Chiefs of Police (IACP) cites such examples and lays out thirteen "lessons" for street cops ("Lesson 8: Handcuff all downed suspects," "Lesson 9: Thoroughly search all downed suspects after they have been cuffed").[15]

What's troubling about all this is that in the rush to militarize our police forces, and to standardize their tactics, we seem to have abandoned the place and value of individual officer discretion. Because cops can fire their weapon in a given set of circumstances, say, a potential assailant who has entered the so-called kill zone with a tire iron, does not mean they must. (Cops are taught that an attacker with an "edged" weapon can, from twenty-one feet away, close to within killing range before the officer can draw and fire. Citizen skeptics in San Diego were disabused of their skepticism when, in a series of public meetings, we simulated attacks on volunteers from the audience: they played cops, we played [plastic] bat-wielding suspects.) Because cops are ordinarily required to cuff downed prisoners does not mean officers cannot size up a given situation and make an informed choice to do otherwise. So long as the officer is willing to live with the consequences of that choice.

In the end, if there is an objectively reasonable chance that failure to handcuff a downed suspect could result in death or injury to oneself, a fellow officer, or an innocent bystander, I'd say optics be damned, and break out the cuffs.

BROOKS UNDERSTOOD, FROM THE cops whose murders he investigated, that a police officer who relaxes too soon (Number 4), or is preoccupied

(Number 9), or apathetic (Number 10), just might pay the ultimate price for "Taking a bad position" (Number 6).

"Position" is crucial to a cop. If you've ever stood next to an on-duty (maybe even an off-duty) police officer, you probably noticed that the officer took great pains to keep you away from his "gun side," to the point that it may have felt like the two of you were engaged in some odd little dance. Most cops finally become explicit about this one: "Look, please stay put. I don't allow anyone, even my bedridden grandmother, on my gun side."

And, finally, "Failure to watch their hands" (Number 7), which just might be the most important of the bunch.

Say you're traveling on the Interstate. You get lit up by an officer who has been following you for half a mile. You pull over and stop. Over the PA, you hear a godlike amplified voice, "Keep your hands on the steering wheel." What should you do? Well, here's my advice: Keep your hands on the steering wheel!

Officers know to watch the hands. Sure, a potential assailant could kick a cop, or deliver a head butt. But most attacks on police are carried out with guns, fists, knives, or other edged weapons. So when the hands move, particularly if they move suddenly, or they disappear, that's cause for an instantaneous reaction. Often involving a service weapon.

In 2000, on his *The Awful Truth* TV show, Michael Moore memorialized the 1999 death of Amadou Diallo. The unarmed, non-English-speaking immigrant had been hit by nineteen of forty-one shots fired at close range by NYPD cops as he removed his wallet, seeking to show them his ID. Moore organized "The African American Wallet Exchange" and attracted a throng of young African American men, plus, I'm guessing, several puzzled and pissed cops. He told the black men he was there, on the street, to "confiscate" their wallets in exchange for bright, glow-in-the-dark orange models. I didn't know whether to laugh or cry (I mean that) as he told them, "Pull your wallets out slowly. Don't make any sudden moves. Now place them on the ground. Step back from the wallets."

OF THE REMAINING TIPS on Brooks's list, Number 1 is self-explanatory (if a cop's car stalls out or his or her gun misfires because of poor maintenance, that could produce a nasty result). And Number 8, "Tombstone courage"? Simply put, it means a "lone-wolf," heroic approach to the job. It means not thinking, not planning, not waiting for backup (when backup is possible).

This raises an important question, one that neither my experience nor the research can answer definitively: Is it more (or less) likely that a cop working alone—versus with a partner—will behave responsibly and in accordance with the law and sound tactics?

In San Diego, in the 1970s, the Police Foundation (funded by the Ford Foundation) studied the differences between one-officer and two-officer patrol units. Researchers examined:

Unit performance: the type, quantity, and quality of services performed.
Unit efficiency: the unit time and cost associated with comparable levels of performance.
Officer safety: the rates of assaults on officers, resisting arrest situations, vehicle accidents, and officer injuries resulting from comparable levels of exposure.
Officer attitudes: the preferences and opinions of assigned patrol officers.

The outcome of the study surprised a lot of people, especially the nation's cops: "Results suggested that two-officer units produced lower levels of service, were less efficient, and were *less* safe than comparison one-officer units [original emphasis]."[16]

Although many variables must be taken into account, including the age of the study (published in 1977), the results do suggest that two cops riding together in the same car will "produce" less work than officers riding in separate cars. That seems to make sense; two cops, two cars, covering twice the ground and theoretically doing their own work should produce more activity (though "activity" should never, ever be equated with good police work). But, really, are two officers less safe working paired than working apart? That conclusion seems counterintuitive, unless one considers the "bravado" factor.

Let's say a cop working alone encounters an ambiguous situation—a figure down a darkened alley at four in the morning. Could be a homeowner taking out the garbage, or a hot prowler (a burglar who breaks in when people are home). Our solo officer is likely to take some time to size up the situation, call for backup, spend additional moments conferring with her cover officer, considering her options. But if her backup is "built in," meaning sitting in the passenger seat, and she's concerned how it might look if she hesitates, she may well rush in, without forethought. And that could get her, her fellow officer, or a citizen hurt.

The bravado factor: there's no room for it in a safe, smart, community-oriented police department—no matter how cool it looks when Detective Danny Reagan of CBS's *Blue Bloods* dashes into a building full of armed terrorists and singlehandedly takes them down. High drama, reckless police work.

POLICE OFFICERS WHO CARE about their citizen partners; who treat the residents as they would like to be treated; who know the law (and are not offended by fellow Americans who question police authority in enforcing it); and who have learned to act safely, conduct themselves with restraint, and stay focused on professional standards—these are the officers who are incredibly valuable to their communities.

In contrast, officers with the attitude I brought to my rookie days—a holier-than-thou arrogance—are a walking, driving liability, an accident or an assault looking to happen. It's because of these kinds of cops that Americans must be thoroughly familiar with and willing to exercise their constitutional rights.

10

FLEX YOUR RIGHTS

IN 1973, ANTHONY HOLMES was led into an interrogation room on Chicago's South Side. Accused of murder, handcuffed and manacled, he awaited his interrogator, Detective Jon Burge.

Burge showed up carrying a small black box, featuring a crank and two wires. He attached one wire to Holmes's wrists, the other to his ankles. The detective then stretched a plastic bag over Holmes's head. When Holmes bit through it in order to breathe, Burge applied another, and twisted it tight. Then he cranked and cranked, and the screams rang out.

As Holmes told prosecutors during a 2006 investigation into Burge's conduct, "When he hit me with the voltage, that's when I started gritting, crying, hollering. . . . It [felt] like a thousand needles going through my body. . . . And then after that, it just [felt] like, you know—it [felt] like something just burning me from the inside, and, um, I shook, I gritted, I hollered, then I passed out."[1]

All the while, according to Holmes, Burge kept demanding, "You going to talk, nigger? You going to talk?"

Later, in 1982, with a couple of cop killers on the loose, Burge personally led the manhunt. As a detective would later describe it, "I don't know what Kristallnacht was like, but this was probably close. [The gang crimes unit's] idea is you go out and pick up 2,000 pounds of nigger and eventually you'll get the right one."[2]

Following five successive days and nights on that job, Burge picked the lock at the home of one of the alleged suspects and arrested, violently, one Andrew Wilson. Burge then personally led the fifteen-hour interrogation that followed. Wilson confessed but, according to the *Chicago Reader*, would later recant, telling "public defender Dale Coventry that he'd been shocked, burned by a radiator, suffocated with a plastic bag, and kicked in the eye and beaten. . . . Coventry had photos of a huge burn on his client's thigh, parallel burns on his chest, and strange U-shaped puncture marks on his nose and ears. Wilson said the marks came from alligator clips attached to wires leading to a hand-cranked electrical device. He said Burge shocked him on his genitals and his back with a second device that resembled a curling iron."[3]

And so it went. For two decades, an American police officer and his sizable posse of like-minded rogue detectives committed gross violations of civil liberties and human rights. Burge personally tortured or otherwise abused as many as two hundred of Chicago's citizens, mostly African American men. And the price he paid for this behavior? Numerous commendations from the brass, and successive promotions, ultimately topping out as detective commander of Chicago's Area 2.

Richard M. Daley, Cook County state's attorney at the time, not only turned a blind eye to Burge's outrages, he commended the detective. Even after having been warned, in 1982, by then police superintendent Richard Brzeczek that a doctor had presented evidence of the torture of Andrew Wilson, Daley, an officer of the court, refused to investigate.

Then Daley got elected mayor of Chicago.

After which he steadfastly discredited a thorough inquiry by a pair of Chicago Police Department Office of Professional Standards investigators who produced a two-section report on (1) a history of Area 2 misconduct allegations and (2) an analysis of the Andrew Wilson case. The mayor's denials, throughout a forty-eight-page deposition from 2006, suggest that both as state attorney and as mayor, Daley refused to believe that Commander Burge could have done what he stood accused of doing.

Later in 2006, when a special prosecutor issued a report confirming the pattern and practice of Burge's torture, Daley announced that he would apologize to all of the commander's victims. Finally, a breakthrough. Or was it? Here's Daley's apology, as he expressed it to the Chicago Independent Media Center:

> "The best way is to say, 'Okay. I apologize to everybody [for] whatever happened to anybody in the city of Chicago'. . . . So, I apologize to everybody. Whatever happened to them in the city of Chicago in the past, I apologize. I didn't do it, but somebody else did it. Your editorial was bad. I apologize. Your article about the mayor, I apologize. I need an apology from you because you wrote a bad editorial," Daley said, laughing.
>
> "You do that and everybody feels good. Fine. But I was not the mayor. I was not the police chief. I did not promote [Burge]. You know that. But you've never written that and you're afraid to. I understand."[4]

That a mayor—first as state's attorney, then as the top elected official of the nation's third largest city—would petulantly, cavalierly brush off responsibility for such breathtaking police abuse is beyond the pale.

Daley's flippant, sarcastic "apology" stands in marked contrast to the way today's city officials, including current mayor Rahm Emanuel, have responded to the travesty—at least on the surface. On May 6, 2015, Emanuel and the city council agreed to $5.5 million in "reparations" for Burge's victims, dating from the early 1970s to the early 1990s. All told, the whole matter has cost the taxpayers of Chicago roughly $100 million in lawsuits against, and in defense of, Mr. Burge.[5]

Regrettably, more recent developments raise fundamental questions about Mayor Emanuel's overall leadership in dealing with patterns of deepseated police abuse within his city's police department. These disclosures raise doubts about the mayor's timing and motives in both the Burge settlement and yet another high-profile police shooting case.

ON OCTOBER 20, 2014, Chicago Police Department (CPD) officers responded to a report of a young man with a knife, allegedly breaking into vehicles in a trucking yard in the 4100 block of Pulaski Road. Upon their arrival, seventeen-year-old Laquan McDonald reportedly slashed a tire on a police car and damaged its window. In a police dash-cam video, we see Officer Jason Van Dyke approach McDonald as the youth walks away from the police. Within seconds—and with McDonald clearly veering *away* from the officers—Van Dyke fires a single round. The teenager drops instantly to the asphalt, whereupon the officer continues to fire, emptying his weapon. Puffs of smoke on the cool evening air can be seen rising from the boy's inert body as Van Dyke fires each of the additional fifteen rounds from his semiautomatic pistol. The first officer on the scene had determined that there was no need to use force, much less lethal force. And none of the at least eight other officers fired a single round. Van Dyke was placed on paid desk duty, par for the course, and months went by as the investigation unfolded.

The year 2015 was a difficult one for the first-term Emanuel. He found himself in a tight, unexpected primary runoff against Jesus "Chuy" Garcia, and the McDonald case loomed large in the minds of voters—who had not yet seen the video. In a March 6, 2015, letter to city officials, a McDonald family attorney wrote: "I submit the graphic dash-cam video will have a powerful impact on any jury and the Chicago community as a whole. This case will undoubtedly bring a microscope of national attention to the shooting itself as well as the City's pattern, practice and procedures in rubber-stamping fatal police shootings of African Americans as 'justified' (file 1, p. 92)."

The parenthetical citation refers to a system created in order to catalog some 3,000 pages of e-mails and other city records provided by the mayor's office in response to open-record requests on the Laquan McDonald shooting. The "catalog," which is referenced in the January 5, 2016, edition of *In These Times,* crediting several contributors who helped the news organization compile it, is damning. It makes clear that the mayor's office knew of the dash-cam footage two months after the shooting—yet failed to make it public until ordered to do so by a Cook County judge. It confirms that the mayor and city council agreed to cut a check for the McDonald family of $5 million, even though the family had not yet filed a wrongful death claim against the city.

The mayor's office released the explosive video on November 24, 2015, shortly after Emanuel was reelected to a second term.

Upon the video's release, and the public's instant outrage over its contents, Emanuel on December 1, 2015, fired his police superintendent, Garry McCarthy. Demands for Emanuel's resignation, as well as that of Cook County state's attorney Anita Alvarez, are growing.

A grand jury indicted Officer Jason Van Dyke on six counts of first-degree murder. On December 29, 2015, he pleaded not guilty to all charges.

Abundant evidence, contained within the catalogued e-mails and other official reports, supports the conclusion that Emanuel and his staff were more interested in political damage control than in getting to the bottom of the shooting.

AND WHAT BECAME OF Jon Graham Burge, the police officer who, more than any other individual, put Chicago's police brutality and corruption on the map? In 2010, the statute of limitations having passed on his violent crime spree, he was convicted only of perjury—reducing all the evidence, all the published findings of his violent behavior to "allegations." Recently released from federal prison after having served just three and a half years, Burge is now living in Florida, where he is supported by a $54,000 per year pension, also courtesy of Chicago taxpayers.[6]

Mayor Emanuel, in announcing the reparations package, said, "Jon Burge's actions are a disgrace—to Chicago, to the hardworking men and women of the police department, and most importantly to those he was sworn to protect. Today, we stand together as a city to try and right those wrongs, and to bring this dark chapter of Chicago's history to a close."[7]

WHAT ARE THE CHANCES this "dark chapter" of the great city's past will be brought to a satisfactory close? A few years ago, I was retained by plaintiffs' counsel in a Chicago case alleging a widespread practice of arresting witnesses. As in handcuffing them, transporting them to police facilities, often against their will, hooking them to concrete benches, withholding food and water, denying access to counsel, as well as family, and holding them for hours if not days. The case went to trial, which ended in a "mixed verdict," although the federal judge did mandate certain changes in the department's handling of witnesses.

In November 2015, I asked Craig Futterman, clinical professor of law, founder and director of the Civil Rights and Police Accountability Project at the University of Chicago Law School, and plaintiff's counsel in the case, for an assessment of how the CPD's practices have changed since the verdict. Here's what he told me:

> From my perspective, Chicago continues to maintain a decades-long practice of denying individuals access to an attorney while they are being held in interrogation rooms—the time that people most need to know about their rights and responsibilities and the time that they are most often vulnerable to abuse. While the means have changed over time (the latest stem from CPD's practice of denying prisoners access to phones until they are placed in lock-up, after an interrogation has been completed), the results have been the same. Virtually no one held in Chicago police stations gets access to a lawyer.
>
> The mistreatment of witnesses was a subset of this broader practice. The CPD often pretended that suspects were "witnesses" to deny them their right to counsel. The consent decree that we won some years back has mostly ended that practice, but the Department has found other ways to deny people their right to lawyers.
>
> Using a lawsuit against the CPD, the *Guardian* revealed the scope of these egregious patterns and practices: Police "disappeared" more than 7,000 people at an off-the-books interrogation warehouse [the notorious Homan Square] in Chicago, nearly twice as many detentions as previously disclosed, the *Guardian* can now reveal.
>
> From August 2004 to June 2015, nearly 6,000 of those held at the facility were black, which represents more than twice the proportion of the city's population. But only 68 of those held were allowed access to attorneys or a public notice of their whereabouts, internal police records show.

The new disclosures, the result of an ongoing *Guardian* transparency lawsuit and investigation, provide the most detailed, full-scale portrait yet of the truth about Homan Square, a secretive facility that Chicago police have described as little more than a low-level narcotics crime outpost where the mayor has said police "follow all the rules."[8]

Please, Mayor Emanuel, you seem to have done the right thing in the Burge case. Political considerations aside, you helped, financially, the family of Laquan McDonald. But no police department anywhere follows *all* the rules. Indeed, the November 2015 release of a study of police discipline within your police department might cause a cynic to ask if *anyone* follows the rules in Chicago.

The nonprofit Invisible Institute (a "journalistic production company" on Chicago's South Side that works to "enhance the capacity of civil society to hold public institutions accountable") and the Mandel Legal Aid Clinic of the University of Chicago Law School battled the City of Chicago for ten years before they were able to bring to light the police department's record of internal accountability.

One subject in the story of police discipline is Officer Jerome Finnegan. In his eighteen years with the CPD, he had amassed a total of sixty-eight citizen complaints, mostly for illegal searches and excessive force. In 2011, he confessed to robbing criminal suspects during his tour with the elite Special Operations Section (SOS). He and other rogue cops committed numerous street robberies, home invasions, and miscellaneous other crimes. Upon learning that a fellow cop intended to turn him in, he ordered a hit on the officer. Finnegan was convicted and sentenced to twelve years in prison.[9]

Jerome Finnegan was but one of thousands of CPD officers who, despite having been the subject of numerous citizen complaints, went unchecked and undisciplined for years.

This is where cops everywhere interject: "We're talking about complaints here, not sustained allegations. Good cops, working in high-crime areas, get complaints. Besides, as every cop knows, lodging a complaint against an arresting officer is a common defense ploy. Get busted, say, for street dealing, why not beef the cop? Maybe the charge goes away, or at least gets reduced."

The problem with that analysis is revealed in the Chicago study's numbers. During a five-year period, 97 percent of the 28,500 citizen complaints of officer misconduct resulted in exactly no discipline. Of the thousands of complaints for 2015, more than 99 percent resulted in no punishment. And, the numbers on racial disparities are as predictable as they are dispiriting: of those few who received discipline, African American cops were punished at twice the rate of their white counterparts for the same offense; and, though black citizens filed most of the complaints, white citizens were much more likely to have theirs' sustained.[10]

It's not just the numbers that should keep Chicago's mayor and police superintendent awake nights. Finnegan had this to say, as he entered his guilty plea: "My bosses knew what I was doing out there, and it went on and on. And this wasn't the exception to the rule. This was the rule."[11]

LIKE FORMER MAYOR DALEY, the much-decorated Burge remains unrepentant. He recently wrote in response to a cop blog, "I find it hard to believe that the City's political leadership could even contemplate giving 'Reparations' to human vermin like them."[12]

It is apparent, given these new revelations, that the "Burge Purge" does not signal an end to the violence done to the citizens of Chicago, their humanity, their civil liberties.

When a police department is shown to be in systemic, if not sweeping violation of its citizens' rights, one can only assume that that agency has elected to rewrite the rules or to throw away the rule book—also known as the Constitution.

JUST AS TOP-FLIGHT DEFENSE attorneys force patrol cops and detectives to become better investigators, so too do citizens who stand up for their constitutional rights.

The police are trying to do a job, and like many others, if there's a dubious or "technical" shortcut that will ease their workload or get them to a quick solution, some will take it. If they meet no resistance, a vacuum is created—into which additional officers are more than happy to step, thereby shaping, indeed corrupting the culture and fostering erosion of civil liberties for all.

And that means it's in everyone's best interest for all citizens to know their rights, and to flex them.

THERE ARE MANY ORGANIZATIONS that can help individuals protect their civil liberties: the ALCU, of course, but also People for the American Way, the NAACP (National Association for the Advancement of Colored People), Cato Institute, National Association of Criminal Defense Lawyers, National Association for Civilian Oversight of Law Enforcement, Friends Committee on National Legislation, The Constitution Project, and hundreds of others, left, right, libertarian, and nonaligned. Some emphasize civil liberties, others civil rights.

The distinction between liberties and rights is not insignificant, although both terms appear in the Declaration of Independence and in the Bill of Rights. *Civil rights* guarantee equal treatment under the law. For example, a person cannot be discriminated against because of age, gender, gender identity, sexual orientation, race, nationality, ethnicity, disability, or religious beliefs. From the beginning, the nation's police have been involved in either helping or, too often, hindering—with crushing efficiency—the progress of civil rights in America.

Civil liberties are most identified with the Bill of Rights, and they include the right to assemble, to engage in free speech, to bear arms (as decided by the "comma" argument of the Second Amendment), and to be free from unreasonable searches and seizures. Again, although American police forces are required by law to protect their fellow citizens' civil liberties, they are often found to be in violation of them.

It may be a little scary, if not terrifying to contemplate, but it is vital that Americans understand and assert their inviolable rights in every encounter with the police. At a very minimum, willingness to report abusive police behavior is essential.

One organization, founded by Steve Silverman, is Flex Your Rights, which has developed "Ten Rules for Dealing with Police."[13] The rules are practical, legally sound, easy to digest. And I'm convinced that the organization's forty-minute film, narrated by acclaimed criminal defense attorney (and actor in *The Wire*) William "Billy" Murphy, will help close the gap between the premise and the practice of civil liberties in this country. The film is available with both Spanish and Arabic subtitles. I've reproduced the "top ten" list below, but I highly recommend watching the movie to see how each plays out in realistic, well-staged, finely performed scenarios. In November 2015, Silverman was kind enough to expand on each of his rules. I've recorded his personal commentary here, in italics:

1. **Always be calm and cool.** *A bad attitude guarantees a bad outcome. If you keep your cool, chances are the officer will, too.*

2. **Cops can lie. Don't get tricked.** *Police are allowed to lie to you. Don't let false threats or promises trick you into waiving your rights.*

3. **Don't agree to a search. Ever.** *Saying "no" to searches is your constitutional right and probably your best move. Cops might search you anyway if you refuse—but your refusal can protect you later if you end up in court.*

4. **Don't just wait. Ask: "Am I free to go?"** *Asking to leave shows that you're not agreeing to the police stop. This can protect you if you end up in court.*

5. **Don't do shady stuff in public.** *Making dumb decisions in public is the easiest way to find yourself in jail. Always think before you act, especially when other people are watching.*

6. **Don't admit anything. Remain silent.** *Cops aren't looking for an explanation; they're looking for evidence. Don't give them any.*

7. **Ask for a lawyer.** *Trying to talk your way out of trouble with police is a big mistake. If you're being interrogated or you're under arrest, calmly and clearly state, "I'm going to remain silent. I want a lawyer." Repeat if necessary.*

8. **Don't let them in without a warrant.** *With few exceptions, police need a warrant to enter your home. Unless you called for help, there's generally no good reason to let police into your home.*

9. **Don't panic. Report misconduct later.** *Pay attention to detail. Write down everything you saw and heard. If you plan to sue or complain, don't tell the officer.*

10. FILM the police! *If you want to prove police misconduct, video evidence is the best evidence. You have the right to record the police in all fifty states.*

We might want to add an eleventh rule: *Never touch a police officer,* and keep your hands in sight. Words to live by.

Friend and colleague Neill Franklin, executive director of Law Enforcement Against Prohibition and retired Baltimore and Maryland state police commander, reviewed a similar film (*BUSTED: The Citizen's Guide to Surviving Police Encounters*) produced by Silverman's organization and had this to say, "I'm a cop. I'm straight from the streets. One of the things I always talked [about] with police academy instructors . . . is to ensure we follow our oath, to serve and uphold the Constitution of the United States. Most people think . . . [the "Ten Rules"] is for kids and [non-cop] grown-ups, but I see it as a great tool for police academies."[14]

So do I. There's value in having new recruits learn about the conduct of cops like Jon Burge and Jerome Finnegan, as a cautionary tale. And for them to understand and appreciate that gross violations of civil liberties almost always start with small, seemingly innocuous acts—along the lines of the "You-don't-mind-if-I-search-your-car?" ploy I employed as a rookie—that have become second nature to so many cops.

PREVENTING CIVIL-LIBERTIES VIOLATIONS AND other police misconduct—and effectively confronting them when they happen—is a critical and multifaceted proposition. And it's complicated by deeply conflicted, real-world priorities. The city of Chicago, for example, is reeling from round after round of gun violence. Its homicide rate in 2015 was up 20 percent over 2014. On November 2, 2015, an adorable nine-year-old fourth-grader, Tyshawn Lee, was shot multiple times in the back and head as he played on a swing, targeted to avenge an earlier gang-related shooting.[15]

Mayor Emanuel's response, in part, has been to blame groups agitating for greater police accountability. Not for the murders, but for creating a "chilling effect" on the initiative of his police officers.

In an October 2015 meeting of top law enforcement and elected officials (a meeting that was to have been closed to the press but which was penetrated by a reporter from the *Washington Post*), the mayor told Attorney

General Loretta Lynch that cops are going "fetal," the result of their fear of being persecuted, or prosecuted, for doing their jobs. I understand the impulse. When people are dying in your city, Mr. Mayor, when babies and elementary school children are being gunned down, you want the cops to do something, to put an end to the violence. But remarks like that one, from the city's top official, aren't helpful.[16]

What is helpful is perspective. The 20 percent increase in murders in 2015? It followed a record low in 2014.[17] It would be nice, of course, if the electorate understood that reality, if the citizens of Chicago understood that crime rates, including murder rates, fluctuate in their city as in every city. That way, perhaps, they would not put undue political pressure on an official whose livelihood is contingent on votes. They would, instead, judge their mayor on his ability to fight crime and keep his cops under control.

Nobody said it would be easy, Mr. Mayor.

HOW DOES A COMMUNITY and its police department, committed both to effective crime fighting and to constitutional, transparent, and accountable policing meet this challenge? The answer is three-pronged: *supervision, peer pressure,* and *external forces.*

11

POLICING THE POLICE

IT WAS ONE OF the most catastrophic failures of police supervision in modern times, and it happened not in New York City, or Philadelphia, or Chicago—political jurisdictions accustomed to cyclical paroxysms of organized lawlessness within the ranks. This time it happened in Los Angeles, home of the squeaky-clean LAPD. Home of Jack Webb's *Dragnet* and Joe Wambaugh's Bumper Morgan, the gruff "Blue Knight" who, though he might have cut a bureaucratic or legal corner here and there, demonstrated his concern for every individual on his beat, grocers and schoolteachers, prostitutes and junkies alike. Growing up in the shadows of Los Angeles, 125 miles to the south, my SDPD colleagues and I heard it often: the LAPD might be a little heavy-handed (case in point, Rodney King), but it's the epitome of a clean police department, known everywhere for its ethics and integrity.

That all changed, big time, in the mid-1990s.

On October 12, 1996, Officers Rafael "Ray" Perez and his partner, Nino Durden, members of the Rampart Division's CRASH (Community Resources Against Street Hoodlums) anti-gang unit, took up an observation post on the top floor of an abandoned four-story apartment building. As they were monitoring gang and drug activity on the street below, a man burst into the darkened room brandishing a Tec-22 semiautomatic pistol. Both cops opened fire. Three rounds struck eighteen-year-old Javier

Francisco Ovando in the chest and neck. To hear them tell it, Perez and Durden were lucky to be alive.

When additional cops and an ambulance crew showed up, Ovando, Honduran born, non-English speaking, a member of the 18th Street Gang known for drug trafficking and vicious murders, was lying in a pool of blood, the gun at his side.

Paralyzed from the waist down and lying on a gurney a few days later, Ovando was wheeled into court, where he was bound over for trial, on seven felony counts. His public defender, Tamar Toister, had no reason to doubt the official version of the incident. Her main concern was the length of the prison term offered by the prosecution: thirteen years. Way too long, she reasoned, for the teenage paraplegic with no criminal record. Having faith that twelve of her fellow citizens would agree, she opted for a jury trial.

Between the preliminary hearing and the trial, Toister had developed nagging doubts about the officers' account of the shooting. For one thing, Ovando offered, through an interpreter, a very different version: he and his friend, "Nene," had been walking down the fourth-floor hallway of the abandoned building when the two plainclothes officers grabbed them, handcuffed them, and took them into the apartment. The cops questioned Nene and let him go. Then, without provocation, they shot Ovando, still cuffed and sitting in a chair. He'd been unarmed, had not threatened the officers, and had no knowledge of the Tec-22.[1]

Additional discrepancies mounted, but the judge rebuffed most of Toister's motions, calling for further investigation. Worse, the mysterious "Nene" was in the wind. No (non-cop) witnesses.

The weeklong trial in February 1997 ended in a guilty verdict, on all counts, and Superior Court Judge Stephen Czuleger sentenced Ovando to twenty-three years in prison.[2]

MEANWHILE, PEREZ'S FORMER CRASH partner, Officer David Mack, was working an off-duty job as a bodyguard for Marion "Suge" Knight, founder and CEO of Black Kapital Records and founder and former CEO of Death Row Records.

On November 6, 1997, Mack did a little additional off-duty work. He robbed a bank. He and three accomplices—a getaway driver, a fellow gunman, and an insider (a bank manager girlfriend of Mack's who had ordered extra cash to be on hand that date)—hit a South Central branch of the Bank of America and got away with $722,000.[3]

As the robbery investigation narrowed, and Mack surfaced as a suspect, LAPD detectives began connecting the dots. Mack's off-duty employer, Knight, had been a "person of interest" in the March 9, 1997, killing of Biggie Smalls (real name Christopher Wallace, stage name The Notorious B.I.G.). Mack was said to be obsessed with the rapper Tupac Shakur and believed Biggie Smalls was responsible for his idol's September 1997 drive-by shooting death in Las Vegas. When the detectives went to Mack's home to arrest him for the bank job, they noticed a 2Pac shrine in his garage. The cop was a bank robber. Was he also a killer?[4]

Digging deeper, the detectives learned that Mack and Perez were very close friends, that they had gone to Las Vegas together two days after the bank robbery. Perhaps to celebrate?

Then in March 1998, officers assigned to the property division discovered that six pounds of cocaine, an $800,000 cache, was missing. When it was learned that Rafael Perez had checked it out for a court case but never returned it, and that there were other irregularities—for example, checking out and not returning drugs from cases he'd never even worked, forging the name of another Officer Perez, replacing coke with Bisquick—Internal Affairs began an undercover investigation, shadowing Perez, gathering evidence. Streetwise and savvy in such matters, Perez was sure he was being tailed. He assumed it was because the investigators thought he was involved in the bank robbery. That caused him to seek out his commanding officer, proclaim his innocence, tell him they were going after the wrong guy.

Early in the morning of August 25, 1998, Perez found out why he'd been tailed. Uniformed and plainclothes officers descended on his home, put him in cuffs, and drove him to jail. In December 1998, he was tried on charges of possession of cocaine for sale, grand theft, and forgery.

The jury deadlocked, 8–4 in favor of conviction.[5]

With a retrial on the horizon, investigators dug deeper, rooting through Perez's financial and other records. It reinforced their growing conviction that the officer was not merely a dirty cop but a major criminal offender. Armed with much more damning evidence, prosecutors squeezed Perez. They offered him five years, and his wife immunity (she was an LAPD employee thought to be in the know about her husband's activities). He agreed to talk.[6]

And talk he did. For fifty hours, over a nine-month period, providing testimony and evidence that ran to 4,000 pages. Although he failed several polygraph examinations and was known as a smooth-talking, stone-cold liar who falsely fingered several of his co-workers, independent investigation supported sufficient cause to overturn 106 CRASH arrests. Ultimately, seventy cops were implicated, accused of either misconduct (mostly for failing to tell what they knew, drinking on duty, other lesser offenses) or criminal behavior ranging from stealing and dealing drugs, doing drugs, planting drugs (and throw-down guns), extortion, robbery, and murder. Twelve officers received suspensions (from seven to thirty days), seven resigned, and five were fired. Fifteen thousand criminal cases were reviewed by defense attorneys and, according to the city attorney, Rampart-related settlements totaled approximately $125 million.[7]

Early in his conversations with the investigators, Perez came clean on the Ovando shooting. It was as the young gangster had described it to his attorney. After the two cops shot him, Durden removed the Tec-22 (he'd previously filed off its serial number) from his backpack, wiped it for prints, and planted it. (The officers had anticipated just such a use for the gun when they'd relieved a gang member of it a few days earlier.) The DA immediately filed a writ of habeas corpus and, three years into his twenty-three-year sentence, Ovando was freed.

Javier Ovando was awarded $15 million, the largest settlement in the history of the LAPD.[8]

ALL THESE YEARS LATER, investigators are apparently no closer to arresting the killers of either Tupac Shakur or Biggie Smalls (though when the topic comes up in the press, Perez, Durden, and Mack get frequent mention in connection with the Smalls drive-by slaying). Nor has David Mack given any hint of what happened to the $722,000 taken in the bank robbery.

SUPERVISION

WHERE THE HELL WAS the sergeant? The lieutenant? The captain? The chief? One would think that with all that rank—upwards of ten tiers in the rank-heavy hierarchy of the LAPD—there would be some semblance of accountability.

Consider the word *supervision*. Conscientious police bosses "super-view" the work of their subordinates. By which I mean, if they're doing their jobs properly, they ride along with their cops, often. They cover their 911 calls. They observe their approach to people, how they talk to them, the actions they take and under what authority. They listen to their language, their tone of voice. They carefully review their reports, checking for understanding of and obeisance to the dictates of law and policy—especially in the arenas of stop and frisk, search and seizure, rules of evidence, laws of arrest, and use of force—and they question them about these activities. They follow up on their officers' contacts. How? Well, one method is to grab a random handful of arrest reports or traffic citations or copies of radio dispatches, then make appointments with those named in the reports and drive out to chat with them: "How did my officer treat you last night?" They listen carefully to the answer and ask meaningful follow-up questions. They sit in court periodically, listening to their officers' testimony.

And they provide feedback to their cops—continuously. Good work is praised, poor performance critiqued, bad conduct rebuked.

How is the feedback provided? How is discipline decided and administered? I've advocated for years a bifurcated system of internal police discipline. Honest mistakes and other obvious performance problems are met with coaching or counseling, perhaps retraining. Willful misconduct, on the other hand, demands punitive disciplinary action: oral reprimand, written reprimand, suspension, termination. Of course, there are times when a well-intentioned but incompetent police officer simply has to be dismissed from the force.

How often does this kind of "super-viewing" supervision take place? In my experience, rarely.

For years, I taught a California POST (Commission on Peace Officer Standards and Training) personnel management class. I would ask my students—sergeants, lieutenants, captains, a sprinkling of chiefs—"How do you know what kind of a job your subordinates are doing?" Answers varied, but the most common? "I look at their 'productivity,' review their reports, check their sick leave, complaints, and commendations." And that was pretty much it, as close to "supervision" as it got.

This experience, reinforced by my own careerlong observations, caused me to conclude that one of society's most sensitive and consequential lines of work goes essentially unsupervised. It's only when a cop does something exceptional—good or bad—that the supervisor acts.

When I laid out a different approach in class, a more thorough, "up-close-and-personal" supervisory modus operandi, the initial response was generally positive. But when I asked why we see so little actual supervision in police work, the kind that would likely prevent a Perez or a Slager, the floodgates opened and out poured a tidal wave of excuses:

I don't have time to follow-up on my officers' contacts—I have other priorities: staffing, scheduling, personnel investigations, performance appraisals, contingency planning.

I don't want to undermine, by "checking up on them," the trust my officers have in me.

My cops are grown men and women, they don't need me breathing down their necks.

[And this is one of my most memorable reactions, from a patrol sergeant of a large agency:] I tell my people: if you don't hear from me that means you're doing a good job.

We have a "court liaison" officer in our department, *she's* responsible for feedback on officers' responsiveness to subpoenas, appearance, testimony (in other words, it's not my job).

I cover calls almost every night, that tells me all I need to know about my coppers' performance.

I conduct *inspections* all the time: uniforms, haircuts and other groom-
ing standards, vehicles, weapons, other equipment, first-aid cards,
driver's licenses . . . if that's not "supervision" I don't know what is.

Oh, and by the way, the last thing a citizen wants is for me to show up
on their doorstep, wanting to talk about a ticket they got yesterday.

Or, a common yet uncommonly voiced excuse: I want my officers to *like*
me. Wanting to be liked is not a bad thing, *needing* to be liked is a fatal
flaw in a leader.

I do not claim, as a "super-viewer" of police work for thirty-one of my
thirty-four years on the job, to have practiced all I've preached here, certainly not at all times. But, by being *conscious* of what it takes to be an able
police supervisor, I was at least aware of those times when I was less than
diligent, less than methodical in my approach.

And, while we're on the topic, a word about one's "approach." Effective
police supervision can be achieved without being a micromanager, or a
horse's ass. In fact, that kind of behavior invariably backfires, causing a loss
of credibility and confidence in the boss. But being open with one's subordinates, enlisting their participation in setting standards, inviting them to
offer suggestions about *how* their work should be supervised builds trust—
and, in the best sense of the word, *compliance* with professional standards.

EARLY WARNING SYSTEM

ANOTHER POTENTIALLY POWERFUL SUPERVISORY tool in assuring
responsible police behavior: the early warning system (EWS). A computer-
based EWS, in use by more than one-third of police departments across
the country, captures key statistical data (citizen complaints, use of force,
police pursuits, accidents, sick leave, and the like). If a certain threshold is
reached by an individual officer, the system, in theory, triggers an analysis
of that officer's conduct.[9]

But doubts have been raised about the efficacy of such systems. For example, in the aftermath of the Rampart scandal, the Los Angeles Police Department began work on a $33 million EWS that was finally implemented

in 2007. Yet LAPD's inspector general concluded in 2014 that the system had apparently failed to detect officers in the early stages of a pattern of bad behavior, officers who ultimately had to be fired. The IG's report examined 748 "alerts" during a four-month period and determined that the department had taken little or no action in the majority of those cases. In only 1.3 percent (ten alerts) was training mandated.[10]

And, across town, the Los Angeles County Sheriff's Department, stung by a 2013 Justice Department investigation that found discrimination against blacks and Latinos (unconstitutional stops, illegal searches and seizures, excessive force), has had to acknowledge problems with its own EWS—though not with the technology. As with the LAPD, the difficulty appears to be a "people problem." "Our diagnostic systems were fine," LASD chief of detectives Bill McSweeney told a reporter in 2014. "Our managerial and supervision response was not fine. It's that simple."[11]

And it almost always is "that simple." Too many police supervisors, at all levels, throughout the nation, are simply not doing their jobs.

EARLIER I POSED THE question of Perez's sergeant, namely, where the hell was he? There can be no substitute for competent daily supervision of police work. But peer pressure, the influence of one's co-workers is, without doubt, the most powerful determinant of police behavior in your city and in mine.

PEER PRESSURE

MOST POLICE OFFICERS START off on the right foot. Swearing an oath to the Constitution of the nation and of one's home state tends to fill new police recruits with a sense of pride, and purpose. I certainly felt it—and believed (naively, as it turns out) in the invincibility of my moral fidelity to that pledge—when on January 14, 1966, the Forty-ninth San Diego Police Academy Class was sworn in. Later, downstairs in the cafeteria, several of us nodded in agreement when Bob Rogers, who would go on to become our class "Honor Man," confessed to the "goose bumps" he'd experienced as we all raised our right hands that morning, took the oath of office, and received our shiny San Diego police badges.

We also swore to abide by the Law Enforcement Code of Ethics—with an extra measure of pride because the code, first adopted statewide by the Police Officers Research Association of California (PORAC) and then by the International Association of Chiefs of Police, had been written by then Lieutenant Gene M. Muehleisen of the San Diego Police Department.

Muehleisen, who went on to become the executive director of the California Commission on Peace Officers Standards and Training (POST), spoke to a PORAC conference on the introduction of his "baby," a special code of ethical behavior for all cops. "It is not enough to merely speak in high-sounding phrases of professionalism. We will not reach our goal until the service we render is truly professional and recognized as such by citizens in all levels of society."[12]

The Law Enforcement Code of Ethics, adopted in the mid-1950s, was ahead of its time. Judging by what's happening today, some six decades later, it is still ahead of its time. Its language, altered little through several iterations by the various national and international organizations seeking to embrace an institution-wide code, is, indeed, full of "high-sounding phrases." But, if anything, it is all the more relevant today:

AS A LAW ENFORCEMENT OFFICER, my fundamental duty is to serve mankind; to safeguard lives and property; to protect the innocent against deception, the weak against oppression or intimidation, and the peaceful against violence or disorder; and to respect the Constitutional rights of all men to liberty, equality and justice.

I WILL keep my private life unsullied as an example to all; maintain courageous calm in the face of danger, scorn, or ridicule; develop self-restraint; and be constantly mindful of the welfare of others. Honest in thought and deed in both my personal and official life, I will be exemplary in obeying the laws of the land and the regulations of my department. Whatever I see or hear of a confidential nature or that is confided to me in my official capacity will be kept ever secret unless revelation is necessary in the performance of my duty.

I WILL never act officiously or permit personal feelings, prejudices, animosities or friendships to influence my decisions. With no compromise for crime and with relentless prosecution of criminals, I will enforce the law courteously and appropriately without fear or favor, malice or ill will, never employing unnecessary force or violence and never accepting gratuities.

I RECOGNIZE the badge of my office as a symbol of public faith, and I accept it as a public trust to be held so long as I am true to the ethics of the police service. I will constantly strive to achieve these objectives and ideals, dedicating myself before God* to my chosen profession . . . law enforcement.

*Reference to religious affirmation may be omitted where objected to by the officer.[13]

Who would have thought the 1950s—the years of the Eisenhower administration, a period predating the civil rights movement, the Kerner Report (on the miserable state of race relations in the United States), and the stormy 1960s and 1970s—would have produced such an auspicious document?

Since then, the IACP added its own Law Enforcement Oath of Honor. It's short, to the point:

On my honor, I will never betray my badge, my integrity, my character or the public trust. I will always have the courage to hold myself and others accountable for our actions. I will always uphold the Constitution, my community and the agency I serve.[14]

And, also from the IACP: the Model Policy on Standards of Conduct, promulgated in 1998 and containing every conceivable benchmark (from handling confidential informants to reporting use of force) by which a police department and its citizens can judge police effectiveness, conduct, and accountability.[15]

For many, including yours truly, the zeal to live by the Law Enforcement Code of Ethics lasted not much longer than it took for the ink to dry on our signatures at the bottom of the swearing-in form. Exposed to the real world, we were soon informed by cynical veterans to "forget all that bullshit they feed you in the academy. You're in the real world now, son."

The biggest lesson from the real world? Protect your fellow officers at all costs. Protect them from physical harm, obviously—but by all means protect them from the snooping, judgmental eyes of the public, the media, the boss (unless, of course, the boss is just another "one of the boys").

Nothing worse than a snitch?

EVERY OCCUPATION, FROM PROFESSOR to priest, judge to general, has its malefactors—and willing co-workers who would shield them from exposure and discipline. Nowhere is this more so than in policing. One of the most pernicious and persistent problems in my former line of work is summed up with the popular phrase, the "blue code of silence."

Paradoxically, the timeworn, film noir notion that there's nothing worse than a snitch has as much currency in the cop world as in the world of bad guys and wise guys. Police officers face danger, together; they drink, tell stories, "process" incidents at end of shift, together. They bond, they build trust based on a common awareness that they need to have each other's backs. For these reasons, peer pressure in police work is especially daunting, and the penalty for breaching it exacting. If one of the brothers or sisters breaks ranks, reports another for some misfeasance, malfeasance, or nonfeasance, the informer will be ostracized, subjected to not-so-friendly pranks, and left hanging when calling for backup. Time and again, police officers lie for one another, cover up wrongdoing for one another. How else did Jon Burge survive, and thrive, in the city of Chicago for so long?

What that city needed, what the LAPD and all law enforcement agencies need today is an army of proud, unapologetic in-house snitches. Cops who understand that tolerating misdeeds in one's fellow officers besmirches their own honesty and integrity, and compromises every aspect of the police service.

Of course, better than after-the-fact accountability is preventing insupportable behavior in the first place. I recall, vividly, officers in San Diego and in Seattle who, because of how they carried themselves, how they communicated with both their colleagues and the people on their beats, commanded great respect. The kind of cops who if they had to tell an inconvenient truth about a fellow officer, told it—without gaps, without varnish. The kind who would wade in to a Rodney King–type beating, at first blow, and save everyone a lot of grief and heartache. The constructive side of peer pressure is an awesome thing to behold.

A virtuous cop who finds himself working alongside a bad cop—a heavy-handed peer, a thief, a racist, an abusive homophobe, a drug dealer, a sexual predator—would do well to heed the message of those ubiquitous signs that started cropping up at airports after 9/11: If you see something, say something.

LYING COPS

POLICE OFFICERS MUST UNDERSTAND that choosing not to confront unethical peers, or bosses, constitutes a form of lying, covering up. And as police administrators understand all too well, a dishonest cop is a liability, in a hundred and one different ways.

Noted defense attorney Alan Dershowitz ignited a continuing debate within policing when in 1994 he wrote about the Mollen Commission's damning report on corruption and cover-up within the NYPD: "As I read about the disbelief expressed by some prosecutors at the Mollen Commission's recent assertion that police perjury is 'widespread' in New York City, I thought of Claude Rains's classic response, in 'Casablanca,' on being told there was gambling in Rick's place: 'I'm shocked—shocked!'" Dershowitz, who went on to encompass the LAPD and all of law enforcement in his indictment of police perjury, concluded:

> For anyone who has practiced criminal law in the state or Federal
> courts, the disclosures about rampant police perjury cannot pos-
> sibly come as a surprise. "Testilying"—as the police call it—has
> long been an open secret among prosecutors, defense lawyers and
> judges.[16]

In 1995, Bill Bratton was said to have agreed with "most of what Dershowitz had to say"—which prompted Richard Bradley, then president of the Boston Police Patrolmen's Association to state, "I find it incredible that he would say that. Every day all over the country, police officers are testifying. Everyone realizes they are testifying under oath. If this was this much a problem, it would have come to light over the years." Bradley told the *Boston Globe* that he had never encountered the practice in his twenty-seven years with the Boston Police Department, a statement that raises doubts about his consciousness or credibility, or both.[17]

And, in 1996, Joseph McNamara, former police chief in Kansas City and San Jose, took note of the peevish if not indignant national police response to Dershowitz's claim and offered an important angle, posing the question, "Has the drug war created an officers' liars club?" McNamara pulled no punches in answering his own question:

> Not many people took defense attorney Alan M. Dershowitz seriously when he charged that Los Angeles cops are taught to lie at the birth of their careers at the Police Academy. But as someone who spent 35 years wearing a police uniform, I've come to believe that hundreds of thousands of law-enforcement officers commit felony perjury every year testifying about drug arrests.[18]

Bratton and McNamara are not the only current or former criminal justice executives to weigh in on the extent to which America's police officers lie on the stand.

More recently, in March 2014, five Cook County police officers—three from Chicago, two from Glenview—took the stand on a drug case and, according to Circuit Court Judge Catherine Haberkorn, a former prosecutor, "All officers lied on the stand today . . . many, many, many, many times they all lied." In what the *Chicago Tribune* called a "Perry Mason moment," the defense attorney had produced a video starkly contradicting the sworn testimony of every one of the five cops.[19]

AS A POLICE ADMINISTRATOR, I was keenly aware of so-called Brady cops: police officers who have demonstrated a willingness to lie, in reports or on the stand. Dating back to a 1963 Supreme Court decision in *Brady v. Maryland*, prosecutors are duty bound to inform defendants and their lawyers of any officer who in his or her official capacity has lied.[20]

Whether we accept McNamara's estimate of "hundreds of thousands" of police perjurers, the number is far greater than most within the field, certainly within the ranks of police union leaders, are willing to acknowledge. In recent years departments in New York, Chicago, Los Angeles, San Francisco, New Orleans, Boston, Philadelphia, Denver, and many other cities, large and small, have suffered scandals involving police personnel fudging the truth or blatantly lying under oath.

THE BEST THING A police department can do when it has screwed up is to say so, loud and clear and as soon as it has assembled the facts.

I'm reminded of the story of the Japan Airlines pilot who, on Flight 2 from Tokyo to San Francisco in November 1968, miscalculated his distance from the runway and put his DC-8 down in San Francisco Bay. It had been an overcast day with the cloud ceiling at three hundred feet and visibility at three-fourths of a mile. None of the ninety-six passengers or eleven crew members was injured. The pilot, Kohei Asoh, with roughly 10,000 hours of commercial flight time in addition to his military experience, missed the runway by two and one-half miles. Testifying before the National Transportation Safety Board, Captain Asoh stated simply, "As you Americans say, I fucked up." The hearing was likely the shortest in NTSB history. Professor Jerry B. Harvey, writing of the episode in his book *The Abilene Paradox and Other Meditations on Management*, labeled the pilot's crisp confession the "Asoh Defense."[21]

One can only imagine the course of American history if certain public figures had invoked the Asoh Defense when confronted with evidence of wrongdoing. Richard Nixon; Bill Clinton; Lance Armstrong; Sarah Palin (her "no thanks" to the "bridge to nowhere" fib); Pete Rose; Lyndon Johnson (Vietnam); Ronald Reagan (Iran-Contra); Bernie Madoff; Hillary Clinton (her heroic evasion of sniper fire in Bosnia); Bill O'Reilly (pick a lie, any lie—from his professional "bona fides" to his personal life); John Edwards; Jayson Blair; Kenneth Lay; Joseph McCarthy; George W. Bush and Dick Cheney, his big kahuna (the "discovery" of weapons of mass destruction); Brian Williams; General Petraeus; Jerry Sandusky; Dennis Hastert; Donald Trump; and so on. And others, so many others.

We humans lie, a lot. Why? Well, fear, of course. And inconvenience, embarrassment, humiliation, hubris, shame. To get what we want, avoid what we don't want. Some lies are big, some small. Some hurt no one, others harm millions.

When it comes to police work, lying can carry grave consequences.

WHEN A COP RAISES his or her right hand and swears to tell the truth, the whole truth, and nothing but the truth, or takes pen to paper or types out an official police report and alters the facts, that cop is committing a crime, one with a likelihood of damaging if not ruining another's life. And, in the process, dealing his or her organization's reputation an awful blow.

In my professional experience, there are too many cops who become habituated to lying (even when they don't "have to"). Even as they put innocent people behind bars, or in the ground.

It starts, I'm convinced, within the organization: dishonesty as a function of heritage, as an artifact of the culture. Indeed, some cops lie their way to the top.

Bill Bratton, in his 1998 book, talks about implementing "Compstat," the NYPD's controversial system of managerial crime-fighting answerability. (Unlike many other critics of Compstat, or "Comstat," I am a fan. Done properly, meaning diligently, respectfully, and with full citizen participation, Compstat—or some similar form of rigorous testing of the police response to crime and other community conditions—is an essential accountability tool.) Bratton cites several examples of commanders who, early on, were caught in "deceptions" as they defended their crime statistics or their strategies and tactics. Two of his most aggressive interlocutors, Jack Maple (Bratton's celebrated idea man) and Chief of Patrol Louis Anemone (who ran most of the Compstat sessions), were ruthless in rooting out slackers and those who would dance around the "facts on the ground":

> Sometimes the grilling got tough. You've heard of the good cop/
> bad cop routine; Maple and Anemone were bad cop/bad cop. You

didn't want to lie or bluff at Compstat—you'd get caught and hung out to dry. . . . Sometimes Maple and Anemone would torment people. The most notable bit of aggression came when Tony Simonetti, who had become chief of Brooklyn South, was reporting, and up on the projection screens behind him appeared a computerized drawing of Pinocchio with his nose growing.

Bratton went on to state that his two henchmen went too far on that occasion. "One of my main rules is: You don't intentionally humiliate people in public, and they had violated that, and they both apologized to Simonetti."[22] Good rule, I suppose. If you're going to humiliate someone, do it in private. On the other hand, police managers who are forthcoming and thoroughgoing on the facts leave no memory, or paper trail, of deception and deceit.

Sadly, deception is all but robotic in many police departments and the only way to stop it, over the long haul, is to set and enforce a policy of truth telling. And by making sure everyone in town understands that liars need not apply, and that those already on board had best make sure their resumes are up to date.

EXTERNAL PRESSURE: THE PROSECUTOR'S ROLE IN POLICE ACCOUNTABILITY

IF YOU'RE A POLICE chief striving for organizational transparency and accountability, there are few things more frustrating than a DA who relies on a finger-wetting, wind-testing interpretation of public opinion or, worse, police union or other political pressure in deciding whether to prosecute a brutal, trigger-happy, or dishonest cop.

If under the same circumstances, charges would be filed against any other citizen, the alleged cop offender must be charged. It's a matter of equal justice, and it sends a message that police officers are not above the law—a message so many communities are aching to hear.

IF A LAW GETS in the way of police accountability, as it sometimes does, that law must be challenged—and changed. Prosecutors here in my home state of Washington (as well as in many other states) often claim, often with good reason, that their hands are tied by state laws when it comes to prosecuting a bad police shooting. In 1986 the Washington state legislature passed a law, the country's most restrictive, that made it all but impossible to prosecute a police officer in a shooting death so long as the officer acted in "good faith" and "without malice" or "evil intent." King County prosecutor Dan Satterberg calls the law an "almost perfect defense to a mistaken use of force."[23] And that's coming from one of the most conscientious lawyers in the country.

Let's return to an event from Chapter 4. On the afternoon of August 30, 2010, Seattle police officer Ian Birk spotted John T. Williams, fifty, walking across a downtown street with a three-inch pocketknife in one hand, a piece of cedar board in the other. Williams, a Nuu-chah-nulth First Nations wood-carver, originally from British Columbia, was homeless, deaf in one ear, and a "public inebriate" who also suffered mental-health problems. He was well known to many in the homeless community and to most of the beat cops in the area.

With both video and audio from Birk's patrol car capturing the officer's initial approach, we see Williams crossing the street with a slow, limping gait. We see Birk get out of his car and approach Williams. Then both men leave our field of view, but the audio continues. We hear Birk shouting, "Hey! Hey! . . . Put the knife down! Put the knife down!" Seconds later, five shots ring out. Four of them strike Williams, and he's dead before he hits the ground.

Birk claimed the pocketknife was open; forensic evidence says otherwise: the knife was recovered at the scene in a closed position. Birk claimed that Williams had a "very stern, very serious, very confrontational look on his face," that he was "in a very confrontational posture," that he exhibited "pre-attack indicators" such as a furrowed brow, a clenched jaw, a "thousand-yard stare."[24] (Perhaps that fixed stare was the result of the alcohol Williams had consumed that day; his blood-alcohol reading was .18.) None of the witnesses on the crowded city street said that Williams, nine feet from Birk at the time of his death, had threatened, much less attacked the officer. It wasn't as bad as the cold-blooded murder of a fleeing, unarmed man shot in the back in South Carolina, but it was bad enough.

Satterberg, citing state law, elected not to prosecute Birk. (The police department's internal shooting-review board, meanwhile, had ruled the shooting "unjustified," and Deputy Chief Clark Kimerer would later call it the most "damning" and "egregious" police shooting in three decades. As the department prepared the paperwork to fire him, Birk resigned.)[25]

Satterberg aptly labels such cases "awful but lawful" and, as head of the statewide prosecutors' association, is considering new legislation that would make it easier to bring a case against law enforcement officers.

Then again, sometimes the problem is not the law but rather the lawyer—a district attorney, for example, who is simply too cozy with the police. It's easy to see how such a relationship develops. Prosecutors are elected officials and, however competent and professional, they all understand the politics of prosecution. Their "batting average"—making cases, taking cases to court, winning those cases—is important to their standing in the legal community. And to reelection. That puts a premium on developing a mutually beneficial, day-to-day working relationship with the local cops, the individuals who conduct preliminary and follow-up investigations; it's hard to assemble and prosecute a case with a sloppy or otherwise deficient investigation.

Many prosecutors have their own investigators and conduct independent investigations into certain alleged criminal offenses, whether involving the police or not. But even with such an arrangement, the relationship between deputy prosecutors and the detectives who feed them cases relies on a high degree of interdependence.

This interdependent relationship between cops and prosecutors—between Rafael Perez, for example, and a deputy DA who handles his cases—with its potential for excessive familiarity and an overreliance on personal loyalties, is extremely problematic when the prosecuting authority must decide whether to file charges against a police officer.

PROSECUTORIAL INDEPENDENCE AND SCRUPULOUS impartiality are essential in deciding whether to charge anyone, but especially a police officer. Both of these qualities appear to have been lacking in the legal review of the Darren Wilson shooting of Michael Brown.

St. Louis County prosecuting attorney Robert P. McCulloch, in office since 1991, has acknowledged his fondness and support for the police in St. Louis County. That is understandable—his father was a St. Louis police officer. When Robert was twelve, his dad was killed on the job, by a black man. His brother, nephew, and cousin also served with the St. Louis police, and his mother worked as a clerk for the department for twenty years. McCulloch had every intention of joining his extended family in law enforcement, but that dream died when, in high school, he lost a leg to a rare form of bone cancer.[26] "I couldn't become a policeman," he told reporters, "so being county prosecutor is the next best thing."[27]

McCulloch, a Democrat and by most accounts very popular in St. Louis County, could have chosen to hand off the Darren Wilson case to a prosecutor with no actual or apparent conflict of interest—a special prosecutor. But, despite intense pressure to do so, he refused to step aside. Indeed, he revealed his bias and passion for the local police when, during the state of emergency following the shooting, he responded angrily to Missouri governor Jay Nixon's decision to place the St. Louis County and Ferguson police forces under the authority of the State Highway Patrol. "To denigrate the men and women of the county police department is shameful," McCulloch said.[28]

This appearance of partiality was bad enough, but McCulloch made an early decision, as he told a local radio station, that he would "be presenting absolutely everything to this grand jury. Every statement that a witness made, every witness, every photograph, every piece of physical evidence. Absolutely nothing will be left out so the grand jury is making their decision based upon absolutely everything and we'll go from there."[29] The statement dropped jaws and turned heads of criminal justice experts from coast to coast. You see, that's not at all how prosecutors present a case to a grand jury.

Prosecutors typically assign a sharp deputy from their office to work up the case, narrowly focus the questions and the evidence, call very few witnesses—rarely the potential defendant—and present their case to the grand jury in tightly controlled fashion. (Grand jurors, twelve in Missouri, are everyday citizens, untrained in the law. They are selected by a circuit court judge from a randomly chosen master jury list. The limited role of the judge, who is not present during the proceedings, is to help ensure, among other things, racial parity in the composition of juries. The Wilson grand jury consisted of nine white and three African American citizens of St. Louis County.)

As a result of McCulloch's decision to throw "everything" at the grand jury, the proceedings lasted months instead of the few hours or couple of days spent on a typical felony case; Darren Wilson himself testified for four hours; and, in a further break from legal tradition, McCulloch promised that if Wilson was not indicted, he would release full transcripts and audio recordings of the grand jury proceedings.

He kept that promise when Wilson walked. The transcripts, capturing a staggering amount of opinion, hearsay, and irreconcilable inconsistencies, stand as evidence of McCulloch's folly.

It may seem that the prosecutor's intention was to be fully transparent. Yet by presenting every piece of evidence, much of it conflicting, confusing, and contradictory, to a group of laypeople, in the midst of unprecedented community tension, he more likely than not obfuscated things. And when that happens rarely does a jury convict, or a grand jury indict.

To be clear, my opinion in the Darren Wilson case is not that the grand jury erred in its decision, but rather that both the circumstances of the incident—Wilson foolishly putting himself in a position where he "had" to fire his weapon—and the highly idiosyncratic manner in which the case was presented to the jurors made the outcome both inevitable and predictable. That view is shared by virtually all legal experts who opined both before and after the jury's decision.[30]

The role of juries in police accountability cases

JURIES, EVEN WHEN PRESENTED evidence that establishes guilt beyond a reasonable doubt, are often unwilling to convict in police cases involving excessive force and unlawful deaths.[31]

In general, jurors have a bias in favor of police;[32] are not aware of evidence that reveals the extent of police false reporting and perjury;[33] are predisposed to side with officers when they consider how difficult or dangerous a cop's job is;[34] and, among white jurors, are much more likely to believe police officers, black or white, when the defendant is black or Latino.[35]

Perhaps, with images of the April 4, 2015, Michael Slager shooting death of Walter Scott in North Charleston, South Carolina, fresh in mind—and increasing numbers of other disturbing police shootings caught on video— these formidable obstacles to conviction just might begin to crumble. It's one thing to read about a police shooting in the newspaper, quite another to see it in living color, with high-quality audio. I recall reading on the day of the shooting an online account of John T. Williams's death at the hands of Seattle police and thinking to myself: sounds like a clean shooting, tragic but justified. Soon thereafter, while reading a follow-up article, I clicked on the accompanying link of Birk's dash-cam video. I played it, several times. What I saw and heard was anything but a clean shooting.

CITIZEN OVERSIGHT

BY WHATEVER NAME, "CIVILIAN" or "citizen" review of alleged police misconduct is a hit-or-miss proposition, at best. Opposition from wary politicians, "anti-crime" and "pro-police" commentators, and especially police unions, is an obvious reason that no single model has established a fully credible, fully effective means of oversight. So, too, are the historical complexities and idiosyncrasies of the local political jurisdiction.

That's not to suggest that the struggle to install effective citizen oversight should be abandoned or that the effort has been a complete failure. Indeed, Sam Walker, emeritus professor of criminal justice at the University of Nebraska–Omaha and nationally recognized expert on police accountability, citizen oversight, and civil liberties, has identified several programs that are inching their way toward greater and greater respectability. In his two books dealing specifically with the subject, he describes modestly impressive developments in the field over the past forty-five years.[36]

His latest work, in particular, traces the progress of "external" means of establishing and sustaining accountability in officer-involved shootings, other uses of force, racial discrimination, citizen complaint investigations, early intervention policies (intended to prevent the growth of "bad habits" in police officers and to catch, as early as possible, signs of disturbing behavior) and other self-monitoring systems, as well as federal "pattern or practice" investigations into police misconduct.

Walker divides citizen oversight into three periods: "Years in the Wilderness" (1920s through 1970), "Years of Growth" (1970 to roughly 1993), and "Years of Consolidation and Development" (1993 to the present).[37]

The first "citizen review" program was created in 1928 in Los Angeles when that city's bar association formed the Committee on Constitutional Rights to receive complaints against police actions. It was a well-intentioned but toothless enterprise.

In 1931, the Wickersham Commission, the first of many national blue-ribbon bodies impaneled to examine patterned police abuse (the latest is the President's Task Force on 21st Century Policing), recommended in its "Lawlessness in Law Enforcement" report that all cities create a "disinterested agency" to help citizens with their complaints of alleged police misconduct.

In the mid-1960s, Chicago police superintendent O. W. Wilson issued an ominous warning: "A review board in this city would destroy discipline in the Chicago Police Department. If we would have a civilian review board, it would create a situation where I, as head of the police department, would be confronted by an adversary group, which the entire department would tend to unite against."[38] Wilson was widely respected in local "good-government" circles, and by the academic community, as well, owing to the fact that before agreeing to the top police post in Chicago he was a professor and the first dean of the School of Criminology at the University of California–Berkeley. Imagine if, instead of opposing citizen oversight, Wilson had used his considerable prestige and influence to help fashion an effective, reputable citizen-review process. Chicago, a city that gave us the "police riot" at the 1968 Democratic National Convention, as well as two decades of Commander Jon Burge's reign of terror, might have served as a national model for police accountability.

Cities across the country entertained the idea of citizen review during those "Years in the Wilderness," but none developed a viable model. The concept was deemed too radical, and each time a local jurisdiction came close to adopting a review process, the cops jumped all over it, claiming it would produce a chilling effect on their crime fighting.

Nowhere was the conflict greater during the "Wilderness" era, or the stakes higher, than in New York City.

IN 1950, A NEW York City coalition of eighteen community-based organizations formed the Permanent Coordination Committee on Police and Minority Relations. The committee lobbied the city, demanding that it address police misconduct generally and "police misconduct in their relations with Puerto Ricans and Negros [*sic*] specifically." In response, the NYPD, in 1953, created the Civilian Complaint Review Board (CCRB). And though Mayor Robert Wagner gave the board marginally greater latitude two years later, all investigations, and all discipline, remained within the exclusive purview of the police department.[39]

In 1965, newly elected mayor John Lindsay appointed former federal judge Lawrence E. Walsh to investigate operations of the NYPD. Walsh's report focused principally on modernization of the agency, but it also concluded that in order to build public confidence in the CCRB, the board should have "civilian" representation. Lindsay agreed and formed a search committee, headed by former attorney general Herbert Brownell. The "outsiders" were selected and soon took seats alongside the deputy police commissioners, the citizens now outnumbering the cops 4–3.[40]

But the police union sprang into action, mounting a voter referendum against the civilian-led CCRB. The Patrolmen's Benevolent Association president at the time, John Cassese, was not reticent about condemning the mayor's board: "I'm sick and tired of giving in to minority groups with their whims and their gripes and shouting."[41]

The PBA had influential allies. William F. Buckley Jr. led the charge on behalf of the conservative intelligentsia, arguing that the civilian review board would "politicize the police." Tamar Jacoby, drawing parallels between historical and modern efforts to introduce meaningful citizen review in New York City, wrote that Buckley's arguments

> went beyond pandering. Crime was rising, [Buckley] said, much
> of it committed by blacks; but poor blacks were also bearing the

brunt of the violence, and they welcomed a tough police presence. It was demagogues who had made an issue of alleged police brutality—a phony charge, he maintained, certain to make life even less safe in the ghetto—and it was being used by militants to whip up racial resentment. At the very least, this presentation seemed convincing to middle-class whites, who had no idea of the different lens through which most blacks viewed cops. Whites in the outer boroughs looked at the issue through their own prism— and, as they saw things, the clear, pressing problem was rising crime.[42]

Opponents also received formidable backing by one of law enforcement's "guiding lights," FBI director J. Edgar Hoover. The original G-Man informed New Yorkers and the rest of the country that such boards "undermine the morale and sap the efficiency of the police. They deter officers in the proper performance of their duties for fear of having charges placed against them, which will be judged by individuals wholly unfamiliar with police work."[43]

The union prevailed and the PBA's referendum passed, at 66–33.[44] Citizen-complaint investigations were, once again, under the exclusive control of the police department.

Still, given the era's concentrated, increasingly aroused and organized opposition to police misconduct, advocates continued to press for greater citizen participation and oversight throughout the 1970s and 1980s. In 1986, the city council passed legislation dramatically restructuring the CCRB. The mayor, with the advice and consent of the city council, would appoint six members to the board and the police commissioner a like number. Again the union groused and grumbled and protested but, in 1987, the new CCRB plan was implemented. Further, the Civilian Complaint Investigations Bureau started hiring non-cops to work alongside and under the supervision of sworn members of the department.[45]

In 1993, the city council "civilianized" the entire CCRB and added a critical new feature: subpoena power. This was a big step forward. But, until the Abner Louima torture case of 1997, the agency was so severely underfunded, it made it impossible for the investigators to stay on top of their caseloads. Evidently, the image of a cop sodomizing a prisoner (an innocent one, at that) with a broom handle in a city precinct house was finally enough to convince the council to adequately fund the promising program they'd created.[46]

Today, the board has thirteen members, the mayor choosing five (including the chair; the council, five (one from each borough); and the commissioner, three. All must live in the city. With the exception of the commissioner's picks, none of the CCRB members can come from a law enforcement background.[47]

With 142 citizen investigators, New York's CCRB is the nation's largest, and arguably the most credible, police oversight agency. It has investigated tens of thousands of complaints, resulting in discipline for thousands of officers.[48] That's all to the good, but until recently, something was missing.

In April 2012, the CCRB, under an agreement with the department, took charge of prosecuting sustained misconduct cases at administrative trials. Such cases had previously been prosecuted by department lawyers. It was an important step, especially in a city whose long battle over citizen oversight has been so grueling and stressful. And it inches forward the argument for true independent prosecutors for police shootings and in-custody deaths.[49]

So, what about the non–New York City part of the country?

Peter Finn's manual, "Citizen Review of Police: Approaches and Implementation," researched and written for the Department of Justice, remains the definitive statement of the four basic types of citizen-review mechanisms in the United States:

Type 1: Citizens investigate allegations of police misconduct and recommend findings to the chief or sheriff;

Type 2: Police officers investigate allegations and develop findings; citizens review and recommend that the chief or sheriff approve or reject the findings;

Type 3: Complainants may appeal findings established by the police or sheriff's department to citizens, who review them and then recommend their own findings to the chief or sheriff;

Type 4: An auditor investigates the process by which the police or sheriff's department accepts and investigates complaints and reports on the thoroughness and fairness of the process to the department and the public.[50]

Kim Hendrickson, writing in "The Conservative Case for Civilian Review" for the American Enterprise Institute (a nonpartisan "limited government" think tank founded in 1938), states, "The days when police departments could claim authority to police themselves are over. The question now for cities is what form of oversight is best. Many police chiefs have embraced civilian review as an acceptable alternative."[51]

So which form is best? The short, largely unsatisfying answer: it depends. On what? Population; department size; history of previous efforts; the local citizenry's dedication to the cause; the governing political body's majority opinion and commitment; the police chief or sheriff's receptivity to the concept; the breadth and depth of local expertise; the attitude and clout of the police union; the editorial leanings and sway of local media; and, of course, how much the local community is willing to invest in the creation and sustenance of citizen review. For example, it's impossible to conceive of a credible "Type 1" oversight process without the considerable financial resources needed to hire and retain top-quality citizen investigators (typically ex-detectives from a variety of federal, state, and local law enforcement agencies).

Having founded Islanders for Collaborative Policing and worked diligently to promote a citizen-review process for Bainbridge Island, Hendrickson has concluded, "after hitting my head against the wall for several years, that small communities like Bainbridge can't have meaningful police oversight. There is too much of a stigma around being 'anti-police,' not enough local expertise to draw from, and too many political obstacles."[52] I'm inclined to agree with her analysis of the barriers to effective (or, for that matter, any) citizen review in small communities. And I'm in agreement with her position that counties, notwithstanding the thorny jurisdictional and political issues involved, should establish a citizen-review process that is binding on all small cities and unincorporated areas in a given county. What type? Whichever the political process of that given county and its small cities and unincorporated areas can agree upon. The most logical, to my mind, is probably Finn's Type 2 model: cops investigate, citizens review the completed reports and present their recommendations for approval or rejection to the chief or sheriff. It's far from an ideal model, but it represents a pragmatic foot-in-the-door strategy for the many smaller jurisdictions across the country that must contend with strong home-rule sentiments, political opposition or timidity, and cross-jurisdictional bureaucratic realities.

And, as I argue later, when it comes to constitutional issues, I believe the federal government must play the leading role in setting and enforcing standards of the citizen complaint and investigation process. That's not going to happen by Tuesday, but the sooner we recognize the primacy of constitutional protections for all Americans—from the farmhand in the Coachella Valley to the computer programmer in the Silicon Valley—the sooner we achieve equal justice under law.

I PART COMPANY WITH Hendrickson when she argues, "The most useful forms of civilian review are concerned with department policies, procedures, and culture, since these are the things that influence officer behavior."[53] She's right, of course: those factors are huge influences in the attitudes and conduct of our cops. But I think we make a big mistake if we reject citizen participation in the investigation into and oversight of police misconduct, especially when such models are finally beginning to flex some muscle, and gain legitimacy.

I do think semantics are at issue in our friendly disagreement, at least in part. As Hendrickson points out, "civilian review" conjures an image of well-intentioned citizen volunteers—amateurs—whose role is essentially passive: examine already completed investigations of complaints, agree or disagree with the findings, and pass along their judgment to the chief or sheriff, at which point the civilian review panel's work, under most such models, is done. This can certainly be the case in Type 2 models. In fact, by design, that is precisely the limited role of citizen participants in police oversight. Of course, there is no such passivity on the part of citizen activists who insist on being heard, who publicize their findings and involve themselves to an even greater degree in oversight efforts beyond the panel's work.

An active, forceful community presence in any of the models is vital to the credibility of the process.

BRIAN BUCHNER, POLICY DIRECTOR for Los Angeles mayor Eric Garcetti's Office of Homeland Security and Public Safety, works with (not *for*) the city's Board of Police Commissioners, the Office of the Inspector General, and the LAPD, all in a non-sworn capacity. He is a nationally recognized expert on police oversight, having worked with Merrick Bobb of the prestigious Police Assessment Resource Center (PARC) and having spent more than eleven years in direct police oversight. Buchner is the current president of the board of the National Association of Civilian Oversight of Law Enforcement (NACOLE) and has reviewed hundreds of police investigations of officer-involved shootings and in-custody deaths. In November 2014, the then mayor and then police chief of Ferguson invited him in to talk with police officers, city officials, and community activists shortly after the Michael Brown shooting and to help them understand the various forms of citizen oversight.

Speaking from his office in Los Angeles in 2015, Buchner provided historical perspective that helps explain the tension within the ranks of oversight activists.[54] He told me, for example, that during the first real impetus for contemporary citizen review boards—a response to police abuses during the civil rights movement of the 1970s—activists were demanding, and in a few jurisdictions were able to bring about, models with a strong community focus. From the early 1990s to about 2000, we saw the emergence of a strong "professional" model of citizen oversight. Independent "auditors" were hired in several cities (including Seattle) to review and comment on completed internal investigations. These auditors were mostly attorneys, and some were also professional mediators (including Seattle).

These "Type 4" forms of oversight are troublesome to some grassroots activists because they are paid positions that, from the critics' point of view, force the auditors to rely on a too-cozy relationship with the police or the local governing body (or both), thus undermining their independence. The professionals, on the other hand, point to the standards and training that have evolved, much of which is driven by NACOLE (which is studiously inclusive of both orientations), and that, in turn, has created more credibility in the eyes of police and elected officials. They point to the lack of standards and training, the continuing "movement" orientation of community-focused initiatives as reasons that they too often fail to achieve credibility with the very people whose cooperation is necessary to effective oversight.

Where does Buchner, clearly a "professional" himself, come down on the argument? Where most sensible people do: there's room for community-driven models and the professional model, room for oversight models that emphasize policies and procedures, and workplace cultural conditions over individual complaint investigations. And, as Hendrickson points out, issues of population, geographical size, and local politics often dictate what kind of citizen oversight, if any, a local jurisdiction can realistically hope to accomplish.

Further, and in a development that bodes well for the field, we're beginning to see a blending of features of the two broad camps, with good potential for success in the real-world laboratory of experimentation and refinement of citizen oversight. Buchner spoke of three jurisdictions that have "returned" to a strong community orientation while maintaining, indeed strengthening, professional oversight: Seattle; Eugene, Oregon; and the Bay Area Rapid Transit (BART) (formed in the aftermath of the New Year's Day 2009 fatal shooting of an unarmed Oscar Grant III).

SEATTLE HAS ITS OFFICE of Professional Accountability (OPA). Formed shortly after I left SPD, but in response to a misconduct case involving several officers during my watch, the office has been led by a succession of three civilians, the first two with no police experience. Since 2013, the office has been led by Pierce Murphy. I met with him early in his tenure[55] and was impressed when he asked, tongue in cheek, that I not "hold it against" him that he's a former cop. He firmly believes people in his position do not require police experience in order to establish credibility and run an effective citizen oversight operation.

One of Murphy's first initiatives was to move the OPA office out of police headquarters in order to create a safe, inviting environment for those with complaints against police officers, policies, or procedures. As a "civilian" ex-cop with an extensive background in citizen oversight (including his own stint as president of the board of NACOLE), Murphy recognizes the value of non-cop investigators and has included in his new budget request the authorization to hire them. He is also leading the effort to create an automated tracking system, along the familiar lines of UPS or FedEx trackers, to keep all parties—complainants, officers, department brass—informed in real time of the progress of an OPA investigation. Given the frustration and dissatisfaction of all parties when complaint investigations drag on (in some cases, in some jurisdictions, for well over a year), such a system is critical to the integrity of the entire citizen oversight function.

The OPA model features a mediation option. A complainant may at any time in the process opt to sit down with the involved officer(s) and a professional mediator and attempt to work out an agreeable outcome. There's no pressure to opt for mediation. but it often produces satisfying results for complainants, as well as cops.

Overseeing the overseer and his internal investigations (whose "sustained" findings are submitted to the police chief for discipline) is an OPA auditor. In 2015, the auditor was the estimable Anne Levinson, former deputy mayor of Seattle and former municipal court judge. Levinson issues two reports a year. Her last, in February 2015, was critical of the department, and of the mayor, for failing to act decisively on her findings and recommendations, particularly on issues of hiring, training, and discipline;[56] she also, while praising the quality of its investigations, called for quicker OPA dispositions of citizen complaints—which should boost Murphy's chances at budget time. Both the mayor and the chief, to their credit, appear to have taken her criticism seriously. At least the second time around.

Seattle has also formed a new Community Police Commission (CPC), a third arm of police accountability.[57] Its members, broadly representative of the city's population, recently took a close look at all existing accountability measures and made a total of fifty-five recommendations for improvement (including provision of an opportunity for citizen complainants in certain cases to "provide information directly to the chief of police" before disciplinary action is taken; creating a system to ascertain whether departmental policies or procedures have contributed to "inappropriate actions" of officers; and drawing a better distinction between "training referrals" and discipline for misconduct). Although the commission was scolded by a federal judge for essentially jumping the gun and encroaching on his hegemony (he's overseeing the city's compliance with a Department of Justice accountability plan), it is evident the CPC has great potential to help improve the community-police relationship in Seattle. And it is heartening that its members are seeking to make the organization permanent.

It's reasonable to ask: Is this multipronged approach to police accountability, a "blended" citizen-professional model, working? Having spoken in the past with Pierce Murphy, Anne Levinson, and more recently, with Harriett Walden,[58] of the Community Police Commission, I believe a qualified yes is in order. Time will tell whether the three elements can achieve greater levels of efficacy, and credibility. And whether the institutionalization of a citizen-professional model is sustainable in other political jurisdictions and climates.

THE EUGENE AUDITOR MODEL, like Seattle's, is completely independent of the police department. Its job is to:

1. Receive and classify complaints of police misconduct;
2. Audit the investigations of these complaints;
3. Analyze trends and recommend improvements to police service.

What distinguishes this model is the sanctioned authority of the auditor to monitor investigations as they are conducted and to sit in on interviews conducted by sworn investigators. The auditor also staffs the city's Civilian Review Board, whose six members are appointed by the city council.[59]

Bay Area Rapid Transit has a Citizen Review Board consisting of representatives of nine geographical districts, an at-large appointee, and a member of the Police Officers and Managers Association, all appointed by BART's board of directors. It also has an Office of the Independent Police Auditor that staffs the Citizen Review Board and is charged with accepting and investigating complaints of misconduct against BART police officers. To date, the Citizen Review Board has received high marks for both effectiveness and efficiency, essential to establishing credibility in the eyes of the citizenry.[60]

SIGNIFICANTLY, ALL THREE OF these "best practices" agencies either allow or require a response to the scene of officer-involved shootings. In the Eugene and BART models, it's the auditor who rolls on shootings and other critical incidents. In Seattle, it's the OPA director. Pierce Murphy made this his personal policy, much to the consternation of investigators at the scene. He told me what took place when he first showed up at the scene of an officer-involved shooting.

"You're not allowed to be present," a Homicide supervisor told him. He told them he couldn't do his job without being present. "Well, you're not welcome here."

To be fair, most cops and all homicide investigators I've ever known are zealous in their protection of a crime scene: trace evidence, perishable evidence can easily become contaminated, or disappear in the wind. Murphy knows this, of course. But he informed the detectives they'd better get used to his presence at police shooting scenes. According to all accounts, these experts have gotten used to what I assume to be Murphy's unobtrusive but diligently observant presence at their scenes.

Putting names of duly authorized oversight officials on the call-out lists represents an important advance in citizen oversight and police accountability. When cops—especially congenitally cynical and suspicious homicide dicks—come to accept the up-close-and-personal presence of oversight agents at scenes of controversial police incidents, the entire process takes on a long overdue element of respect.

IF AMERICANS UNDERSTOOD THE extent to which policing fails to supervise itself, fails to rid the system of corrupt or corrosive cops, they would likely be shocked. In any case, given the sensitivities of the moment, there's never been a better time for policing's citizen partners to demand an end to unsupervised police work.

Given the way the institution is organized, it won't be easy.

12

THE COMMUNITY AS DMZ

IN MANY AMERICAN CITIES, the wall between community and police might as well be made of poured concrete and rebar. Instead, it is constructed of a paramilitary-bureaucratic structure—and mentality, as rock-ribbed and impermeable as that new Zetix anti-car-bomb, blast-proof fabric.

Informed by a military-like anatomy and trappings—top-down, "command-and-control" decision-making, military titles, a reflexive us-them mindset, an overreliance on SWAT, and arcane, militarily influenced nomenclature—the archetypical law enforcement agency is designed to keep the citizenry as far removed from the inner workings of the agency as possible.

And its undeniable success in doing so will continue until such time as we develop the wisdom and the will to change the system, fundamentally.

As previously observed, when something bad happens in police work— for example, a cop shoots a fleeing, unarmed man in the back—the tendency is to fixate on the incident, often ignoring the organizational *structure* that produces the *culture* that gives rise to the *event*.[1] This tendency is understandable: we're angry in the moment, and probably more than a little bewildered that a police officer would do such a thing. The citizens demand "accountability" for what's happened, and they are owed it.

But unless the citizenry is willing to engage in a searching, systemic analysis of the organizational influences that led to the event—and to then work with all stakeholders to reengineer that system—it'll never change it. A year or two from now, we'll be agonizing anew over how this "something bad" could possibly have happened, again.

TRIGGERED BY THE RODNEY King incident and the public's subsequent outrage, elected officials and police administrators, even the most defensive, bureaucratic-minded among them, set about rewriting policies. They rolled out new training for their officers. They installed stronger accountability measures. Cops, up and down the chain of command, and across the country, were informed that "bystandership" was no longer acceptable. Witness a fellow cop misbehave? Put a stop to it immediately, then report it. Or pay the consequences.

Good intentions, good policies, sensible training. But, what effect have they had? Even in Los Angeles, scene of the infamous 1991 beating, a few short years later, in 1998, the department was enmeshed in one of the biggest brutality and corruption scandals in the history of policing—a scandal that made "Rodney King" look like a fraternity hazing.

Why was it that after the King internal investigation; the exhaustive Christopher Commission inquiry ("Ugly incidents will not diminish until ranking officers [are] held responsible . . . ");[2] the swapping out of police chiefs (from Daryl Gates to Willie Williams to Bernard Parks); and all the other hand wringing, teeth gnashing, and soul searching, the LAPD was incapable of detecting, much less preventing, the undisguised behavioral patterns and trends that led to the Rampart scandal?

Here again, the glaring deficiency in all of the postmortem diagnoses and ultimately ineffectual prescriptions was failure to pay attention to the very structure of the department, the way policing was organized.

The LAPD, and every other domestic law enforcement agency, operates as a paramilitary-bureaucratic organization. And that all but guarantees a host of persistent organizational ills: dreadful internal communication that distorts important, sometimes critical information; the shielding of bosses from bad news; a dysfunctional disciplinary system; resistance to external (read "community") influences; and much more.

"YOU GUYS ARE LIKE the military, right?" The speaker is a fellow police-science major at Southwestern Community College (eleven months into my rookie year, I've gone back to school). We're on break, hanging around the coffee and cigarette machines. I'm the only cop in the crowd, a novelty. He continues, "I mean you both wear uniforms, right? You both carry guns, right?"

I hadn't thought about it that way. "I suppose."

"And you both go after the enemy, right?"

I couldn't argue with his assessment. Sure, I knew there were plenty of good people on my beat in East San Diego (hell, my grandparents lived there), but, yes, the "bad guys" on Beat 35 were indeed the "enemy." And as I drove out of headquarters five nights a week to do battle with them, I was prepared for war.

In the months ahead, a confluence of influences caused me to question my fellow student's assumptions, and my own. It started with a run-in with a deputy prosecutor: reviewing an arrest I'd made (for public drunken-ness, of a nineteen-year-old drunk who wasn't drunk). He wanted to know whether the US Constitution meant anything to me; within a few brief mo-ments, I shifted through a range of emotions, from anger to embarrassment to shame.[3]

I was also starting to be affected by other influences, by my non-police-science classes, for example: history, sociology, psychology, political sci-ence. And by fellow students, people my age who in the mid-1960s were all about challenging racism; white privilege; middle-class values that made little room for women, gays, lesbians, and other "minorities"; American im-perialism; and, horror of horrors, "police brutality." Also, I was influenced by several fellow officers who, unlike my early role models, showed me it was possible to be a tough crime fighter *and* a decent human being.

And I met a woman, a woman who would become my wife and best friend, and whose passion for social justice was highly contagious.

In short, I came to conclude that *no*, cops are *not* like the military. At least they're not supposed to be.

Images of the "Battle in Seattle," of the streets of post–Michael Brown Ferguson and post–Freddie Gray Baltimore notwithstanding, the differences between soldiers and cops are profound: soldiers follow orders for a living, cops make decisions for a living—important decisions like freedom or arrest, life or death; the military's mission is to win wars on foreign soil, the job of police officers is to help their citizen partners stay safe, and to protect civil rights and civil liberties on the streets of America. We simply cannot achieve those ends through military means.

IT ALL STARTS WITH the mission. A beat cop will tell you she is here to "protect life and property." A textbook answer, but she believes in it.

How is her work, and that of her co-workers, organized to accomplish this mission? Well, understanding there are wide variations from one jurisdiction to the next, she is assigned to a geo-based *squad*, working for a *sergeant* who reports to a *lieutenant* who reports to a *captain* who reports to a *major* (or "commander" or "inspector") who reports to an *assistant chief* who reports to a *deputy chief* who reports to the *chief of police* (or to a *sheriff* in county law enforcement). In smaller jurisdictions, the smallest of the small, there may be only one cop, total: no bureaucracy to speak of, paramilitary or otherwise. In larger jurisdictions, the LAPD, for example, with its layer upon layer of "supervision" (Captain I, Captain II, Captain III, for instance) the communication links can run to ten levels. So in the language of communications experts, that means ten "relays"[4] through which information must pass from the streets to the corner pocket, the office of the chief. Or vice versa.

Even assuming the best of intentions, people, being people, will add to, subtract from, or otherwise warp the information they pass up or down the chain of command. Or both up and down and laterally, through the specialists of police work: a dozen different brands of detectives—burglary, robbery, homicide, intelligence, sexual assault, domestic violence, child abuse, anti-terrorism, bomb squad, auto theft, narcotics, vice, forgery, and the list goes on. Then there are the traffic officers, collision investigators, scene reconstructionists, DUI, and hit-and-run specialists, other experts in the realm of traffic flow, traffic safety. And within patrol: mounted, SWAT, harbor, K-9, search and rescue, mountain, beach, and other specialized units, anti-crime details—think buy-bust operations in open-air drug markets, think LAPD's now-defunct CRASH, or Chicago's disbanded SOS, the Special Operations Section. And there are numerous other specialists, sworn and non-sworn, working in as many as four to seven bureaus, with their respective divisions, precincts, sections, teams, or squads. Some are scientists of the CSI-forensics variety, some are crime- or systems-analysts, budget wizards, records keepers, dispatch phone operators, radio operators, and so on.

The point is, information that must pass through seemingly endless bureaucratic relays will get distorted, will be "incrementally whitewashed" (cleansed of its meaning, cleansed of its affect), and will, on occasion, be intentionally misrepresented. And we haven't even begun to overlay the range of personalities you'll find in any police department: the rigidly bureaucratic captain, the laissez-faire sergeant, the fiercely militaristic lieutenant, the bigoted detective, the absentee chief, and the like. You've played the telephone game? To humorous effect, no doubt? Now, imagine the game, played for real, with much higher stakes, its effects multiplied exponentially.

Much organizational angst can be chalked up to the paramilitary mandate: everybody will adhere to the "chain of command." At all times. Naturally, enterprising individuals find "work-arounds," ways to break the chain of command, without having their legs broken. And enlightened leaders do find ways—"vertical staff meetings" (everyone in the chain assembled together, same time, same room, same agenda), or ride-alongs in which, say, the beat cop and the bureau chief cover calls and shoot the shit for a shift . . . informal communication that can break down barriers and allow both parties to gain knowledge and insight. Assuming neither lets rank get in the way—not always a safe assumption, in my experience.

Also, "work-arounds" tend to piss people off, especially bosses who feel undermined; and they do little to foster the day-to-day flow of critical information within a police department.

And they do absolutely nothing for the citizen on the outside looking in.

THAT FORTRESS OF A police building down on Main Street? Designed for maximum security, its uniformed representative scowling from behind a bulletproof window? That can be downright intimidating for the average citizen. As can cops muscling 5,000-pound machines around your neighborhood (cop cars pack an additional 1,000 pounds, from bumper to bumper, than those coming off the assembly line). Also intimidating? Cops glaring out at the world from behind mirrored shades. Add the equipment and weaponry we talked about in Chapter 7, cops who speak in code ("I'll handle the 11–10 of that 245, 246 after I drop off my 10–16 at Point 7"), or who never smile. The picture that emerges is that of a secretive if not otherworldly force. Pity the citizen who has come to the stationhouse or hailed such a cop with a request, a question, a complaint, even a commendation.

IF YOU'RE A MAYOR or a city council member, a community activist or a police chief dedicated to improving community-police relations (even as you back effective crime fighting, officer safety, and readiness to deal with "critical incidents" such as riots and terrorists' bombs), you might want to take inventory of the extent to which bureaucratic or militaristic tendencies of your local PD are undermining your efforts.[5]

ONE POWERFUL MEANS OF demilitarizing and humanizing a police department is to feminize it. In the 1970s, women constituted about 2 percent of sworn police officers. Today that number hovers at around 12 percent, a fivefold increase—but still a sorry commentary on the state of American policing,[6] particularly when one considers that every study of note over the past four decades shows that women perform at least as well as men in all categories and better in some.

A definitive roundup of these studies, a "meta evaluation," was done in 2003 by the National Center for Women and Policing (NCWP). The absence of more recent, on-topic studies might suggest that women have achieved parity in police work, a judgment certainly not borne out by the numbers. Further, women of color remain disproportionately underrepresented at both the entry-level and management ranks.[7]

Still, the dearth of contemporary research does suggest that questions about women's basic suitability for the work, all the rage in the early 1970s, have been put to rest. Supported by over one hundred research citations (removed from the following text, which is that of the NCWP, but available in the referenced document), the NCWP study, excerpted here, found six "advantages for law enforcement agencies that hire and retain more women":[8]

1. **Female officers are proven to be as competent as their male counterparts.**

   Research has shown no meaningful difference between male and female officers in: their activities or productivity on patrol; their commitment to law enforcement organizations; their response to violent confrontations; their performance evaluations received both at the academy and on the job; their level of job satisfaction; and their participation in training and other professional development activities.

   In fact, some studies indicate areas of police performance in which women excel. There is evidence that women officers tend to use a style of policing that relies more on communication than physical force, and that they are therefore more likely than their male counterparts to deescalate potentially violent situations and avoid excessive use of force.

2. **Female officers are less likely to use excessive force.**

   "Police work used to be like a laborer's job [wrote Timothy Egan in the *New York* Times] . . . the only requirement was that you had to be tough. Now, that's not what we're looking for. . . . [The job] is all about knowing how to talk to people. We screen for drug use, criminal background, but we don't do much screening for people who can get along with other people. . . . A good cop knows how to defuse the situation by talking it out."

   . . . men and women are equally likely to use force during the course of routine professional duties. . . . Yet research unequivocally demonstrates that women are less likely to be involved in employing both deadly force and excessive force....

... one recent study of seven major U.S. police departments indicated that female officers are named in only 5 percent of citizen complaints for excessive force and 2 percent of the sustained allegations of excessive force.

... the question of physical strength lies at the heart of the traditional reluctance to hire women into policing. A number of studies document that police officers and community members are both concerned that women are not strong enough or aggressive enough for police work. Yet physical strength has not been shown to predict either general police effectiveness or the ability to successfully handle dangerous situations.

... According to the National Law Enforcement Memorial Fund, the vast majority of police officer fatalities are caused by gunfire and automobile accidents. Physical strength does not play a primary role in these tragedies, nor does it explain why men are disproportionately more likely than women to be killed in the line of duty....

Research demonstrates that female officers not only exhibit more reasoned caution than their male counterparts, but also that they increase this tendency in their male partners....

3. **Female officers implement "community-oriented policing."**

Community policing represents a new approach to modern law enforcement, emphasizing communication and cooperation with citizens as well as informal problem solving. It is therefore important to note that women officers receive more favorable evaluations and fewer citizen complaints than their male counterparts.

... For their part, female officers report greater support for the principles of community policing than their male colleagues and are less cynical and more respectful in their view of citizens....

There is also evidence that women in law enforcement are less likely to be involved in various forms of misconduct. It is no wonder, then, that some have suggested hiring more female officers as a way of improving the public image of the police department. Several police agencies in Mexico and Latin America have even established a corps of women-only to handle traffic violations because they are less likely to accept bribes and engage in other forms of corruption.

4. **More female officers will improve law enforcement's response to violence against women.**

Research indicates that 2-3 million women are physically assaulted each year in the U.S. by their male partners. In addition, the most recent national estimates indicate that 1 out of 6 American women will be sexually assaulted and 1 out of 12 will be stalked during their lifetime. Clearly, the extent of the problem highlights the critical importance of police response to crimes of violence against women.

. . . the benefits of success are . . . substantial. For example, effective police response has been found to both improve the self-esteem of battered women and increase the likelihood that they will leave abusive relationships.

. . . female officers have long been viewed as more effective in this area than their male counterparts. This perception is shared by the community, police training instructors, and female officers themselves.

. . . it is insufficient to discuss the police response to violence against women without addressing the possibility that responding officers have committed these crimes themselves.

. . . Increasing women's numbers in the ranks of law enforcement also has the potential for lessening the chance that crimes of violence against women will be handled by an officer who has perpetrated such a crime.

5. **Increasing the presence of female officers reduces problems of sex discrimination and harassment within a law enforcement agency.**

Study after study documents that women in law enforcement continue to face a variety of obstacles, including negative attitudes, gender discrimination, and sexual harassment.

. . . women enter and remain in the policing profession for many of the same reasons that men do, including the desirable pay and benefits, the challenges associated with the job, desire for promotion, and the opportunity to help others.

However, they often leave for reasons that are very different, including unique stresses not faced by their male counterparts. Among these are problems with co-worker gossip, training, lack of promotional opportunity, inflexible working patterns, and administrative policies that disadvantage female officers.

Women face the extra burden of having to "prove themselves" beyond what is expected of men, and they are often isolated from the networks that provide an officer with needed information, support, mentoring, and protection. Women of color face additional difficulties based on the intersection of sexism and racism in police agencies.

. . . increased representation of women can also have the benefit of transforming the very climate within a law enforcement agency, and reducing the prevalence of gender discrimination, under-utilization . . . and at least one study has found that some of the problems with tokenism experienced by female officers are particularly pronounced in departments with a smaller representation of sworn women.

6. **The presence of women can bring about beneficial changes in policy for all officers.**

Lewis Sherman envisioned as early as 1973 that police departments would be held liable for their under-representation of female officers, and that hiring more women would not only bring them into compliance with the U.S. Constitution but also yield improvements in the procedures for selection, recruitment, and retention of all sworn personnel.

. . . these [improvements] would inevitably benefit both female and male employees within law enforcement. The Police Foundation similarly noted in 1974 that:

"The introduction of women will create an incentive . . . to examine many management practices which are less acceptable now that they must be applied to men and women alike. This may result in the development of improved selection criteria, performance standards, and supervision for all officers."

[The Police Foundation] further concluded that [an] expanded supply of police personnel, the reduced cost of recruiting, and better community representation were additional benefits of hiring of more female officers.

Pop quiz: Of all the controversial officer-involved shootings in the past two years, how many women officers pulled the trigger? If you answered none, you're right. True, because of notoriously spotty agency reporting, it's hard to be absolutely certain. But we do know, according to Bureau of Justice Statistics, that male officers are responsible for 98 percent of all police shootings.[9] And, because women are underrepresented in the higher ranks, that means most female officers are on the streets—where officer-involved shootings, naturally enough, are most likely to take place.

Generalizations are always risky, including this one: in my professional experience, women supervisors, managers, and executives tend to do a better job, overall, than their male counterparts. They are more community-oriented, more inclusive, more inclined to identify and work to solve "personnel" problems, more likely to meet deadlines and produce a higher-quality work product. They are also more likely to confront bigotry, excessive force, corruption, and male officers' inattention, apathy, or worse in the face of violence against women.

So that means if America's cities are looking to reduce if not eliminate racism, sexism, homophobia, dishonesty, brutality, and unjustified officer shootings, and to demilitarize their police forces, they could do a lot worse than to hire more women, promote more women, and appoint more women police chiefs. Generally.

13

COMPASSIONATE COPS

"*FEELINGS* WILL GET YOU killed, kid." Thus spoke my first "senior officer," who today would be called a field-training officer, or FTO—a pivotal
guru and tone setter in the life of the neophyte cop.

"Feelings?"

"Yeah, you know, like compassion, feeling sorry for someone."

It was obvious "Bob" had thought about the subject or had remembered
well what he had been told in an earlier day.

"You can't let compassion for others get in the way of your decision-
making, or your actions. You'll become distracted, lose sight of your priorities . . . wind up in the hospital, or the morgue."

Bob had a point, to a point. In my time in policing, I did observe a small
number of officers who took what might carelessly be called a compassionate or, more accurately, a sentimental, softheaded approach to police work,
and whose spiritual or religious beliefs about the basic decency of others
jeopardized their own safety and the safety of those around them. What,
exactly, are these dangerous beliefs?

It's a short list, at the top of which is the idea that all people are good,
all people are rational, all people will act not only in their own interest but
selflessly in the interests of their families, friends, and the whole community. What this belief ignores, of course, is that not everyone is wired for
reason, or goodness—that some people are devious, evil, unburdened by

conscience. Without prejudging anyone, cops need to know this about certain of their fellow human beings.

Moreover, they must be able to deal alertly, expertly with people who are mentally ill, suicidal, under the influence. And quite possibly, armed. The "under the influence" diagnosis may involve alcohol or other drugs, of course, as is often enough the case (usually once or twice a shift for cops on busy beats in big cities). But police also regularly come into contact with people who are under the influence of fear, triggered often enough by unexpected contact with the police or by any of the many other sources of fear: jealousy, insecurity, sorrow—emotions that may have nothing whatsoever to do with the cop standing in front of them at the moment but rather the everyday maddening, irritating, or tragic facts and circumstances of their lives. These emotions are guaranteed to affect behavior.

People are human, just like cops.

Therefore, we may ask, by way of example, whether it is reasonable that a police officer whose spouse has just left him might feel a little something for the weeping or raging person who has suffered the same fate. Yes? No? Maybe? It's complicated. But as Bob told me, getting distracted, losing sight of one's purpose and priorities as a cop can get you killed.

Or, as we learned in Cleveland, Ohio, the person who gets killed just might be a lonely child trying to entertain himself on a snowy deserted playground.

TO HIS NEIGHBORS, TIMOTHY Loehmann was a good guy. Described as quiet and respectful, he'd wanted to be an NYPD police officer just like his father, who had served for twenty years. Loehmann did become a cop, though not in New York.[1]

In 2012, he joined the Independence (Ohio) Police Department, where he lasted six months before being asked to resign (or before he was "constructively terminated," meaning he would have been fired had he not quit). Seems Loehmann fell apart on the pistol range, after having fallen asleep during a training session. He and his on-again, off-again girlfriend had been having problems. For months, according to the officer's own statements to his sergeant, he wept often on the job. His mother told the same sergeant that her son's academy papers "would be soaked in tears nightly for three months."[2]

When he became "distracted" and "weepy" at the range; when he "could not follow simple directions, could not communicate clear thoughts nor recollections"; when his "handgun performance was dismal"; when the department's deputy chief concluded, in a written report, that neither "time, nor training, will be able to change or correct the deficiencies," young Loehmann was given his marching orders. This was on December 4, 2012.[3]

In March 2014—having made only one phone call to a human resources person in Independence, but without benefit of a background investigation, without even knocking on the door of the Independence PD, some eighteen minutes away—Cleveland hired him.[4]

Several months later, on November 22, 2014, Officer Loehmann was riding shotgun with his partner, Frank Garmback, when they were dispatched to a snowy field at the Cudell Recreation Center. A citizen, sitting in the park, had called in a qualified suspicion: there was a boy, "a juvenile," playing with what looked like a fake handgun. The caller repeated, twice, that the gun was "probably" fake. (This information was never transmitted to the officers, another strike against the Cleveland Police Department's record of efficiency and professionalism.)[5]

Garmback pulled up to twelve-year-old Tamir Rice and slid to a stop. Loehmann bailed out and, in less than two seconds, shot and killed the boy.[6]

AN IMPORTANT DIGRESSION. THIS tactic, pulling right up to the source of a potentially lethal threat, is reminiscent of Ian Birk's rash, deadly encounter with Seattle wood-carver John T. Williams on August 30, 2010. And Ferguson officer Darren Wilson's reckless approach to Michael Brown in the August 9, 2014, fatal shooting. That event was similar to a tragedy, addressed below, that stemmed from the May 2, 2015, attempted stop of Demetrius Blackwell in Queens Village by NYPD officer Brian Moore and his partner.[7]

Blackwell, who had been "adjusting his waistband," pulled a revolver and murdered young Moore before he could get out of his police car. From an officer safety point of view, the smart tactic is to park far enough away from the subject, and to approach slowly, cautiously. If a weapon is spotted or there are signs of aggression, the officer can take evasive action (a clever, not a cowardly move), perhaps using the police car for cover. This rush-to-judgment, macho tactic we're witnessing over and over is foolhardy and deadly. It's got to stop.

THE KILLING OF YOUNG Rice begs the question: What was the officer's mental state at the time?

Of course, there's nothing to suggest that Loehmann's "weepy," sensitive mien translated into "compassion." On the contrary, it suggests the personality of an excessively self-absorbed individual, one not inclined, or able, to empathize with others. Making him utterly unsuitable for police work.

What exactly is compassion? The *Oxford English Dictionary* (*OED*) defines it as "Sympathetic pity and concern for the sufferings or misfortunes of others [as in]: 'the victims should be treated with compassion.'" Some synonyms: "pity, sympathy . . . fellow feeling, care, concern, solicitude, sensitivity, warmth, love, tenderness, mercy, leniency, tolerance, kindness, humanity, charity."

Average police officers would gag on this list. These qualities, they would argue, may be appropriate for the priesthood or hospice workers. But not for cops, definitely not cops.

But what of police officers who exhibit "fellow feeling," who act out of genuine concern and kindness for the citizens on their beats? Am I suggesting this should disqualify such people from becoming police officers?

Of course not.

In fact, such candidates, possessed of other essential qualities—self-discipline, the physical and mental wherewithal needed to defend themselves and others, and a sufficient supply of moral rectitude—would likely prove to be ideal cops. Their everyday acts of kindness establish them as caring police officers . . . who can also take care of themselves, and innocent others. In short, precisely the kind of candidates law enforcement should actively pursue.

There has been much talk lately of replacing the "warrior" mentality of police officers with a "guardian" mindset. I've followed for several years this "ping-pong" conversation with fascination, partly because in my previous book, *Breaking Rank*, I defended the path of the warrior:

> When I picture warriors I don't see the "jarheads" described in Anthony Swofford's 2003 chronicle of the Gulf War. I see: Nelson Mandela, Joan of Arc, Martin Luther King, Jr., Mahatma Gandhi, Harriet Tubman, Vaclav Havel, Eleanor Roosevelt, Viktor Frankl, Sojourner Truth, Branch Rickey, Rosa Parks, Franklin Delano Roosevelt, Mother Teresa, Anne Frank. Men and women who went into battle armed only with a moral compass and a passion for justice. They changed the world, these warriors.[8]

When Sue Rahr, former sheriff of King County, stepped down from that post and took over the Washington State Criminal Justice Training Commission in 2012, she was determined to "demilitarize" academy training, to eliminate certain military protocols that had been in place for years, and to encourage recruits to think for themselves and embrace a strong community orientation. (Police recruits come to Burien, Washington, from all over the state, including Seattle and King County, to undergo nineteen weeks of entry-level training.)

In searching for a unified, and unifying, theme to capture the philosophy of a new approach to policing (and hence to training), Rahr told a reporter that her "history-major son suggested the guardian model referenced in Plato's 'The Republic'—which describes guardians who are gentle with citizens but fierce against enemies."[9]

One problem with the analogy is that in *The Republic*, the guardian class is responsible for ruling the city; they are the "philosopher kings." Plato divides a good and just society into three classes: the guardians; the producers (of goods and services); and the auxiliaries, or the warrior class whose job is to defend the city.[10] Of course, though deemed by some the best philosophical and political theory of all time, the work *was* written in 360 BCE, and I'm sure Rahr had a more literal, more modern version of "guardian" in mind.

But there's another problem. Let's call it the "fierce against enemies" clause.

I'm guessing that labeling criminal offenders "enemies"—and urging police officers to behave ferociously toward them—is also not what Rahr was thinking when she adopted the term. In fact, in that same *Seattle Times* article, reporter Steve Miletich wrote appreciatively of a class he had observed on the searching of suspects:

> The instructor, Raphael Park, a Bellevue police officer told of a gang member who became belligerent about a search of his backpack. The gang member, Park said, didn't want police to see photos of his premature baby who had died, as well as the baby's mother.
>
> It was important to remember, Park said, that gang members have "their own lives and their own issues."
>
> Showing "respect and compassion," he said, is "going to make your job much easier."[11]

Park's story, particularly its punch line, is an exquisite example of how a modern police officer, always ready to protect the public, always ready to defend himself or herself, can both neutralize criticism of cops and make the work safer, more effective, and more satisfying on a human-to-human level.

On the issue of "guardians" versus "warriors"? I'm willing to concede the latter label has accumulated hefty baggage in recent years (thanks, in large part, to Radley Balko's insistence on naming his superb 2013 book *Rise of the Warrior Cop*)[12] and the numerous pejorative references to "warriors" in the wake of "Ferguson." That said, I continue to adhere to a belief that the warrior model, one that embraces disciplined peacekeeping while rejecting base aggression, is a worthy concept. As is "guardian," though of a distinctly non-Platonic hue: the police are not here to rule.

Semantic differences aside, police experts and critics are likely in agreement: good cops are empathetic cops. In other words, they have the capacity to put themselves in the shoes of the people they encounter, regardless of circumstances. What if we were to embed empathy in a police officer's job description, setting standards for its exercise in daily practice and establishing a level of competency as a condition of employment?

OED's definition of *empathy*, "The ability to understand and share the feelings of another," is simple and straightforward. It's actually a skill that can be developed, observed, reinforced through practice—and brought to bear in everyday police work, to the benefit of all.

A community that demanded empathetic police officers would let all comers know: If you want to be a cop in this town you must demonstrate your ability to listen to and understand others. (Of course, this presupposes direct citizen involvement in the hiring process, long overdue.) Which is to say, to a would-be police officer, you must be verifiably able to see others, and capable of understanding what's going on with them.

Bill Bratton reinforced this view when, according to a reporter, he told an audience at the Greater Allen African Methodist Episcopal Church in Queens that the NYPD "needs to face the hard truth that in our most vulnerable neighborhoods we have a problem with citizen satisfaction. We are often abrupt, sometimes rude, and that's unacceptable." He later told the reporter, "We want cops to be able to see the people they're policing. In this department, and maybe in a lot of American policing today, unfortunately, too many members don't treat people appropriately."[13]

Bratton is on to something here. In "The Inexplicable: Inside the Mind of a Mass Killer," Karl Ove Knausgaard wrote of the mass murderer Anders Behring Breivik:

> The most powerful human forces are found in the meeting of the face and the gaze. Only there do we exist for one another. In the gaze of the other, we become, and in our own gaze others become. It is there, too, that we can be destroyed. Being unseen is devastating, and so is not seeing. . . . Breivik remained unseen, and it destroyed him.[14]

Knausgaard's description evokes memories of cops over the course of my career who could not, or would not, "see" the people they encountered, even to make eye contact with them.

If being unseen is devastating, so, too, is being unheard. Therefore, when a cop ignores a motorist's explanation or a mother's questions about her detained daughter, when that cop fails to acknowledge the mother's very existence and to hear what she has to say, that adds to the all-too-common perception that our nation's police officers are automatons, not fully human.

There is a wonderful photograph, by Eric Thayer for Reuters, that accompanies a January 8, 2015, Jonathan Capehart editorial in the *Washington Post*.[15] In it, two smiling hipsters face off with an unnamed NYPD uniformed officer. They're in midtown Manhattan, part of a crowd protesting police actions in the Eric Garner death on Staten Island. The officer's expression is priceless. As the two protesters attempt to convey their feelings, the cop reacts with closed eyes, his large, marvelous face contorted into an expression that reads, "No way, my friends. I am not listening. But if I were, I would say to you, 'You're full of shit. You don't understand the real world. You got it all wrong.'" And, because I'm mind reading here (and indulging a sweeping generalization from a two-dimensional black-and-white photo), I would go on to say that this guy strikes me as the kind of cop—in a different organizational culture, with new and improved expectations based on the values Bratton claims he wants to instill in the NYPD—who could very well set a standard of empathetic listening. A fully human cop. With a sense of humor yet.

A VIRTUE OF MAKING empathy a job requirement is that it can be taught, just like any other skill. And it can be tested; we can assess a police candidate's ability to "see" others. A cop wannabe says, "I'm a good listener, I care about what people are telling me." The background investigator insists on proof, goes out to talk with family, friends, neighbors, classmates, co-workers of the candidate, asking, "Does this applicant listen to others? Show concern?" However imprecise the replies, this feedback is vital.

In my work as an expert witness on police misconduct cases, I will occasionally read the report of a background investigation that leaves me shaking my head. Some individuals with a pre-hire association with the candidate might say something like, "Well, Philbert's kind of standoffish."

Or, "He can come across as disinterested, or aloof." If only one person says something like that, it may not tell you a whole lot about Philbert, but if several say the same thing? Especially coming from people who've never met one another? You're likely looking at a character trait. Someone who, in Bratton's eyes, doesn't "see" the other person. Someone, in short, who shouldn't be a cop.

I've heard police officers say, "Okay, so empathy's important. But why don't 'they' (the citizenry) show us some empathy first?" After I get over my initial now-that's-a-real-mature-attitude attitude, I treat the question as actual versus rhetorical, and answer it along these lines: Because you work for them. Because showing empathy begets empathy. Because it makes your job easier, and safer, and more satisfying. And, by the way, Officer, while citizens are required to obey the law, they're under no obligation to love you. Though it might be nice, nowhere is it written that they must demonstrate empathy or respect toward law enforcement. If you genuinely want to gain your critics' trust and support, you will ignore slights and insults, learn to de-escalate tension, and attend to the business of "seeing" everyone.

ALL RIGHT THEN, HOW does a community and its police department go about hiring candidates with strong potential for professional competence and ethical, empathetic, compassionate conduct? We're talking about officers who get the job done, care about the citizenry, and who, when confronted with dishonest or brutal colleagues, are unafraid to act on their convictions? Hint: *ask the community.*

The community knows.

True, an unpaid, untrained citizenry cannot be relied upon to create, staff, or finance a recruitment campaign; devise and administer fair, reasonable, job-related, nondiscriminatory entry-level testing, including medical and physical fitness exams; conduct polygraph exams; complete thorough background investigations into each candidate's life history, his or her work and academic performance, and relations with others: family, friends, neighbors, fellow students, co-workers; check criminal, driving, medical, and financial records; and administer sophisticated psychological testing. *All* of which must be accomplished before an agency takes the calculated risk to hire a candidate. (We can only assume that had the Cleveland Police Department been half this thorough in the screening of Timothy Loehmann, Tamir Rice would likely be a teenager today.)

THOUGHTFUL, NON-COP CITIZENS KNOW what qualities they want in a cop. And because they know, and because the officers selected will be working in their neighborhoods, and because the police belong to the people, America's citizens simply must participate in deciding who gets hired, and who doesn't.

In addition to sitting on oral-interview boards, citizens can and should participate as actors in testing simulations (for instance, mock scenes, or role playing, covering a range of key scenarios that cop wannabes will encounter in the real world), and in any other mutually agreed upon candidate-screening capacity.

Of course, it's always possible that a request for community partnership in selecting the best candidates will be met with skepticism, if not outright opposition. "Why?" critics ask. "Why would we want to collude with or be exploited by a department that behaves like an occupational force, disrespects our community, violates our civil liberties?"

The short answer is that because if all those things are true—and, make no mistake, they are true for many people, in all cities—what's most urgently needed is to turn that perception around. And perceptions won't change in the absence of (1) legitimate, structural reforms in policies, procedures, and practices, and (2) high-quality people picked to become tomorrow's police officers: cops who reject racism, brutality, militarism. It's kind of a chicken-and-egg argument, to be sure. But, even as a given jurisdiction commits itself to long-haul, major structural reform, it must simultaneously go after the very best of the right kind of officers.

To do that, the citizens' participation, in full partnership with police and human resources experts, is essential.

And all parties should probably agree on what they're looking for.

THE COMMUNITY POLICING CONSORTIUM, supported by the US Department of Justice Office of Community Oriented Police Services and headed by noted police and public-safety psychologist Dr. Ellen Scrivner, conducted an important research project on police recruitment and hiring.[16] The project identified the following core competencies for all law enforcement officers, paraphrased and annotated here:

Good judgment and problem-solving skills. As Will Rogers once said, "Good judgment comes from experience, and a lot of that comes from bad judgment"—of the type threaded throughout these pages. In police work, as in medicine, bad decision-making can have terrible consequences. But you already know that.

What you may not know is that systematic, disciplined *problem solving* is at the core of true community policing. First introduced by Professor Herman Goldstein at the University of Wisconsin–Madison, "Problem-oriented policing (POP),"[17] and its expanded model, originated by William Spelman and John Eck in work for the National Institute of Justice,[18] provides a simple, effective framework for cops and citizens to work together. Doing what? Enhancing public safety, building mutual trust, and strengthening the community-police relationship. Spelman and Eck brought us the "SARA" model: *scanning* (identification of crime and other community problems); *analysis* (studying those problems, coming to a common definition); *response* (working together, developing strategies and tactics to solve or reduce the identified problems); *assessment* (evaluation to determine whether the response worked, or is working).[19] Regrettably, these acronyms make great targets, lending themselves to both lighthearted mockery and mean-spirited attacks by status quo preservationists within the cop culture ("Pop and Sara walk into a bar . . . "). Nonetheless, POP works, SARA works.

Empathy and compassion. As suggested earlier, compassion is a nice quality for a cop to have, empathy a requisite skill. If you've had any interaction at all with an empathy-challenged cop, you'll likely remember it with a bad feeling for a long time. Conversely, contact with an empathetic or compassionate cop is likely to leave a lasting, feel-good impression.

Will we ever forget the story of NYPD officer Larry DePrimo, who on a frigid November night in 2012 bought a pair of $75 insulated boots and warm socks for a homeless, shoeless man?[20] Captured in a photo by a tourist from Arizona, the twenty-five-year-old Sixth Precinct cop knelt down and put the footwear on the man. DePrimo said at the time, "I had two pairs of wool winter socks and combat boots, and I was cold." Some may recall that following this sweet act of kindness, cynics came out of the woodwork to proclaim the homeless man a con artist, someone who preferred to walk the mean streets barefoot, who hid his new boots and angled for a "piece of the (publicity) pie," who wasn't homeless at all—suggesting that DePrimo was duped. Possible? Sure, just as it's possible that the generous deeds by police officers I've personally witnessed in San Diego and Seattle—collecting money to help feed and clothe a poor family, pitching in to clean up the dilapidated, unsafe property of a shut-in, giving an elderly pensioner a lift across town to a doctor's appointment (the examples go on and on; they do)—might also be derided by doubters. But so what? Cops who care are worth their weight in goodwill.

Am I suggesting that police officers have a duty to do what DePrimo did? No. That's what made it special.

Capacity for multitasking. Most jobs demand some degree of multitasking mastery. Police work is no exception, and the new cop's first assignment—patrol—puts those skills to the test right out of the academy. Say that "Elena Delgado," a new cop on a busy beat (the larger the jurisdiction's population, the busier the beat), finds herself rushing to an armed robbery of a mom-and-pop convenience store, dodging traffic the whole way, monitoring radio transmissions, dialed in for a description of the suspects and weapons and vehicles and time element and direction of travel, eyes peeled for suspects hotfooting it toward a darkened alley or speeding away in a getaway car. And, once at the store, assuming the robbers made good on their escape plan, administering first aid as necessary, then shifting quickly into preliminary investigation mode: protecting the crime scene; politely keeping the clerk (Mom?) from ringing up, in the midst the investigation, the attempted purchase of a customer's Cheetos, Fritos, or Doritos, or calling Pop at home to fill him in on every detail while the officer cools her heels; clearing out the store, except for potential witnesses; separating those witnesses and interviewing them and the clerk; obtaining and putting out over the air additional suspect information and other details, especially on weapons, so that colleagues in the area have a shot at capturing the suspect(s), and staying safe; collecting, identifying, and preserving evidence; gathering all relevant information for the preliminary report and getting it to robbery detectives in a form and fashion that meets their particular needs . . . and so on and so on.

And, in the back of her mind our officer is playing over ways to nail the daytime residential burglars who have been carrying away her beat during her off-duty hours; putting together a SARA plan to deal with persistent, repeat calls to landlord-tenant disputes at the big apartment complex at the south end of her beat; mentally rehearsing her testimony for tomorrow's auto theft/chop-shop trial; mulling gift ideas for her partner's upcoming birthday; and so on.

Multitasking: it's what cops do. Every shift.

Courage and demonstrated willingness to take responsibility. For all my finger-wagging lectures about the need for cops to show restraint, take evasive action, wait for backup, there are moments when fearless, decisive measures are called for. For example, at a time when most rational people would run from danger, cops run toward it—active-shooter situations come to mind. As do tall parking structures and high bridges—from the Golden Gate to the Verrazano-Narrows—with suicidal strangers dangling from railings. Not to mention the all-too-frequent if-I-can't-have-her-no-one-can 911 calls featuring a man with a gun to the head of someone he claims to love.

The physical risks in police work are all too real. So are the emotional ones. Risks that test a cop's moral sensibilities, his or her sense of responsibility, his or her guts. To stand up to a peer, or a boss, who's done or is planning to do the wrong thing.

Resourcefulness and initiative. Judge this story as you see fit, but it definitely is an example of police resourcefulness and initiative. Not to mention chutzpah.

Years ago, in San Diego, we put together a fugitive detail composed of a sergeant and several detectives. The idea was to go after scofflaws, people who had skipped bail, who were wanted on warrants. "Scofflaw" sounds almost quaint, evoking images of ninety-three-year-old shoplifters, oblivious parking violators, minor offenders. But for this detail we had prioritized major violators, with an emphasis on those who had done violence to others—outlaws who, unless captured, would likely reoffend and maybe do permanent damage to a fellow human being.

Sergeant Gordon Redding and his squad of gung-ho sleuths had their sights on one such elusive offender. As I remember it, they'd developed extensive information on the man's comings and goings, learned he would be in the hospital on such-and-such a date for such-and-such a surgical procedure. Imagine the bad guy's shock when into the OR strolled Doctor Redding and his surgical crew, decked out in scrubs and masks, a stethoscope draped around the "chief surgeon's" neck, a clipboarded arrest warrant in hand. The real doc, apparently hungry for diversion or wanting to help out in the capture of a dangerous fugitive, may or may not have violated his Hippocratic oath when he agreed to the conspiracy. Redding informed his patient—while he was still lucid—that the real doc would perform the procedure, but upon completion, and with sufficient time for recovery, under guard, said patient would be transferred to the care of the county jail, hospital ward. Judge it as you will, but it's an illustration of a police officer's undeniable resourcefulness and initiative.

Assertiveness. It used to be called *aggressiveness*. And it was a label all newbies aspired to. I know I did. So I went out of my way to earn the mantle "aggressive cop." Like the time I marched into a tavern on Adams Avenue, under the watchful, judging eye of my senior officer, to answer a closing-time disturbance call involving shitfaced pool players, cue sticks, pitchers of beer, and what Tom Waits would call a whole lot of "visual and verbal insubordination."[21] Having seen how it was done by the pros, I lined up all the big, burly drunks, arrested the biggest and the burliest, hooked him up, escorted him to our cage car and drove him to jail. I booked him, retrieved my cuffs, wrote the report, recapped the criminal arrest on our daily, and, a week later, basked in the glow of a performance evaluation that cited the incident and extolled my "aggressiveness." It was the highest praise a rookie could get. And it "incentivized" me to get more.

After my "come-to-Jesus" moment with that principled prosecutor at the end of my rookie year, I began to seriously consider what it means to be a good cop. I realized a fundamental truth about policing: there's no room in it for aggressive police officers. But there's plenty of room for assertive cops: beat officers, detectives, sergeants, chiefs who know their jobs, have mastered the attitudes and skills necessary to live up to their job descriptions, and do just that. They're not out to prove anything. They're just wise, skilled, patient. So when they assert themselves, it's done in such a way that the job gets done, competently.

Integrity. With all due respect to Dr. Scrivner, who, as noted, assembled this list of core cop competencies, and who, while using a perfectly fine definition of "integrity," might have wanted to draw a distinction between integrity and "ethics."

Over the years, working with literally thousands of cops, I came to realize that the difference between ethics and integrity is really important: integrity is doing what you say you're going to do. If you say you're going to cheat, steal, and lie and you cheat, steal, and lie, you get points for high integrity. Ethics, on the other hand, is knowing the difference between right and wrong, and choosing the former over the latter.

I've worked with some police officers—not a lot, but certainly too many—who were proud of their integrity, by which I mean they proclaimed and boasted of their intention to kick ass and take names, and did precisely that—inflicting their "integrity" on the people they were hired to protect and serve. What they needed, what all our communities need, is a commitment to ethical police behavior.

Teamwork and ability to collaborate. Effective, dignified, constitutional police work in a free, pluralistic, multicultural society cannot be achieved as a solo performance. It requires a large orchestra of strings, woodwinds, brass, percussion or, if you prefer, a full-throated chorus of people: black, white, Latino, Native American, Asian, gay, lesbian, bisexual, transgender, queer, questioning, straight, old, young, male, female, poor, wealthy; those with and without physical or mental disabilities; those of varying political, ideological, religious or nonreligious orientations; those who are or who have been in the military; those who are in this country legally and those who are not; those who appreciate the police, those who do not. In other words, today's community-oriented police work requires cops to partner with people who are different from them, and who are entitled to respectful treatment and equal protection under law.

Inside the ranks, the same principles apply. Patrol officers and detectives, the brass and rank-and-file cops, sworn and non-sworn personnel working collaboratively, seamlessly among themselves, in all their manifold differences, and with the citizenry to achieve safe communities. It's all about partnership.

14

ACTIVISTS AND COPS: PARTNERING TO CONTROL PROTESTS

Michael Brown was shot to death on August 9, 2014. From August 13 through December 29 of that year, I was interviewed ninety-one times on the topic of "Ferguson."

Reporters, commentators, and podcasters from radio, television, print, and cyberspace wanted my take on police militarization, police training, police use of lethal force, police misconduct. From my home, from studios in Seattle and New York (for *The Colbert Report*, where Stephen "accused" me of playing the "America card" because of my condemnation of police violations of civil liberties), I talked to reporters from throughout the United States and from around the world.

Of all the questions I fielded, the most frequently posed was a surprise. Was it about laws governing police use of lethal force? Was it about Pentagon and Homeland Security giveaways of instruments of war to local law enforcement, the increasing militarization of domestic policing? "Loose-cigarettes, quality-of-life, broken-windows" policing? Stop and frisk? SWAT policies and procedures? Racial tension in the community-police relationship, or within the ranks?

No. The number one question was this: What should the police do tonight on the streets of Ferguson to "contain" the protesters, to stop the rioting?

My unspoken response? *Why the hell are you asking me, of all people?*

I'm the guy who presided over the "Battle in Seattle," the 1999 anti–World Trade Organization (WTO) riots that produced mass arrests of contested constitutionality, left the city awash in broken glass and tear gas, demoralized my cops, and pissed off anti-globalization protesters and business owners alike. I'm the last guy the press should have been pressing for wisdom about police tactics during times of civil unrest.

I thought we were ready for the thousands of WTO ministers, trade officials, secretaries and heads of state (including the American president), the international press—and the tens of thousands of protesters. We were not.

I thought our officers had received ample, relevant training. They had not.

I thought our pre-event strategy, our policies, procedures, tactics, and equipment were all "state-of-the-art, good-enough-to-write-home-about, best-practices." They were not.

I thought we had sufficiently brought "the community" (particularly anti-globalization protesters) into pre-event planning. We had not.

I thought, having invoked mutual-aid assistance from other law enforcement agencies in advance, we had plenty of personnel on hand. We did not.

In short, as I confessed after the event, I got "snookered in Seattle."

So the best I could muster when asked by reporters what the police chief should do in Ferguson was, "Well, for gosh sakes, not what I did!"

THE LAST DAY OF November 1999. A cold, rainy morning. Both my field commander and my operations commander believed we needed to clear the intersection of Sixth and Union near the Sheraton in downtown Seattle. Demonstrators had been occupying it for an hour or so, seated on the wet asphalt, arms linked, defying orders to get up and leave. With additional contingents of protesters converging on the area and, with additional tens of thousands of labor marchers soon to be added to the mix, we made it official.

The field commander informed the occupiers that their failure to disperse would subject them to arrest. And that "chemical agents," a euphemism for tear gas, would be used if they refused the lawful order. I was standing on the far side of the intersection in order to hear with my own ears whether his warning was audible (check), unambiguous (check), and repeated a sufficient number of times to make clear the consequences of noncompliance (check).

The field commander warned them repeatedly. Then warned them again, then gassed them.

I watched through stinging, gas-filled eyes as the demonstrators stood up, coughing and hacking, and staggered out of the intersection.

Mission accomplished?

Hardly. Our use of tear gas against nonviolent, indeed nonthreatening demonstrators—a decision I blessed—was an unnecessary act of aggression against our fellow citizens.

And it had the utterly predictable effect of escalating tension and violence, turning thousands of protesters who, for the most part, had been supportive of our early efforts against the cops.

ON A BOOK TOUR in 2005, a middle-aged man came up to me after an Elliot Bay Books reading at Seattle's Town Hall. I was prepared to sign his copy, Sharpie at the ready. But he held no book.

"I used to respect you," he said, quietly. He went on to tell me why he had admired my work, which was kind of him. "But, no longer."

"I'm sorry to hear that." I thought I'd done a fair job at the reading, addressing relevant topics from the book, including key sections of the chapter on the week that left my legacy in tatters. "Care to tell me why?"

"You know why. You talked about it tonight. You used tear gas on peaceful protesters, Chief. I was one of those protesters. We weren't hurting anyone. We weren't destroying property. We weren't looting or throwing objects at your officers. We weren't torching cars or buildings." All of which would eventually transpire, of course—after my fateful decision to allow the gassing.

I knew we'd get nowhere, he and I, debating the merits of the decision. My thinking hadn't changed over the past five years: we did what we had to do that morning. And there were some eighty-five people in line to have their books signed. "Well, I'm sorry," I told him. "I guess we'll just have to agree to disagree."

He nodded, subtle but genuine disgust registering on his face, and he left the building. I wasn't used to that. I'd been holed up in my cabin year-round, writing, living the life of a part-time recluse, visiting occasionally with friends and family. Now, I was back in the real world. The man's comments stung.

Still, I do remember thinking, *If only he understood police work.*

Over the course of the tour, on both coasts, after meeting dozens of anti-globalization activists who had come to Seattle in 1999 and listening to their complaints of what my cops did to them—of what *I* did to them—I began to feel the rumblings of a tectonic shift.

A LONG-HELD FOUNDATIONAL VIEW of policing, one that in my case dated back to the civil rights insurrections, campus activism, and anti-war demonstrations of the1960s, began to crumble beneath my feet. You see, it had been axiomatic in those days, from Watts to Newark, San Diego to St. Petersburg: if you were outnumbered, if you didn't want to get rocked-and-bottled into submission, witness your city go up in flames, you had no choice but to trot out a generous supply of CS gas and apply liberally.

That was a situation we had sincerely tried to prevent that morning outside the Sheraton Seattle Hotel.

But we peered into our murky crystal ball and predicted a dire outcome if we didn't gas the protesters out of that intersection. It was the cop and not the police chief in me who made that decision—for one thing, how could we possibly get emergency vehicles through that crowd, should there be a need?

I blew it, the biggest mistake of my thirty-four-year career.

WITH THAT, MY PITY party is over. I'm done beating myself up. My goal now is to help other police officials and communities from making the same mistake. Yet from Ferguson to Oakland, from anti-police brutality demonstrations to the Occupy Movement, the institution seems hell-bent on repeating my mistakes.

I mean, my lord, is there anyone in the country who didn't see the You-Tube of the University of California–Davis police officer pepper-spraying those students in 2011? The protesters, like those in Seattle, were completely nonviolent and nonthreatening, seated as they were, arm in arm, heads bowed. Yet, one Lieutenant John Pike casually shook his industrial-sized canister of aerosol oleoresin capsicum spray, as if to build drama, then, working the line, proceeded to apply the burning bright-orange product like he was watering his lawn or spraying his roses.

The university (that is, California's taxpayers) paid handsomely for the police overreaction. The protesters settled for $1 million. And Pike received a $38,000 worker's comp settlement for depression and anxiety brought on by death threats against him and his family.

So, how do we handle the next "Battle in Seattle" or "Battle of the Bronx" or "Battle at Harpers Ferry"?

As with every other suggestion in this book, it all starts with the citizenry and their police establishing an authentic, mutually respectful partnership—and working together. The partners' job in this context? To ensure protection of First Amendment and other Bill of Rights guarantees and to prevent violence and property destruction during both planned and unanticipated demonstrations.

And all of this should be reduced to writing, in a document we'll call "The Agreement."

The Agreement is just that: all stakeholders agreeing to the scope and nature of the theoretical and literal meaning—and the practical and political implications—of *co-policing* "critical incidents."

A genuine partnership is a 50–50 proposition. Citizens, as selected not by the police but amongst themselves, must have an equal say in how events are policed, whether planned a year in advance or materializing spontaneously. Given that neither side gets to decide unilaterally, a tremendous amount of soul searching, philosophizing, questioning, and practical, hard-core planning is essential. That includes the discipline of learning from the successes and failures of other jurisdictions.

Partnership assumptions:

- Whatever faults and other historical baggage the police might bring to the partnership, they also bring considerable knowledge, wisdom, and skills. Moreover, they contribute weapons, badges, uniforms, vehicles, and specialized emergency equipment—all the trappings of coercive authority, which on occasion is essential to the cause of protecting life, property, and, yes, civil liberties. Consider if the first responders to the November 2015 terrorist attacks in Paris were not so equipped, were not identified by their badges and uniforms.
- How this coercive authority is exercised must be negotiated between the partners. To the maximum extent possible, effective "self-policing," that is, internal security, should be arranged in advance.
- It must be understood that where self-policing breaks down and violence erupts or is imminently threatened, it's time for the unarmed, non-uniformed citizen partners to take a back seat to traditional police authority—exercised, of course, in accordance with the values, stipulations, and specific procedures of The Agreement.
- Each side of the partnership must commit to continuous learning, taking stock of the response to all major events, including natural disasters, industrial accidents, fires, and political protests and demonstrations.

NONE OF THIS IS new, or at least completely new. Indeed, then Seattle Police captain Jim Pugel (now undersheriff of King County) had met in advance with self-identified WTO protest leaders to craft an agreement for how police and protesters would operate. Among other things, provision was made for a choreographed, photo-op event that would feature staged (but very real) "mass" civil disobedience arrests. Unfortunately, these plans lasted but a day before they had to be jettisoned, for reasons outlined above.

But, envisioned here is something much more ambitious: police and citizens co-planning, co-preparing, and co-policing, to the maximum extent possible, all major events, including especially those with high potential for conflict.

I realize this could be a pipe dream. The police, for one, can be expected as an institution to resist mightily. As can the protesters, especially in light of a relatively new phenomenon in political activism and protest organizing. Those pre-event meetings of the type Pugel and demonstration leaders held in 1999? They might very well have already become a thing of the past, a victim of today's "leaderless" protests. It used to be that police officials, at least in a few cities, would routinely reach out to readily identifiable individuals who "put themselves out there" (typically in pre-event interviews with traditional media) as demonstration leaders. Today, with an appreciation of decentralization and autonomous action, of consensus decision-making and rejection of hierarchy, of an explosion of social networking, and of on-site communication, such as use of the "people's mic" (someone at the front of a crowd calling for a "mic check!" protesters near the front repeating, "mic check!" and the speaker, in short phrases, going on to say what's on his or her mind, the information being passed along, in waves, to the back of the crowd), there is no need for a "leader with a bullhorn." Literally, no one is in charge.

I saw these dynamics at play in October 2011. Friends and I had gone to New York to check out the theater scene and the city's eateries and drinkeries. During the day, we wandered all over the city and happened upon the Occupy Movement's encampment in Zuccotti Park (this was a month before the mayor, under pressure from local business owners and upscale, high-rise condo residents, ordered the public park cleared). The park was jammed on that sunny October day, from Liberty Street to Cedar Street, Trinity Place to Broadway, and it was apparent that there was no headquarters, no nerve center . . . no one in charge.

On November 18, 2015, Melina Abdullah was a guest on Tavis Smiley's late-night PBS talk show. One of the founders of Black Lives Matter, Dr. Abdullah offered a different take on the question of leaderless political movements. Smiley noted that some critics believe the Occupy Movement "fizzled" in large part because it had no leaders. Wouldn't Black Lives Matter meet the same fate?[1]

Abdullah's response was that the Black Lives Matter movement is far from "leaderless." It is "*leaderful*," she said. Adopting a "group-centered" leadership style of the type practiced by the early civil rights activist Ella Baker, Black Lives Matter has "thousands of leaders," "organizers" from around the world.[2]

I hold out hope that protest organizers will overcome any reservations—including an all-too-understandable fear of being co-opted by police—and insist on a seat at the table as the local community plans for "crowd management" at all future demonstrations.

A YEAR AFTER MY Elliot Bay reading, I was speaking at an ACLU-sponsored forum in the cavernous Kane Hall at the University of Washington. I told the audience that, upon reflection, I'd made a huge mistake on that November 30, 1999, morning in Seattle, and I apologized.

Afterward, out in the lobby, I spotted a familiar face. As the man approached, I recognized him as the individual who "used to respect" me. He smiled and shook my hand as we agreed to agree.

15

COMMUNITY POLICING?

MOST OF US CAN imagine "community policing" thriving in a small, homogeneous town where everybody knows everybody and, like the residents of Mayberry, get along famously with one another. But what of New York, Chicago, Houston, Paris, London, Berlin, and other big cosmopolitan cities with vast socioeconomic, demographic, and political diversity, cities with a long history of neighborhood, racial, and ethnic divisions, and long-standing, seemingly intractable tension between police and community?

In New York, the country's biggest city with the country's biggest police force, Mayor de Blasio and Police Commissioner Bratton announced on June 25, 2015, "One City: Safe and Fair Everywhere," essentially a "new and improved" version of community policing. Rolled out at a major press conference, the two men called "Safe and Fair" a "comprehensive approach designed to fully engage community as *coequal partner* to keep neighborhoods safe, support officers, and keep crime at historic low levels [emphasis added]."[1] The "central pillar" of the department's "broad plan" consists of the "Five Ts":

- **Tactics:** A neighborhood-policing plan that is rooted in local communities and tied to local concerns.

- **Technology:** A revolution in NYPD technology, bringing its full capabilities to police officers in the field.
- **Training:** Field training for recruits and recurring training for veterans, imparting the skills to manage the human encounters that are the fundamental business of street policing.
- **Terrorism:** Strengthened investigative enforcement efforts with federal, state and local partners, as well as significantly enhanced critical-incident response capabilities in evolving overseas conditions that have altered the local threat picture.
- **Trust:** A compact with both the communities and the cops to deal fairly and respectfully with one another.[2]

One worrisome sign is that in embracing the Five Ts, there is virtually no attention to the challenge of overcoming deep-seated friction and resentment between the city's communities of color (and police critics of any color) and its police department. "Trust" is unlikely to result from a plan that addresses it in a single sentence, and that seems to suffer from a lack of comprehensive community involvement in developing (and, indeed, in announcing) that plan.

My criticism, or skepticism, is based on a well-established habit of police everywhere to tell the community what's best for the community, and to announce its unilateral intentions. That is *not* community policing.

The mayor and his police commissioner did take pains to line up non-cop supporters (seventeen, in all) in advance of their formal announcement. But, to an individual, these endorsers are congressmen and congresswomen, city council members and borough presidents, state senators and state assembly members. If you happen to favor a definition of undiluted representative democracy, this exclusive reliance on the "electeds" to advance your initiatives makes some sort of sense. But my hunch is that very few of those official leaders who jumped onto the "Safe and Fair" bandwagon have had up-close-and-personal problems with police neglect or abuse. Where are those voices, the voices of people who have been forsaken or otherwise mistreated by their police, and who have much to say about police practices? What would it have cost the city to reach out to Eric Garner's widow or to any of countless candidates from the ranks of young black men who have been victimized by the department's aggressive stop-and-frisk policies and practices?

IN ITS PUBLICITY ROLLOUT of "Safe and Fair Everywhere," the NYPD had this to say:

> Today the NYPD is reinventing the way cops and community, public and private entities, all work as one team to fight crime even more effectively and, ultimately, to prevent crime from happening in the first place.[3]

So the biggest police department in the country, steeped in a paramilitary-bureaucratic tradition dating back 166 years, having undergone persistent waves of corruption, contractually obligated to an intransigent union, and notoriously resistant to change, has, as of June 2015 "reinvented" itself?

Allow me to repeat my skepticism. Had there been even a hint that critics had been invited to participate, had we seen the fingerprints of the Black Lives Matter organization in the "reinvention of the NYPD," I might be more upbeat about its prospects.

Short of radical restructuring, short of the people putting themselves in the driver's seat, true community policing is not going to happen in Ferguson or North Charleston, South Carolina, much less New York City. True community policing has the *citizens policing themselves,* with a little help from their friends in blue.

Mychal Denzel Smith advocates a period at the end of "citizens policing themselves." In a provocative April 2015 article, he advanced the idea of abolishing America's police forces:

> When I say, "abolish the police," I'm usually asked what I would have us replace them with. My answer is always full social, economic, and political equality, but that's not what's actually being asked. What people mean is "who is going to protect us?" Who protects us now? If you're white and well-off, perhaps the police

protect you. The rest of us, not so much. What use do I have for an institution that routinely kills people who look like me, and make it so I'm afraid to walk out of my home?

My honest answer is that I don't know what a world without police looks like. I only know there will be less dead black people. I know that a world without police is a world with one less institution dedicated to the maintenance of white supremacy and inequality. It's a world worth imagining.[4]

I'm not an advocate. Too much violent crime, too many emergencies. However, I do favor a genuine co-policing model, one that puts "community"—with all its internal contradictions, its social and political divisions, its competing and colliding priorities—behind the wheel: the senior partner in the community-police partnership. The police don't go away, under my system, they don't even fade into the background. Instead, they become a true *people's police*—fully partnered with the people who pay their salaries.

ARE WE A REPUBLIC? A direct democracy? A representative democracy? All of the above, none of the above? The debate rages—among perhaps 1 percent of Americans (most aligned with ideologues from left and right, and whose intellectual arguments are generally ignored by the masses). Yet how we choose to govern ourselves is an important question, and in the context of community policing, a critical one.

I do believe the framers made clear (though I did not check with the late Justice Scalia for confirmation) that the United States is, indeed, a representative democracy. The "people" elect representatives—from town and city councils and special districts (water, fire, utilities, and the like) to the US Congress and the presidency.

Case-by-case exceptions to representative democracy can be noteworthy, a way for people to exercise their will under the rubric of "direct" or "pure" democracy. For example, the electorate has recalled governors and mayors; the people have passed marijuana legalization statutes; the people have reduced state taxes; and the people have made gay marriage a reality (in discrete states, in advance of the Supreme Court's historic 2015 decision to make same-sex marriage legal in all fifty states).

But even in California, where the people in 2003 recalled Governor Gray Davis and replaced him with Arnold Schwarzenegger, the "representative" approach to lawmaking is far more common than the "direct" approach. In fact, fewer than half the states (plus Washington, DC) allow some form of direct democracy.

Why and how is this important to the furtherance of an authentic people's police? Because in both small and large jurisdictions, the people face a formidable structural and political challenge in changing the way their local police department is organized and run. If they want to be part of a successful change movement, something this book argues is both necessary and urgent; they have to figure out a way.

One such path follows.

STRUCTURALLY, I ENVISION INTERESTED citizens within a given city's census tracts electing individuals from within those boundaries to represent them in all police matters. (The population of a typical census tract is about 4,000, though tracts can range from 1,000 to 8,000 people.) These individuals would work, in an official capacity, part-time and unsalaried, at least at first, but supported by tax-funded stipends to cover expenses (a model in use in several cities, including San Diego and Seattle, although only in narrowly defined ways). They would function as members of sanctioned police boards on: policy making; program development; crisis management; hiring and promotion panels; entry-level and in-service training; budget and priority-setting; citizen oversight of police misconduct investigations; shooting-review panels—in short, *all* significant police operations.

Given that census tracts generally align well with recognized neighborhoods, it's reasonable to project a level of grassroots community representation in these critical police activities that is both fair and meaningful.

Although neither San Diego nor Seattle has achieved the ideal, both cities' police departments, at least at the executive levels, have taken important steps toward welcoming greater citizen participation in policing.

During my time in San Diego, for example, the city council authorized formation of a fifteen-member Citizens Advisory Board on Police/Community Relations and made it law. Municipal Code Section 26.0802 states, in part:

> This Board shall promote and encourage open communication and cooperation between the Police Department and residents of the City. The Board shall also develop and make recommendations directed toward informing the community of its rights and responsibilities when coming into contact with police officers.... It is further intended that this Board shall function as a method of community participation in recommending and reviewing policies, practices and programs designed to make law enforcement sensitive, effective and responsive to the needs of the City. It shall actively encourage and foster citizen participation in crime prevention activities.

The ordinance speaks to composition of the board, requiring one representative from each of the nine city council districts. The other slots are reserved for a police union representative, a human relations expert, an "expert on youth," a member of the judiciary, and two members chosen from the fields of social service, corrections, probation, or "other related fields." The city manager, police chief, and police psychologist serve as ex-officio members, and the city attorney is required to provide "appropriate legal services at each meeting."

It is obvious the Citizens Advisory Board on Police/Community Relations does not comport with the grassroots model I advocate. It speaks of "crime prevention," not policy making. Its members are appointed by politicians, its allotted slots filled by bureaucrats and "experts," its meetings scrutinized by a city lawyer. However, in practice, the advisory board did help usher in a whole new era of expanded citizen participation in day-to-day police operations in San Diego.

As one of a cadre of "progressive" San Diego police administrators when the board was formed, I can attest to the effect it had in opening up the police bureaucracy to the presence and perspectives of grassroots activists.

I recall, in particular, overhearing a conversation one afternoon among veteran detectives in the coffee shop. It went something like this:

"What the hell is this world coming to?"

"What are you talking about?"

"All these civilians." Two tables over sat one of our community-relations officers, the department's first openly gay cop, chatting with three or four citizens. Across the room were a half dozen other citizens, enjoying a cup without benefit of a sworn chaperone.

"Yeah?"

"Just the other day I walked out of our office and bumped into a snot-nosed kid. Seventeen, eighteen. Tatts and metal everywhere, including one of those goddamn nose rings. Baggy pants, ass-crack showing. So, I challenge him. 'Who are you? What are you doing here?' 'Just going to the bathroom,' he says. 'Let me repeat,' I say. 'Who *are* you? What are you doing here?' Tells me he's at a 'meeting' in the captain's office. Something about 'improving relations between cops and kids.'"

I understood the culture shock. But the department was, in fact, undergoing a significant shift. Same in Seattle, where the presence of citizens of all ages, races, gender identities, sexual orientations, and other forms of human diversity was becoming increasingly commonplace in offices and hallways of the old Public Safety Building—where citizens were taking seats on key internal panels, like officer-involved shooting boards.

BUT THAT WAS IN the late 1990s. Then the terrorists struck. And the barriers went up. And "community policing" took a backseat to "homeland security." And military madness.

My own sense is that SDPD and SPD did not retreat as much as other law enforcement agencies in the aftermath of 9/11. But the bunker mentality—I'm not talking about smart, reasonable security precautions—was evident throughout the land, and doors slammed shut.

Although it's crucial to maintain those smart, reasonable security measures, it's also vital that police departments reopen those doors. And that they keep in mind that in the best of times, in the worst of times, they still belong to the people.

BEYOND ALL THAT, IF the people want to police their own streets, the cops have no right to deny them. Indeed, as I see it, they have an obligation to help them.

I'm a fan of the admittedly controversial practice of citizens patrolling their own streets. I'm not talking about armed George Zimmerman–like zealots but rather everyday citizens dedicated to making their communities—from the streets to the schools and workplaces, to churches, temples, and mosques, day-care facilities, parks and recreation centers, private dwellings and public housing—safe and fair for all.

I recall a group of San Diegans in 1992 taking the initiative to organize and mobilize themselves in order to confront a vicious gay-bashing robbery-murder series—that peaked with the beating-stabbing death of a seventeen-year-old. Long story short, citizen patrollers (whom we had offered to train and to equip with cell phones) spotted the suspects and called it in. From a safe distance, they kept an eye on the murderous skinheads. Moments later, their cop partners showed up, swooped in, and made the bust.

I can't help but think that if Reverend Clementa C. Pinckney and his parishioners had been more attuned to the potential danger posed by twenty-one-year-old white supremacist Dylann Roof at the Charleston Emanuel African Methodist Episcopal Church on June 17, 2015; had individuals within the prayer group that horrible night taken reasonable precautions as they observed Roof's escalating agitation; had individuals, other than Tywanza Sanders (who dove in front of his eighty-seven-year-old aunt and took the first bullet), acted en masse; had they swarmed Roof as he reloaded—*five times* (with hollow points, designed to cause maximum damage)—during that massacre, that some, perhaps all of the nine slain would have been spared.

I realize how ridiculous, if not unfeeling, this might all seem: innocent citizens, six women, three men, inclusive Christians (accustomed to welcoming strangers), in a house of worship, engaged in prayer and Bible study—pitted against a twisted racist with a .45-caliber semiautomatic, a fanny pack full of extra clips, and a fervent desire to start a race war. How could they have known? How could they have been prepared?

But given what this country has witnessed throughout its history, particularly in attacks on black churches (the 1963 Ku Klux Klan bombing deaths of four girls at the Sixteenth Street Church in Birmingham, the torching of black churches throughout the mid-to late 1990s, the racially motivated burning of a black church in Massachusetts the day Barack Obama was inaugurated as the country's first black president), Americans of all colors must be ready to stand against violence, and to protect themselves, their families, and other members of the community.

This is what the African Methodist Episcopal (AME) national church has attempted to do in the aftermath of the Charleston slaughter. All member churches have been given copies of the newly crafted "Twelve Considerations for Congregational Security," a sensible how-to plan both for personal safety and for buildings and grounds security.[5]

The "security zealots" of the world can be a problem, to be sure. In San Diego, the Hillcrest citizens understood this and worked with us to create rules and guidelines for participation in the citizens' patrol. Further, they asked for and voluntarily agreed to submit to a rudimentary National Crime Information Center (NCIC) background check. Communities can do much to ensure the success of such grassroots policing, enhancing public safety and protecting human rights. The police have a key role in helping to provide structure, as well as training, for this effort. But so, too, do the community's other partners: community-based organizations (CBOs), academics, subject-matter experts, other branches of local government, and neighborhood activists.

Of course, it all starts with the right attitude.

ON AUGUST 22, 2015, Spencer Stone was in deep sleep on a high-speed train traveling from Amsterdam to Paris when his friend Alek Skarlatos hit him on the shoulder and said, "Go!" Joined by a third friend, Anthony Sadler, the three Americans sprinted up the aisle and jumped a man who had come out of a bathroom with an AK-47 and opened fire. A radical Islamist, the man was also packing a Luger pistol, a box cutter, and eight magazines of ammunition—enough firepower to kill dozens of passengers. Stone tackled the man, sustaining significant wounds to the back of his neck and the near-loss of his left thumb. Joined by a British businessman, the three Americans, pals since middle school in California, were able to subdue the suspect and hold him until authorities arrived. Stone, who later said he barely felt his own injuries, turned his attention to a wounded fellow passenger who had taken a bullet to the throat. He stuffed two fingers into the wound and stanched the bleeding until paramedics arrived. Two days later, French president François Hollande awarded the men the Legion of Honor, France's highest form of recognition.[6]

Community policing, on a speeding train.

I know, I've heard it: sure, but two of these guys were military—young, fit, trained. How would regular citizens have fared if they'd attempted to disarm the terrorist? Given what the man was packing, and the carnage he could easily have exacted, maybe the better question is what would have happened if all the passengers had remained in their seats?

I know it's tough to wrap our minds around the horror of mass murder and rampage violence. But, what is it about us, as a people, that we cede to law enforcement the authority to exercise 100 percent responsibility for the safety of our bodies, our well-being, our rights? What's wrong with citizens taking prudent but direct action in the face of threats to their own lives, liberty, and pursuit of happiness? Or such threats to their loved ones, their neighbors?

Not a damn thing. And done well, eschewing the pitchforks-and-torches mentality, everyone's safety is enhanced. It's also useful, I think, to keep in mind the statistical picture and draw at least some small comfort from it. From 2000 to 2014, the United States recorded 133 mass shootings. Yes, that's a lot of murders, particularly when compared to most other countries in the world, whose mass shootings over the same period numbered in the single digits. And mass murders have definitely been on the rise, but the 133 shootings translates into a rate of 0.15 per 100,000 population.[7]

NOT ALL FORMS OF communal initiative are heroic or life-saving, and most are not: citizens who band together to help a mentally ill homeless person get shelter and medical attention, or escort potential assault victims from office to car, or help an aggrieved citizen file a complaint against police abuse, or patrol a park to let would-be child sexual predators know they're not welcome there, or lend moral and other support to a victim of domestic violence, and so on.

Hedrick Smith was, for twenty-six years, a correspondent for the *New York Times* in Washington, Moscow, Cairo, Saigon, Paris, and the American South. He won the Pulitzer Prize for International Reporting for his work from Russia and Eastern Europe and was part of the Pulitzer Prize–winning team that produced the Pentagon Papers series in 1971. For twelve years he was the Washington bureau chief for the *Times*. Most Americans probably know him best as an Emmy Award–winning producer and correspondent for PBS's *Frontline*. He is also an independent filmmaker, with his producer-wife, Susan Zox, and is the author of several best-sellers, including his 2012 *Who Stole the American Dream?*[8]

A recurring theme, running through Smith's entire body of work, is the pivotal importance of community.

I spoke to Smith in his home in Washington, DC.[9] "The word 'community' is so important," he said. "Obama [commenting on Ferguson] keeps saying, 'This is not who we are.' But tragically, it *is* who we are. Community is about relating to other people, particularly younger people, but what happens? Well, we've all been caught for speeding, or for parking illegally, or for having a taillight out. For solid, middle-class professional people you pay the fine, or get a friendly warning, and move on. Poor people can't do that. They get chucked in jail, and have a criminal record. So the next time they get stopped they get nailed worse. The money multiplies, their problems with the law multiply. A bank vice president gets caught for jaywalking, the officer tells him, 'Watch yourself,' and goes on his way. A black teen with a hoodie goes to jail. It's not just inequality, it's unfairness."

And it stands in the way of building "community."

"As a reporter," Smith said, "I understand what you learn from people by walking and talking and listening." That's something he's done everywhere he has gone, including Chicago's Uptown neighborhood. "What we saw there were community organizations, community networks holding down crime." He cited several examples, from a newly formed softball league to numerous community-based nonprofits to, most important, grassroots efforts to make the culturally diverse neighborhood safe. "There's this idea that 'community policing' is soft, liberal, 'airy fairy.' Not so. Community policing is absolutely essential to lowering crime rates."

(I agree with Smith and have all kinds of anecdotal evidence to support his assertion. However, because of wide variability in defining "community policing," and owing to numerous other crime-reporting complications, the best evidence is that community policing is responsible for a reduction, albeit a statistically insignificant reduction, in crime.)[10]

Smith reflected on the "iconic moment" when that Baltimore mother in bright yellow waded into a street protest (in response to the 2015 Freddie Gray killing), looking for her son. Violence was escalating when Toya Graham recognized her sixteen-year-old, Michael, under a hoodie and behind a mask, brick in hand. "Drop that brick!" she said. She then slapped him around, pulled him from the crowd, and slapped him some more. "Two wrongs don't make a right," she later told her son

"People laughed at that," Smith said. "Like it was great entertainment. But here was a mother, like so many we met [in Chicago] who would literally stop fights. We heard it all the time, 'You want me to tell your mom?'"

It wasn't just the image of that prototypical (if not stereotypical) strong black mother exerting authority over her own child in Baltimore that captured the attention of the nation.

Toya Graham expressed respect for the police, and one of her daughters wants to become a Baltimore cop. But without getting too psychological here, it was also obvious that her intense anger (young Michael later described it as "like World War III") masked a deep fear—of the police. Mother and son appeared on several news broadcasts, during which Michael admitted to being embarrassed, as any sixteen-year-old would be if his mother slapped him around on national TV. But when CNN's Anderson Cooper asked him if he'd return to future riot scenes "and do it again," he made it clear that he would not.

"Why not?" Cooper said. "Is it because your mother is standing right here?"

"No," he said. It was because when they got home that day, "She told me she didn't want me to be another Freddie Gray." He would protest, he concluded, on reflection, but would "do it the right way."[11]

16

STRENGTH
IN NUMBERS

IF YOU'RE OUT TO fundamentally change an entire institution and think you can do it solo, you might want to reconsider. Particularly when the forces of the status quo outnumber, outweigh, and outflank you. Which means they'll outlast you.

Certainly, one person can make a big difference in this world. A single individual, without conscious thought or deliberation, can launch the spread of a deadly globe-circling disease, or destroy every tree in a forest, or consciously and deliberately exterminate millions. And on the credit side of the ledger, individuals such as Mahatma Gandhi, Betty Williams, Chief Joseph, Martin Luther King Jr., Aung San Suu Kyi, Nelson Mandela, Oskar Schindler, and Harriet Tubman were able to bring about indelible social, political, and human rights advances.

Yet when it comes to healing entrenched institutional ills, flying solo—whether as cop or citizen—is like writing a book without an editor, fielding a major league ball club with no bullpen, or presiding over a nation with no cabinet. Good people with good ideas need help to get those ideas circulating and poised to land in the right place at the right time, with at least half a chance to succeed. And it doesn't hurt to have folks around who can provide caring criticism as well as emotional support.

Those who would change a resistant institution need structured opportunities to air personal as well as professional challenges, their highs, their lows. They need moments to exchange information and wisdom, and to share reassurances with individuals experiencing the same or similar psychological and political pressures.

Deborah Jacobs is a justice advocate and former ACLU executive director in both Missouri and New Jersey. She lives in St. Louis, consults on race and gender equity issues, and serves on the Steering Committee of the Don't Shoot Coalition. I spoke with her during a July 2015 visit to Washington state.[1]

She pointed out that most of the protesters in the movement for police accountability in Ferguson and throughout the country are young, "mostly in their twenties or younger." She spoke of their sacrifices and challenges. "Some have dropped out of school. They've decided their lives are at greater risk if they *don't* organize and protest." She believes local universities throughout the country should "create and track a system for protesters," providing "leadership training" that encourages "first-person stories" of their experiences on the streets. "Some will survive and thrive, some will not. But there is tremendous potential out there for leadership training that focuses on concrete takeaways."

We agreed that similar leadership training for beat cops as well as chiefs is also necessary. It's hard for many in my old profession, for example, to understand, or accept, the fundamental nature and value of protests that "disrupt." "If protesters are not peacefully disturbing, unsettling things, there is no protest," Jacobs said.

I had to remind myself of that hard-to-hear truth as I watched footage of protesters shutting down Bernie Sanders's speech on the Democratic presidential campaign trail at Westlake Park in downtown Seattle in the summer of 2015. Bernie was just beginning to speak when two young women, Black Lives Matter activists, climbed onto the stage, grabbed the microphone, and demanded that Sanders be held "accountable." Some in the crowd booed, yelling at the protesters to let Sanders speak and demanding that the women leave the stage. Twenty minutes into it, Sanders was again pushed back and denied the mic when he tried to speak. The event's organizer finally called an end to it, and Sanders left, fist raised high in a salute to the crowd.[2]

You know you're into painful but rich educational territory when your own values are duking it out in a pitched internal battle. Airing these conflicts is essential to resolving them, or at least to keeping what's left of one's sanity.

FOR POLICE CHIEFS PARTICULARLY, such opportunities are few indeed. Although organizations like the International Association of Chiefs of Police, the Major Cities Chiefs Association, the Police Executive Research Forum, and the National Sheriffs' Association provide a professional forum for members to confront controversial issues and to share insights born of tough personal experiences, none offers a safe harbor for raw, bone-honest conversations about the troubles facing reform-minded executives. That's not their purpose.

There's another problem with these organizations.

The public profiles of certain members of the sheriffs' group, for instance, individuals like David Clarke of Milwaukee County, Wisconsin, Joe Arpaio of Maricopa County, Arizona, and Paul Babeu of Pinal County, Arizona, are leading opponents of progressive change; they're hardwired to fight, not lead, institutional reform. In fact, they are preservationists of the conservative law-and-order mentality, pandering to the reactionary impulse on issues of race, police use of force, gun violence, and immigration. They're the Bill O'Reillys of the cop world. Clarke is probably the most dangerous of them all. A charismatic, well-spoken African American, and a regular on *Fox and Friends* who believes President Obama has been a "nightmare" for the country, he predicted in an October 27, 2015, tweet that Black Lives Matter (or Black Lies Matter, as he calls the organization) will soon join forces with the Islamic State of Iraq and Syria (ISIS) and bring down the republic.[3] He claims that charges of police racism and brutality are fallacious, that "we ended that back in the '60s," as he told a *Fox News* commentator.[4] He went on to cite a Harvard study that showed there is no racism in the hearts of police officers. According to blogger Daniel Bice, Harvard officials are still trying to "track down any studies on the hearts of police officers."[5]

YET ANOTHER LIMITATION OF these programs is that they're designed for bosses: supervisors, managers, executives. They ignore the fact that effective leadership in a police agency can be, and often is, exercised multidirectionally. In other words, though "leading down" the chain of command (too often nothing more than flexing one's *authority*, not leadership) is the norm, individuals at the bottom of the pyramid can "lead up," that is, influence the views and behaviors of their superiors.

Peer leadership is also a powerful form of influencing behavior in a police department. One need look no further than the implicit rules that govern the police "code of silence" for a Sandbox 101 example of the extraordinary power of peer pressure.

Recognizing the need for advanced, nonsupervisory education and training in leadership, community policing, ethics and standards, and change-agent skills, as well as opportunities that encourage honest self-reflection and personal growth, Nancy McPherson developed a plan for an officer-level program she named the Institute for Developing Police Leaders (IDPL).

McPherson, a friend and colleague for almost three decades, had been a "civilian" assistant police chief in San Diego, Seattle, and Portland, where she fought tirelessly for the creation of a true community-influenced police practice. As a consultant, trainer, and citizen monitor of Justice Department consent decrees in other jurisdictions, and, more recently as the newly named state director of the American Association of Retired Persons–California, she continues the fight for social and economic justice.

Although supported by the University of Southern California's School of Public Policy, Planning, and Development, the IDPL, conceived over ten years ago, never got off the ground.

Interviewed at her home in Sacramento, California,[6] McPherson pointed to poor timing as the explanation: the country was preoccupied with post-9/11 homeland security—and the widespread (erroneous) perception that our police agencies were doing "just fine." Then there was her own decision to make a career change and move, first, to Louisiana as that state's director of AARP.

We agreed that times have indeed changed, that the nation is no longer in the paralyzing grip of "homeland security mania," that recent crises in police use of force, discipline, and credibility must be met head on, and that the dream of an institute for the development of progressive police leaders is an idea whose time has arrived.

What is most exciting about McPherson's original idea is that it focuses not on chiefs and sheriffs, or their supervisory underlings, but on America's promising front-line cops who see a need for institutional change and want to help bring it about. Envisioning these officers as future leaders of the institution, she believes the IDPL would create a safe yet exacting place for them to gather and to build a research-driven, esoteric body of knowledge on police organizational change; to question basic assumptions of modern police work; to build relationships with others who are not afraid to challenge their peers or question their superiors; and to unite with the community and like-minded cops to transform police work.

As McPherson asked in the executive summary of her proposal, "Who will develop the next generation of police leaders? Who will help them embrace the ideals of a healthy community in a free society? Who will encourage them to shape policing in a positive way?" In the report, she clarifies and amplifies the essence of the IDPL:

> The Institute's purpose is to help build healthy communities in democratic societies by preparing rank-and-file police officers for ethical and effective leadership. This is accomplished by creating a "learning culture" outside the officer's own agency where each participant is challenged to develop, intellectually and emotionally, in five areas: leadership, problem solving, healthy communities, social justice, and personal wellness. Participants begin with a two-week immersion experience and continue through virtual education and individual coaching for a full ten-year period; this ensures the kind of ongoing support typically lacking after a

"mountain-top" educational experience. A research program supports the graduates as they return to their practitioner roles, and it informs the police profession as well. Policing effectively in the 21st century will require increased competence in leadership and criminology, and personal character that is unwavering against the powerful undercurrent of the police culture. Street cops who are prepared for these demands early in their careers are far more likely to lead positive changes that benefit our communities.[7]

McPherson's plan, crafted in conjunction with multidisciplinary experts from throughout the country, envisions the enrollment of up to three hundred new officers each year, each committed to a full ten-year program of professional development and personal growth. At the time she wrote the proposal, she anticipated a "collaborative funding effort," with revenues generated from business, philanthropy, and government sources.

I agree with McPherson's statement that "the potential for looking internally to rank-and-file officers as 'agents of change' is enormous and untapped"—with the caveat that full and sustained participation by community activists and leaders would also be essential to the success of the enterprise.

Given what's happening in the world of policing, given the need to support good cops, it's time to dust off McPherson's proposal and create a national Institute for Developing Police Leaders.

FIXING AMERICA'S POLICE: MORE BIG GOVERNMENT, PLEASE!

THERE ARE 18,000 LAW enforcement agencies in the nation but only one constitution. As the "secular bible" of the land, the US Constitution is binding on every law enforcement agency—federal, state, and local—and on each of the nation's 1 million sworn officers. All people, whether in huge urban centers or tiny rural hamlets, are entitled to the full protection of the country's most basic laws, its civil liberties. Yet, as we have seen, there is evidence of patterned police abuse throughout the United States. The costs of this abuse, in lives lost, violations of human rights, strained community-police relations, and civil-suit settlements (over $1 billion in just ten cities, in the past five years)[1] are truly staggering.

We must turn, I believe, to the Department of Justice to operationalize law enforcement's upholding of the Constitution.

When Thomas Jefferson wrote, "We hold these truths to be self-evident, that all men are created equal, that they are endowed by their Creator with certain unalienable Rights, that among these are Life, Liberty and the pursuit of Happiness," the Second Continental Congress was seeking to "consecrate" a future of specific, permanent, inviolable liberties for all citizens.

The United States Constitution, introduced eleven years after the Declaration of Independence, was meant to govern, not merely guide, the everyday work of those who would become the nation's police officers.

Although police recruits receive instruction in constitutional law during their academy training, the workplace "acculturation" process soon begins eroding any postgrad zeal for the deliberate practice of safeguarding civil liberties and human rights. Such is the way of the cop world.

New Ferguson police officers, for example, are given forty-one hours of constitutional law instruction, including "an explanation of the significance of the U.S. Constitution and the Bill of Rights." This happens during their 916 hours at the St. Louis County and Municipal Police Academy. But, as has been made clear in "The Ferguson Report: Department of Justice Investigation of the Ferguson Police Department," published by The New Press (with an excellent introduction by noted civil and human rights attorney Theodore M. Shaw),[2] the city's new cops are quickly absorbed into a culture that is both "banal and toxic."

What happened in Ferguson, what is happening throughout the nation, is not good for the country, and it's not legal. The federal government—with respect, but no apologies, to my libertarian friends—is the logical place to turn for leadership, and compliance.

AFTER THE MICHAEL BROWN killing, the uprising in Ferguson, and the many other controversial deaths at the hands of police, President Obama created a task force on December 18, 2014, whose purpose was to "strengthen community policing and trust among law enforcement officers and the communities they serve—especially in light of recent events around the country that have underscored the need for and importance of lasting collaborative relationships between local police and the public."[3] The task force, co-chaired by Charles Ramsey, Commissioner of the Philadelphia Police Department (at that time), and Professor Laurie Robinson of George Mason University, two colleagues for whom I have the highest respect, consisted of nine additional experts: Deputy Chief Operating Officer for Public Safety Cedric L. Alexander, DeKalb County, Georgia; Lead Organizer

Jose Lopez, Make the Road New York; Walton Hale Hamilton Professor of Law Tracey L. Meares, Yale Law School; Executive Director Brittany N. Packnett, Teach for America, St. Louis, Missouri; Executive Director Susan Lee Rahr, Washington State Criminal Justice Training Commission; Co-Director Constance Rice, Advancement Project, Washington, DC, and Los Angeles; Director and Chief Counsel Sean Michael Smoot, Police Benevolent and Protective Association of Illinois; Founder and Executive Director Bryan Stevenson, Equal Justice Initiative, Montgomery, Alabama; and Chief of Police Roberto Villaseñor, Tucson Police Department.

Members of this distinguished body held "listening sessions" and teleconferences with the public. They took testimony from law enforcement, critics, academics, and experts, and they solicited and received voluminous written comments. In its final report, issued May 2015, the task force divided its recommendations into six "pillars":

Building Trust and Legitimacy. Promoting trust and ensuring legitimacy through procedural justice, transparency, accountability and honest recognition of past and present obstacles.

Policy and Oversight. Developing comprehensive and responsive policies on key topics while also implementing formal checks/balances and data collection/analysis.

Technology and Social Media. Balancing [the] embrace of technology and digital communications with local needs, privacy, assessments and monitoring.

Community Policing and Crime Reduction. Encouraging implementation of policies that support community-based partnerships in the reduction of crime.

Training and Education. Emphasizing the importance of high quality and effective training and education through partnerships with local and national training facilities.

Officer Wellness and Safety. Endorsing practices that support officer wellness and safety through the re-evaluation of officer shift hours and data collection/analysis to help prevent officer injuries.

The group presented fifty-nine concrete recommendations. Anyone interested in police reform would do well to give it a thorough read. I'm generally supportive of those recommendations, and generally opposed to Tim Lynch's position, as expressed in *Cato at Liberty*:

> I want to highlight the numerous ways in which the [presidential task force] report would expand the role of the federal government. By way of background, policing is supposed to be the near-exclusive province of state and local government under the U.S. Constitution.[4]

It's reasonable to expect libertarians like Lynch to oppose what they (and most Republicans) call President Obama's "big government" agenda. But it is also reasonable, I submit, to ask how long we, as a nation, will continue to permit policing to be the "near-exclusive province of state and local government under the U.S. Constitution," when so many of those same agencies as a matter of course violate the letter and spirit of that very document.

I BELIEVE THE PRESIDENT'S task force, for all its fine, historic work, falls short of the bold institutional changes necessary to solve the country's "police problem."

I believe enjoyment of safe and healthy neighborhoods, homes, schools, places of work, and all other public and private spaces is an essential human right; and that the police and the citizenry of every political jurisdiction have an interdependent responsibility, and opportunity, to create and sustain these safe communities.

Informing the sweeping recommendations that follow is an asserted moral imperative that the federal government set and enforce standards for policing in America—much as it has done for air traffic control through the Federal Aviation Administration, agricultural products through the US Department of Agriculture, and pharmaceuticals through the US Food and Drug Administration.

Unlike the president's task force recommendations, which, of necessity, speak of what the president, Congress, law enforcement, community-based organizations, and others *should* consider, the following proposals are framed as initiatives of a proposed aggressive populist campaign aimed at what the aforementioned individuals and groups *must do* in order to fundamentally reform American policing:

1. The campaign will persuade Congress to pass legislation transforming the Department of Justice's traditional, largely reactionary police accountability role to one that sets and enforces binding national standards for police conduct. Such standards will govern police hiring and training; use of force policies and procedures; stop-and-frisk and arrest standards and procedures; investigations into use of force; ethical conduct; leadership and supervision; citizen complaint policies and practices; and citizen oversight.

2. DOJ will establish a program of standards-based certification of both law enforcement agencies and individual officers and will exercise concomitant authority over decertification, based on established cause, of both agencies and individual officers.

3. Special, federally trained and certified teams of regional (not federal, not local) investigators will investigate all homicides at the hands of police, including in-custody deaths, regardless of circumstances. Independent prosecutors will replace grand juries in all such cases. Criminal proceedings, if justified by the facts, will be heard by local courts and in accordance with existing rules of evidence. Moreover, all local, state, and federal law enforcement agencies will report every officer-involved shooting and in-custody death and injury to the Department of Justice, which, in addition to serving as a clearinghouse for statistical data, will order investigations, as appropriate.

4. Every police officer in the country will undergo intensive, ongoing classroom and "experiential" training in shoot/no-shoot scenarios; body-camera policies and procedures; use of less-lethal weapons and other defensive tactics; nondiscriminatory police practices; crisis

intervention; de-escalation techniques; response to civil disorders; ethical behavior; and policing in a democratic society. Citizens will be invited and encouraged to attend training sessions, and local jurisdictions will be obligated to welcome and accommodate them.

5. Citizens will be involved in all aspects of police operations: policy making; program development; police oversight; use of lethal-force review panels; police officer recruitment; candidate screening and hiring; academy and in-service training; co-planning, co-preparation, and co-policing of all scheduled and spontaneous events that carry potential for neighborhood and citizen-police conflict.

6. The Department of Justice will, in conjunction with community activists, community-based organizations, representatives of local police departments, academics, and subject-matter experts, develop and host a national, ongoing community-police leadership academy for America's promising beat cops and detectives.

7. Congress—with the grassroots support of the people—will end the War on Drugs and replace prohibition with a rigorously enforced regulatory system, thereby dramatically reducing mass incarceration, particularly of young people, poor people, and people of color.

8. The tens of billions of dollars saved by ending the drug war will be used in three ways: to finance a drug-use regulatory system and provide resources for local drug education, abuse prevention, and treatment; to underwrite the costs of a comprehensive realignment of Department of Justice functions and resources; and to develop and enforce constitutional standards of police performance and conduct in every political jurisdiction throughout the country.

Obviously, this "manifesto" rejects a "tweaking," "tinkering," or otherwise incremental-improvement approach to policing in America. It is, rather, a demand for an exhaustive overhaul of the institution, as we know it. If I thought for a moment that our nation had the financial means, legal basis, and political will to "federalize" the institution—along the lines of the United Kingdom's Metropolitan Police Service—I would urge that course.

There *is* the matter of that pesky Tenth Amendment, namely: "The powers not delegated to the United States by the Constitution, nor prohibited by it to the states, are reserved to the States respectively, or to the people."

THE BRITISH SYSTEM, WHILE far from perfect, encompasses—and enforces—national benchmarks. It provides for uniformity and consistency in "police administration": the promulgation of organizational mission-, vision-, and values-setting; candidate recruitment and selection; entry-level and ongoing education and training; unit and individual performance and conduct standards; unit and individual performance appraisal; supervision and leadership; discipline; transfers, assignments, and promotions; budgeting and fiscal controls; and all other facets of organizational responsibility, transparency, and accountability.

The strength of a national system against a backdrop of constitutional guarantees, that standardizes performance and conduct, and consistently enforces those standards, cannot be denied. The British come closer to this ideal and, I maintain, do a far better job of it than we Americans.

That said, "The Met" is far from perfect. Having spent a week at the College of Policing in Bramshill (in 1999), and having studied the British model of national law enforcement, it is clear that our law enforcement counterparts in England and Wales are almost as resistant to opening their doors, and their minds, to the ideal of a true "people's police" as we are.

I AM NOT UNMINDFUL of the practical, political, and fiscal obstacles— not to mention the fundamental philosophical disagreements—this agenda presupposes. But by adopting national standards, and by implementing the specific proposals contained herein, I'm confident we can dramatically improve police effectiveness, citizen and officer safety, and the community-police relationship throughout the nation.

With homicide and other crime rates rising in many cities, with cops shooting and killing unarmed black men, with police officers themselves being ambushed, and with the chasm between many citizens and their officers growing deeper by the day, the need for fundamental reform has never been greater. Or more urgent.

ACKNOWLEDGMENTS

With deepest appreciation to family, friends, and colleagues whose support and critical feedback have made this book possible: Deborah Jacobs, Teri Black, Joe Brann, Anita Castle, Merrick Bobb, Vanna Novak, Neill Franklin, Kim Hendrickson, Ethan Nadelmann, Jack Mullen, Barbara Raymond, Don Drozd, Peter Morrison, Dirul-Islam Samshid-Deen, Nancy McPherson, Hedrick Smith, Harriet Walden, Steve Casey, Brian Buchner, Jack Cole, Matt Stamper, Jim Poe, Adrienne Casey, Susan Zox, Keith Stroup, Lisa Belsky, Bill Geller, Larry Stamper, Norm Rice, and Nancy Gray.

Particular thanks to Darby Beck of Law Enforcement Against Prohibition, whose tireless help and media savvy in the aftermath of the Michael Brown shooting in Ferguson were indispensable.

Thanks, too, to my agent, Sarah Smith of the David Black Agency, and to my publishing team at Nation Books: Clive Priddle, publisher of PublicAffairs; Jaime Leifer; Melissa Raymond; Lindsay Fradkoff; Tony Forde; Julie Ford; Sally Jaskold; François Trahan; and designer Timm Bryson. A special thank-you to copy editor Michele Wynn, whose eagle eye caught an embarrassing number of bushleague constructions and grammatical errors.

And very special thanks to editorial director Alessandra Bastagli of Nation Books, whose encouragement, wisdom, and persistent, spot-on questioning were invaluable from start to finish.

NOTES

PREFACE

1. The statements of Dorian Johnson and Darren Wilson, from this point forward, appear in the transcripts of the "Grand Jury—Ferguson Police Shooting," *State of Missouri vs. Darren Wilson*, which convened for three months in late 2014.

2. According to KMUW, in August 2014, after the Michael Brown shooting death, Wichita's mayor, city manager, and deputy police chief, joined by community activists, convened a series of "No Ferguson here" sessions. Citizens of North Charleston, South Carolina, following the shooting death of Walter Scott did the same, in an effort to prevent "another Ferguson" (*Washington Post*, April 8, 2015). A state legislator in Alabama has invoked "no Ferguson here" language in an effort to generate support for enactment of stronger laws against racial profiling in traffic stops (AL.com, May 17, 2015). And the "Ferguson effect"—higher crime rates thought to be caused by so-called de-policing—has been hotly debated within law enforcement, academic, and larger community circles (*Atlantic*, November 21, 2015).

CHAPTER 1

1. "Investigation of the Ferguson Police Department," *Civil Rights Division of the Department of Justice*, March 4, 2015.

2. Norm Stamper, *Breaking Rank: A Top Cop's Exposé of the Dark Side of American Policing* (New York: Nation Books, 2005).

3. Jason Hancock and Dugan Arnett, "'Outside Agitators' Worsening Unrest in Ferguson, Mo., Residents Say," *Kansas City Star*, August 18, 2014.

4. Patrick Howell O'Neill, "NYPD Keeps Tight Control of Eric Garner Protests," *Daily Dot*, December 3, 2014.

5. J. David Goodman, "Bratton Says New York Police Department Must Dismiss Bad Officers," *New York Times*, October 2, 1014.

6. Noah Berlatsky, "When Chicago Tortured," *Atlantic*, December 27, 2014.

279

7. Goodman, "Bratton Says New York Police Department Must Dismiss Bad Officers."

8. Clifford Krauss, "Corruption in Uniform: The Overview; 12 Police Officers Charged in Drug Corruption Sweep; Bratton Sees More Arrests," *New York Times*, April 16, 1994.

9. William Bratton and Peter Knobler, *The Turnaround: How America's Top Cop Reversed the Crime Epidemic* (New York: Random House, 1998).

10. Jonathan Blanks, "National Police Misconduct Reporting Project," Cato Institute, Washington, DC, November 24, 2015.

11. "The Counted: People Killed by Police in the United States in 2015," *Interactive*, Guardian, at http://www.theguardian.com/us-news/series/counted-us-police-killings.

12. Julie Tate et al., "How the Washington Post Is Examining Police Shootings in the U.S.," *Washington Post*, June 30, 2015.

13. Robert C. Kennedy, "The Big Chief's Fairy Godmother: Mr. Devery Tells 'Where He Got It,'" *Harper's Weekly*, excerpted from the *New York Times*, "On This Day," September 6, 1902.

14. Adam Walinsky, "The Knapp Connection," *Village Voice*, March 1, 1973.

15. Selwyn Raab, "New York's Police Allow Corruption, Mollen Panel Says," *New York Times*, December 29, 1993.

CHAPTER 2

1. "End of Watch," Officer Down Memorial Page, Cornelius Hogeboom, Sheriff, Columbia County Sheriff's Office, New York, October 22, 1791.

2. Peter Moskos, "History of Police, Department of Law, Police Science, and Criminal Justice Administration," John Jay College of Criminal Justice, lecture series, August 27, 2015.

3. "Metropolitan Police Act of 1829," *Encyclopedia of Community Policing and Problem Solving*, ed. Kenneth J. Peak (Thousand Oaks, CA: Sage Publications, 2014), 11.

4. "Creeden's Captaincy Cost Him $15,000," *New York Times*, December 15, 1894.

5. San Diego Police Historical Association. The association's website also notes that of the first twelve officers hired, eight were Republicans, four Democrats. None of them would get a day off until 1891. See www.sdpolicemuseum.com/HISTORY.html.

6. Kenneth E. Vanlandingham, "Municipal Home Rule in the United States," *William and Mary Law Review* 10 (2) (1968).

7. Joseph Goldstein and J. David Goodman, "A London Guide for 1 Police Plaza," *New York Times*, April 15, 2014.

8. Susan Page, "Poll: Whites and Blacks Question Police Accountability," *USA Today*, August 26, 2014.

CHAPTER 3

1. Emily Dufton, "The War on Drugs: How President Nixon Tied Addiction to Crime," *Atlantic*, March 26, 2012.

2. Andrew Glass, "Reagan Declares 'War on Drugs,' October 14, 1982," *Politico*, October 14, 2010.

3. Walter Hickey, "Marijuana Has Won the War on Drugs," *Business Insider*, April 4, 2013.

4. "Get the Facts," 2015, online at Drug War Facts website, http://www.drugwarfacts.org/cms/#sthash.XZ1dP7RU.dpbs.

5. "The Drug War, Mass Incarceration and Race," Drug Policy Alliance, June 12, 2015.

6. Kathryn Hanson and Deborah Stipek, "Schools v. Prisons: Education's the Way to Cut Prison Population," *San Jose Mercury News*, June 16, 2014.

7. David Shapiro, "Banking on Bondage: Private Prisons and Mass Incarceration," American Civil Liberties Union, November 2, 2011.

8. Andrea Jones, "The Nation's Shame: The Injustice of Mandatory Minimums," *Rolling Stone*, October 7, 2014.

9. "The War on Drugs: Causing Deforestation and Pollution," 2014, at http://www.countthecosts.org/sites/default/files/Environment-briefing.pdf.

10. Brianna Lee, "Mexico's Drug War," Council on Foreign Relations, March 5, 2014, at http://www.cfr.org/mexico/mexicos-drug-war/p13689.

11. Rebecca Gordon, "The Failed War on Drugs in Mexico (and the United States)," March 27, 2015, Moyers and Company (appearing originally at TomDispatch.com, March 22, 2015).

12. Mary Jane Borden, "Global Illicit Market Value," at DrugSense.org, June 2, 2012.

13. "The War on Drugs at a Glance," Law Enforcement Against Prohibition, 2015, at http://www.leap.cc/for-the-media/the-war-on-drugs-at-a-glance.

14. "Racial Justice: Stop and Frisk Data," New York Civil Liberties Union, 2015, at http://www.nyclu.org/content/stop-and-frisk-data.

15. "Floyd, et al. v. City of New York, et al.," Center for Constitutional Rights, 2013, at https://ccrjustice.org/home/what-we-do/our-cases/floyd-et-al-v-city-new-york-et-al.

16. Harry Levine, Loren Siegel, and Gabriel Sayegh, "One Million Police Hours: Making 440,000 Marijuana Possession Arrests in New York City, 2002–2012," Drug Policy Alliance, March 2013. See also: Harry G. Levine and Deborah Peterson Small, "Marijuana Arrest Crusade: Racial Bias and Police Policy in New York City 1997–2007," New York Civil Liberties Union, April 2008.

17. Jen Hayden, "Former Philadelphia Police Officer: I Planted Drugs Too Many Times to Count," *Daily Kos*, April 14, 2015.

18. Robert Allen and L. L. Brasier, "Lawsuits Against Inkster Cop Go Back for Years," *Detroit Free Press*, March 27, 2015.

19. Allan Lengel, "Ex-Inkster Cop William Melendez Guilty in Beating of Motorist," *Deadline Detroit*, November 19, 2015.

20. Tim Stelloh, "Detective Is Found Guilty of Planting Drugs," *New York Times*, November 1, 2011.

21. "Asset Forfeiture," 2015, see DrugWarFacts.org.

22. Ibid.

23. Sarah Stillman, "Taken," *New Yorker*, August 12 and 19, 2013; http://www.newyorker.com/magazine/2013/08/12/taken.

24. "Asset Forfeiture," 2015, see DrugWarFacts.org.

25. Jack Cole, "Everyday Citizen," undated entry online at Jack Cole's Blog.

26. Jeffrey Miron and Katherine Waldock, "The Budgetary Impact of Ending Drug Prohibition," Cato Institute, September 27, 2010.

27. Rick Anderson, "Seattle Activist Plans Mobile Drug Haven to Encourage Safe Use," *Los Angeles Times*, January 11, 2016.

CHAPTER 4

1. Amy S. F. Lutz, "You Do Not Have Asperger's: What Psychiatry's New Diagnostic Manual Means for People on the Autism Spectrum," *Slate*, May 22, 2013.

2. Sarah Lane, "Ostling v. City of Bainbridge: The Trial Begins," *Inside Bainbridge*, May 15, 2012.

3. Brian, Roach, Kelsey Echols, and Aaron Burnett, "Excited Delirium and the Dural Response: Preventing In-Custody Deaths," *FBI Law Enforcement Bulletin* (July 2014).

4. Jonathan Martin and Ken Armstrong, "Two Cops, an Ax and Many Questions on Bainbridge," *Seattle Times*, February 25, 2012.

5. Laura Usher, "Saving Lives, Changing Communities," *National Alliance on Mental Illness*, October 4, 2013.

6. Amy Goodman et al., "Memphis Model: Police Pioneer Use of Crisis Intervention Teams to Deal with Mentally Sick," *Democracy Now!* October 22, 2013.

7. Betsy Vickers, "Memphis, Tennessee, Police Department's Crisis Intervention Team," Bulletin from the Field: Practitioner Perspectives, *Office of Justice Programs, DOJ*, July 2000.

8. Ibid.

9. Timothy Williams, "Long Taught to Use Force Police Warily Learn to De-escalate," *New York Times*, June 27, 2015.

10. Neal Thompson, "The Carver's Life," *SeattleMet*, April 22, 2011.

11. Ryan J. Reilly, "Police Group Makes a Big Admission About 'Justifiable' Police Shootings," *Huffington Post*, August 19, 2015.

12. "DeEscalation," undated, CIT International, at http://www.citinternational .org/training-overview/61-deescalation.html.

13. Ibid.

14. Brian Kelly, "Attorney Asks Jury to Send a Message with Ostling Verdict," *Bainbridge Island Review*, June 1, 2012.

15. "Any Mental Illness (AMI) Among Adults," *National Institute of Mental Health*, 2013, at http://www.nimh.nih.gov/health/statistics/prevalence/any -mental-illness-ami-among-us-adults.shtml.

16. Thomas Insel, "Director's Blog: Mental Health Awareness Month: By the Numbers," *National Institute of Mental Health*, May 15, 2015.

17. "How Common Is PTSD?" undated, *U.S. Department of Veterans Affairs, PTSD: National Center for PTSD.*

18. Ibid.

19. Sarah Takushi, "Obesity Is a Sizable Problem for Police Officers," *Liberty Voice*, April 10, 2014.

20. Steven Greenhut, "Police and Fire Continue to Promote 'Early Death' Fiction," *Public Sector Inc.*, August 4, 2014.

21. Daniel Clark, Elizabeth K. White, and John M. Violante, "Law Enforcement Suicide: Current Knowledge and Future Directions," *Police Chief* (May 2012).

22. "A Psychological Force Behind the Force," *American Psychological Association* (June 2002).

23. Tad Sooter, "Two Years After Shooting, Ostling Family Advocates," *Kitsap Sun*, October 27, 2012.

CHAPTER 5

1. Jamelle Bouie, "Michael Brown Wasn't a Superhuman Demon: But Darren Wilson's Racial Prejudice Told Him Otherwise," *Slate*, November 26, 2014.

2. Seth Stoughton, "How Police Training Contributes to Avoidable Deaths," *Atlantic*, December 12, 2014.

3. Jacquelyn Smith, "America's Deadliest Jobs," *Forbes*, August 22, 2013.

4. "9/11 by the Numbers," *New York* (September 2014).

5. L. Tay and E. Diener, "Needs and Subjective Well-Being Around the World," *Journal of Personality and Social Psychology* 101 (2) (2011).

6. "The Rodney King Affair," *Los Angeles Times*, March 24, 1991.

7. Melissa Pamer, "Los Angeles 1992 Riots: By the Numbers," *NBC4 News*, April 20, 2012.

8. Seth Mydans, "Rodney King Is Awarded $3.8 Million," *New York Times*, April 20, 1994.

9. Zusha Elinson and Dan Frosch, "Cost of Police-Misconduct Cases Soars in Big U.S. Cities," *Wall Street Journal*, July 15, 2015.

10. Linda Deutsch, "Police Officer: 'I Haven't Beaten Anyone This Bad in a Long Time,'" Associated Press News Archive, March 19, 1991.

CHAPTER 6

1. Celeste Fremon, "Forty-first and Central, 1969—The Black Panther Shootout and the Birth of SWAT," *Witness LA*, April 6, 2011.

2. Miles Corwin, "The Shootout on East Forty-fifth Street: Violence: Twenty years Ago, the LAPD and the Symbionese Liberation Army Exchanged Fire at a Home in South-Central," *Los Angeles Times*, May 18, 1994.

3. Rick Orlov, "North Hollywood Shootout, Fifteen Years Later," *Los Angeles Daily News*, February 27, 2012.

4. Greg Toppo, "Ten Years Later, the Real Story Behind Columbine," *USA Today*, April 14, 2009.

5. ACLU Foundation, "War Comes Home: The Excessive Militarization of American Policing," American Civil Liberties Union, 2014.

6. Peter Kraska, e-mail exchanges, July 12–14, November 28, 2015.

7. Taylor Wofford, "How America's Police Became an Army: The 1033 Program," *Newsweek*, August 13, 2014.

8. Jonathan Martin, "Why Do Small Police Departments Need Eighteen-Ton Armor-Plated Assault Vehicles?" *Seattle Times*, December 8, 2014.

9. Lecia Bushak, "Eighty Percent of Police Officers Are Overweight; Why They're More Likely to Die from Heart Disease Than Fighting Crime," *Medical Daily*, August 16, 2014.

10. Michael Kunzelman, "Little Oversight as Small-Town US Police Departments Get Discarded Military Gear," Associated Press, July 31, 2013.

11. Ibid.

12. Max Ehrenfreund, "The Biggest Question About Police Militarization Obama Hasn't Answered," *Washington Post*, May 21, 2015.

13. Hank Johnson, "Rep. Johnson Reintroduces Bipartisan Bill to Demilitarize Police," March 4, 2015, at http://hankjohnson.house.gov.

14. Adrienne LaFrance, "America's Top Killing Machine," *Atlantic*, January 12, 2015.

15. Tom Zirpoli, "More Guns Equals More Deaths," *Carroll County Times*, March 25, 2015.

CHAPTER 7

1. Craig Wolff, "New York City Police to Replace Revolvers with Semiautomatics," *New York Times*, August 21, 1993.

2. Ibid.

3. Cindy Chang, "Rise in Accidental Gunshots by L.A. County Deputies Follows New Firearm," *Los Angeles Times*, June 13, 2015.

4. Ibid.

5. "Cop Cleared in Deadly Shooting," *ABC, KGTV 10 News*, July 20, 2001.

6. "Jack Cover: Inventor of the Taser Stun Gun," *Independent*, October 22, 2011.

7. Oliver Laughland, Jamiles Lartey, and Ciara McCarthy, "Bolts from the Blue," *Guardian*, November 5, 2015.

8. Ibid.

9. "Man with Knife Tasered by Port Clinton Police," *ABC 13 News*, August 7, 2015.

10. Michael E. Miller, "Miami Cops Misuse Tasers, with Deadly Results," *Miami New Times*, December 30, 2014.

11. Suzanne Trimel, "Amnesty International Urges Stricter Limits on Police Taser Use as U.S. Death Toll Reaches 500," Amnesty International, February 15, 2012.

12. Daniel A. Gross, "The Forgotten History of Mace, Designed by a Twenty-Nine-Year-Old and Reinvented as a Police Weapon," Smithsonian.com, November 4, 2014.

13. Christian Nordqvist, "What Is Pepper Spray? Is Pepper Spray Dangerous?" *Medical News Today*, November 25, 2011.

14. Conor Friedersdorf, "Did Police in Salinas Use Excessive Force?" *Atlantic*, June 10, 2015.

15. "What Walkie-Talkies Do the Police Use?" *Walkie-Talkie World*, January 21, 2015.

16. Kristina Davis, "Weapons Packed with a Punch but Rare," *Union-Tribune San Diego*, October 7, 2006.

17. The end of the story: Anderson survived, was convicted of robbery and first-degree murder, and sentenced to die. His sentence was commuted to life in prison when the California State Supreme Court, citing *People v. Anderson*, declared the death penalty unconstitutional. The decision also commuted the death sentences of Charles Manson and Sirhan Sirhan. Anderson was paroled in 1967 after eleven years in San Quentin and, at last report, was living quietly, on Social Security, in Seattle.

18. "The Patrol Rifle: Considerations for Adoption and Use," International Association of Chiefs of Police, *Police Chief* (February 2007).

19. Stanley Coren, "Do Some Dog Breeds Have Better Noses and Scent Discrimination Than Others?" *Psychology Today*, January 15, 2011.

20. Aliza Nadi, Jim Seida, and Tracy Connor, "Porn-Sniffing Dog Helped Bring Down Subway Star Jared Fogle," *NBC News*, August 26, 2015.

21. "Canine Use in Law Enforcement," *Private Security Professionals of America*, May 25, 2015, at https://www.mypspa.org/article/more/canine-use-in-law-enforcement.

22. Talal Ansari, "Deadly Heat: Police Dogs Die When Left in Patrol Cars," *BuzzFeed News*, June 2, 2015.

23. Ibid.

24. Ibid.

25. Ibid.

26. Ibid.

27. Bruce Nolan, "K-9 Officer Fired After Dog's Death Is Reinstated by Appeals Court," *Times-Picayune*, May 4, 2012.

28. Terrence McCoy, "Tear Gas Is a Chemical Weapon Banned in War. But Ferguson Police Shoot It at Protesters," *Washington Post*, August 14, 2014.

29. Amy Goodman and Juan González, "Scott Olsen, U.S. Vet Nearly Killed by Police Beanbag at Occupy Oakland, Settles Lawsuit with City," *Democracy Now!* March 21, 2014.

30. Jim Brunner, "Claim Filed over Officer's WTO Kick," *Seattle Times*, June 29, 2000.

31. Mandi Milligan, "Toddler Severely Burned by Flash Bang in Habersham Co. Drug Raid," *CBS46 Atlanta*, May 30, 2014, updated July 22, 2015.

32. Julia Angwin and Abbie Nehring, "Hotter Than Lava: Every Day, Cops Toss Dangerous Military-Style Flashbang Grenades During Raids, with Little Oversight and Horrifying Results," *ProPublica*, January 12, 2015.

33. As I confessed in my first book, I "misused" the sleeper hold during my rookie days. But the misuse took the form of applying it when circumstances didn't justify it (or when I'd manufactured "justification" by baiting individuals into taking a swing at me). I'd behaved badly, but the method I employed was proper, and no one died.

34. Daniel Bethencourt, "Guy Impersonating a Cop Flees from Real Ones on I-96," *Detroit Free Press*, July 2, 2015.

35. Jay Stanley, "Police Body-Mounted Cameras: With Right Policies in Place, a Win for All," American Civil Liberties Union, March 2015.

36. Ibid.

37. Chuck Wexler and Ronald L. Davis et al., "Implementing a Body-Worn Camera Program: Recommendations and Lessons Learned," Police Executive Research Forum and Office of Community Oriented Policing Services, 2014.

38. Barak Ariel, William A. Farrar, and Alex Sutherland, "The Effect of Police Body-Worn Cameras on Use of Force and Citizens' Complaints Against the Police: A Randomized Controlled Trial," *Journal of Quantitative Criminology* (September 2015).

39. Office of the Attorney General, "Justice Department Announces $20 Million in Funding to Support Body-Worn Camera Pilot Program," *United States Department of Justice*, May 1, 2015.

40. "Considering Police Body Cameras," *Harvard Law Review*, April 10, 2015.

41. Jonathan Kaminsky, "Seattle Police Plan for Helicopter Drones Hits Severe Turbulence," Reuters, November 27, 2012.

42. "Seattle Mayor Says No to Drones," Homeland Security News Wire, February 12, 2013.

43. Christine Clarridge, "Protesters Steal the Show at Seattle Police Gathering to Explain Intended Use of Drones," *Seattle Times*, October 25, 2012.

44. Ibid.

45. "Domestic Drones," undated, American Civil Liberties Union, at https://www
.aclu.org/issues/privacy-technology/surveillance-technologies/domestic-drones.

46. Ibid.

47. Ibid.

CHAPTER 8

1. Shafaq Hasan, "Tone-Deaf Police Group Declares Anniversary of Michael
Brown Shooting 'Darren Wilson Day,'" *Nonprofit Quarterly*, August 13, 2015.

2. Jake Halpern, "The Cop," *New Yorker*, August 10, 2015.

3. Camara Phyllis Jones, "Levels of Racism: A Theoretical Framework and a
Gardener's Tale," *American Journal of Public Health* (August 2000).

4. Michelle Alexander, *The New Jim Crow: Mass Incarceration in the Age of Colorblindness* (New York: The New Press, 2010).

5. Interview with Dirul-Islam Shamsid-Deen, May 12, 2015, Eastsound,
Washington.

6. Ken Auletta, "Fixing Broken Windows," *New Yorker*, September 7, 2015.

7. Ansel Herz, "Seattle Police Union President to Cops: Get With the Times or
Get Out of This City," *Stranger*, February 18, 2015.

8. Ibid.

9. Informal conversation with Kathleen O'Toole, NACOLE Conference, February 6, 2015, Seattle University.

10. "Pat Lynch, Who's the Enemy in Your NYPD Union's War?" *New York Daily
News*, December 19, 2014.

11. Andy Cush, "How Mayor de Blasio Warned His Own Son About His Police
Force," *Gawker*, December 3, 2014.

12. Ross Barkan, "Bill de Blasio Defends 'Dante' Remark After PBA Boss Blasts
Him Again," *New York Observer*, December 4, 2014.

13. John Del Signore, "Unhinged NYPD Union Boss Urges Cops to Fight De
Blasio's 'Revolution,'" *Gothamist*, December 18, 2014.

14. Benjamin Mueller and Al Baker, "Two N.Y.P.D. Officers Killed in Brooklyn
Ambush; Suspect Commits Suicide," *New York Times*, December 20, 2015.

15. Andrew Hart, "NYC Police Union Chief Blames Mayor, Protesters for Police
Killings," *Huffington Post*, December 21, 2014.

16. Anthony M. Destefano, "NYC PBA Media Ad Blitz Aims to Push for Better
Contract," *Newsday*, October 9, 2014.

CHAPTER 9

1. Kevin Rector, "Baltimore Police Recruits Receive Cognitive Training to
Better Handle Stress," *Baltimore Sun*, August 24, 2015.

2. Ibid.

3. Ibid.

4. Ansel Herz, "The Seattle Police Department Fires Officer Cynthia Whitlatch," *Stranger*, September 15, 2015.

5. Steve Miletich, "SPD Officer in Golf-Club Case Pushed Prosecutors to File Charges," *Seattle Times*, February 5, 2015.

6. George Thompson, "Seven Things Never to Say to Anyone, and Why," *Police-One*, November 11, 2005, at https://www.policeone.com/communications/articles /120708–7-things-never-to-say-to-anyone-and-why-Part-1.

7. Ibid.

8. Thomas Frank, "Feds Fail to Track Deadly Police Pursuits," *USA Today*, September 29, 2015.

9. Michael Taylor, "Obituary—Pierce Brooks," *SFGate*, March 4, 1998.

10. Pierce R. Brooks, " *. . . officer down, code three*" (Chicago: Motorola Teleprograms, 1976).

11. Legal Information Institute, *Terry v. Ohio*, Cornell Law School, June 10, 1968, at https://www.law.cornell.edu/supremecourt/text/392/1.

12. Joseph Goldstein, "Judge Rejects New York's Stop and Frisk Policy," *New York Times*, August 12, 2013.

13. Aviva Shen, "White People Stopped by New York Police Are More Likely to Have Guns or Drugs Than Minorities," ThinkProgress.org, May 22, 2013.

14. Al Baker, "Handcuffing the Wounded: A Police Tactic Hits a Nerve," *New York Times*, November 18, 2007.

15. David Klinger, "Dealing with Downed Suspects: Some Lessons from the VALOR Project About How to Properly Manage the Immediate Aftermath of Officer-Involved Shootings," *Police Chief* (May 2012).

16. J. E. Boydstun, M. E. Sherry, and N. P. Moelter, "Patrol Staffing in San Diego—One-or Two-Officer Units," Police Foundation.org, 1977.

CHAPTER 10

1. John Conroy, "Tools of Torture," *Chicago Reader*, February 4, 2005.

2. John Conroy, "The Persistence of Andrew Wilson," *Chicago Reader*, November 29, 2007.

3. Michael Miller, "Cop Accused of Brutally Torturing Black Suspects Costs Chicago $5.5 Million," *Washington Post*, April 15, 2015.

4. "Daley Issues Sarcastic Apology for Torture," Chicago Independent Media Center, October 23, 2008, at http://chicago.indymedia.org/archive/newswire /display/84323/index.php.

5. Hal Dardick, John Byrne, and Steve Mills, "Mayor Backs $5.5 Million Reparations Deal for Burge Police Torture Victims," *Chicago Tribune*, April 14, 2015.

6. Flint Taylor, "Jon Burge, Torturer of Over 100 Black Men, Is Out of Prison After Less Than Four Years," *In These Times*, October 2, 2014.

7. Aamer Madhani, "Chicago to Pay Reparations to Police Torture Victims," *USA Today*, April 15, 2015.

8. Craig Futterman, e-mail response to inquiry, November 11, 2015, University of Chicago Law School.

9. Annie Sweeney, "Twelve Years for Chicago Cop at Center of Scandal: 'I Can Hold My Head High,'" *Chicago Tribune*, September 8, 2011.

10. Timothy Williams, "Chicago Rarely Penalizes Officers for Complaints, Data Shows," *New York Times*, November 18, 2015.

11. Lauren Chooljian, "Former Chicago Cop Gets Twelve Years in Prison," *WBEZ91.5*, September 8, 2011.

12. Fran Spielman, "Disgraced Chicago Cop Breaks Silence, Condemns $5.5 Million Reparations Fund," *Chicago Sun-Times*, April 17, 2015.

13. See the website, at www.flexyourrights.org.

14. "High School Teachers Suspended After Showing 'Know Your Rights' Film," *HeadCount Blog*, June 3, 2010, at http://www.headcount.org/high-school-teachers -suspended-after-showing-know-your-rights-film.

15. Steve Schmadeke, Jeremy Gorner, and Rosemary Regina Sobol, "Tyshawn on Swing When Gangbangers out for Revenge Targeted Him: Prosecutors," *Chicago Tribune*, November 27, 2015.

16. Aaron C. Davis, "Here's the 'Fetal' Police Quote Causing Grief for Chicago Mayor Rahm Emanuel," *Washington Post*, October 15, 2015.

17. Michael Lansu, "Chicago's 2014 Murder Total on Track for Another Low, but Shootings Rise," *Chicago Sun-Times*, December 28, 2014.

CHAPTER 11

1. Lou Cannon, "One Bad Cop," *New York Times Magazine*, October 1, 2000.

2. Ibid.

3. David Rosenzweig, "Ex-LAPD Officer Sentenced in Bank of America Robbery," *Los Angeles Times*, September 14, 1999.

4. Randall Sullivan, "The Unsolved Mystery of the Notorious B.I.G.," *Rolling Stone*, January 7, 2011.

5. "Rampart Scandal Timeline," *PBS Frontline*, March 18, 1997–December 17, 2001.

6. Ibid.

7. Ibid.

8. Ibid.

9. Joel Rubin, "Report Questions LAPD Program to Flag Misconduct," *Los Angeles Times*, August 25, 2014.

10. Ibid.

11. "Departments Use Technology to ID Troubled Officers," *Newsmax*, September 4, 2014.

12. Rick Baratta, "The Law Enforcement Code of Ethics," undated, International Police Association Region 29, at http://websitesbycook.com/ipa29/le-code-of-ethics.

13. "Law Enforcement Code of Ethics," undated, California Commission on Peace Officers Standards and Training, at https://www.post.ca.gov/commission -procedure-c-3-law-enforcement-code-of-ethics.aspx.

14. "Law Enforcement Oath of Honor," undated, International Association of Chiefs of Police, at http://www.theiacp.org/portals/0/pdfs/oath_honor_adobe.pdf.

15. "Model Policies," undated, International Association of Chiefs of Police, at http://www.iacp.org/Model-Policies-Alphabetical-Order.

16. Alan M. Dershowitz, "Controlling the Cops; Accomplices to Perjury," *New York Times*, May 2, 1994.

17. "Dershowitz: Cops 'Designated Liars,'" UPI Archives, November 15, 1995, at http://www.upi.com/Archives/1995/11/15/Dershowitz-cops-disignated-liars /7792816411600.

18. Joseph D. McNamara, "Law Enforcement: Has the Drug War Created an Officer Liars Club?" *Los Angeles Times*, February 11, 1996.

19. Steve Schmadeke, "Five Cops Caught in Lies on Witness Stand, Judge Says," *Chicago Tribune*, April 15, 2014.

20. Jeff Noble, "Police Officer Truthfulness and the Brady Decision," *Police Chief* (October 2003).

21. HW, "Shiga into the Bay," *Historic Wings: Flight Stories*, November 22, 2012.

22. William Bratton and Peter Knobler, *Turnaround: How America's Top Cop Reversed the Crime Epidemic* (New York: Random House, 1998).

23. Rick Anderson, "Why It's Nearly Impossible to Convict a Killer Cop in Washington State," *Seattle Weekly*, September 28, 2015.

24. Christine Clarridge and Steve Miletich, "Officer on Fatal Shooting: 'No Doubt . . . Attack Was Coming,'" *Seattle Times*, January 11, 2011.

25. Steve Miletich and Jennifer Sullivan, "Officer Birk Quits After SPD Rebuke," *Seattle Times*, February 16, 2011.

26. Rich Schapiro, "Cold as Ice: Ferguson, Mo., County Prosecutor Has Deep Ties to Police," *New York Daily News*, November 25, 2014.

27. Ibid.

28. From staff reports, "McCulloch Blasts Nixon," *St. Louis Post-Dispatch*, August 14, 2014.

29. Dylan Scott, "Special Report: Brown Family and Prosecutor Bitterly Divided over Grand Jury Probe in Ferguson," *TalkingPointsMemo (TPM)*, October 1, 2014.

30. Paul Cassell, "The Michael Brown Grand Jury Process Was Fair," *Washington Post*, November 25, 2015.

31. Kimberly Kindy and Kelly Kimbriell, "Thousands Dead, Few Prosecuted," *Washington Post*, April 11, 2015.

32. Tony Norman, "Grand Jury System Tainted by Police Bias," *Pittsburgh Post-Gazette*, December 5, 2014.

33. Christopher Slobogin, "1037 Testilying: Police Perjury and What to Do About It," *University of Colorado Law Review* (Fall 1996), online at Constitution Society, http://www.constitution.org/lrev/slobogin_testilying.htm.

34. "Indictments in Police Shootings Rare; Convictions, Even Rarer," *Statesman*, May 12, 2014.

35. German Lopez, "The Trial of Ex-Cop Daniel Holtzclaw: Why an All-White Jury Is Such a Huge Problem," *Vox Identities*, November 5, 2015.

36. Samuel Walker, *Police Accountability: The Role of Citizen Oversight* (Belmont, CA: Wadsworth Publishing, 2000), and Samuel Walker and Carol Ann Archbold, *The New World of Police Accountability* (New York: Sage Publications, 2013).

37. Ibid.

38. Jack R. Green, ed., "Civilian Review Boards," in *The Encyclopedia of Police Science* (London: Routledge, 2006).

39. New York City Civilian Complaint Review Board, "History," at www.nyc.gov/html/ccrb.

40. Ibid.

41. Ibid.

42. Tamar Jacoby, "The Uncivil History of the Civilian Review Board," *City Journal* (Winter 1993).

43. William G. Bailey, ed., "Civilian Review Boards," in *The Encyclopedia of Police Science* (London: Routledge, 1995).

44. New York City Civilian Complaint Review Board, "History."

45. Ibid.

46. Ibid.

47. Ibid.

48. Ibid.

49. Ibid.

50. Peter Finn, "Citizen Review of Police: Approaches and Implementation," *National Institute of Justice* (March 2001).

51. Kim Hendrickson, "The Conservative Case for Civilian Review," American Enterprise Institute, October 15, 2013.

52. Kim Hendrickson, telephone interview and e-mail exchanges, June 2, 2015.

53. Ibid.

54. Brian Buchner, telephone interview and e-mail exchanges, summer and fall, 2015.

55. Pierce Murphy, in-person interview, October 11, 2013.

56. Ansel Herz, "Auditor: Reforming the Seattle Police Department Remains an 'Aspirational Goal,'" *Stranger*, February 26, 2015.

57. Steve Miletich and Daniel Beekman, "'We've Waited Too Long': Frustrated Groups Say Seattle Police Fixes Needed Now," *Seattle Times*, December 1, 2015.

58. Harriett Walden, informal conversation, NACOLE Academic Symposium, February 6, 2015, Seattle University.

59. See the Eugene, Oregon, Civilian Review Board website, at http://www.eugene-or.gov/policeauditor.

60. See the site for the Bay Area Citizen Review Board, at http://www.bart.gov/about/policeauditor.

CHAPTER 12

1. My views on organizational theory have been significantly influenced by the works of Peter Senge, particularly his *The Fifth Discipline: The Art and Practice of the Learning Organization* (New York: Doubleday, 2006).

2. "The Christopher Commission on Tuesday Issued a 228-Page Report on the Activities of the Los Angeles Police Department," *Los Angeles Times*, July 19, 1991. This piece contains extensive excerpts, chapter by chapter of the report.

3. Norm Stamper, *Breaking Rank: A Top Cop's Exposé of the Dark Side of American Policing* (New York: Nation Books, 2005).

4. jpsmith: Just Another Center for Information and Communication Sciences site, "Theory of Human Communications," October 26, 2008, at http://centerforics.org/jpsmith/2008/10/26/theory-of-human-communications.

5. In *Breaking Rank* (2005), I presented additional contrasts between the institutions of the military and the police, and I offered, as well, an account of my singular failure to "demilitarize" supervisory titles within the San Diego Police Department. Opposition was overwhelming—and from a variety of sources, including the hometown newspaper, which editorialized against the lunacy of "Normanclature."

6. Peter Horne, "Policewomen: Their First Century and the New Era," *Police Chief* (September 2006).

7. Kathy Spillar, "The Nation's Police Have a Sex-Discrimination Problem," *Ms. Magazine*, September 30, 2014.

8. Kim Lonsway et al., "Hiring and Retaining More Women: The Advantages to Law Enforcement Agencies," *National Center for Women and Policing* (Spring 2003).

9. "Policing and Homicide, 1976–1998," Bureau of Justice Statistics, at http://www.bjs.gov/content/pub/pdf/ph98.pdf.

CHAPTER 13

1. Sasha Goldstein, "Tamir Rice, Twelve, Shot Dead by Cleveland Cop Who Had 'Dismal' Gun Skills and 'Weepy' Demeanor at Previous Police Department," *New York Daily News*, December 4, 2014.

2. Adam Ferrise, "Cleveland Officer Who Shot Tamir Rice Had 'Dismal' Handgun Performance for Independence Police," *Northeast Ohio Media Group*, December 3, 2014.

3. Ibid.

4. Shaun King, "No, Police Killing Pre-Teen Tamir Rice Wasn't Reasonable—It Was a Heartless Murder Backed by Lies," *Daily Kos*, October 12, 2015.

5. Jaeah Lee, "How Cleveland Police May Have Botched a 911 Call Just Before Killing Tamir Rice," *Mother Jones*, June 24, 2015.

6. Ibid.

7. J. David Goodman and Al Baker, "Brian Moore, New York Police Officer Shot in the Head, Dies," *New York Times*, May 4, 2015.

8. Norm Stamper, *Breaking Rank: A Top Cop's Exposé of the Dark Side of American Policing* (New York: Nation Books, 2005).

9. Steve Miletich, "Police Academy 2.0: Less Military Training, More Empathy," *Seattle Times* (July 13, 2013).

10. *The Republic of Plato*, trans. Allan Bloom (New York: Basic Books, 1991).

11. Miletich, "Police Academy 2.0."

12. Radley Balko, *Rise of the Warrior Cop: The Militarization of America's Police Forces* (New York: Public Affairs, 2013).

13. Ken Auletta, "Fixing Broken Windows," *New Yorker*, September 7, 2015.

14. Karl Ove Knausgaard, "The Inexplicable: Inside the Mind of a Mass Killer," *New Yorker*, May 25, 2015.

15. Jonathan Capehart, "Police and Protesters Must 'See' Each Other," *Washington Post*, January 8, 2015.

16. Ellen Scrivner, "Innovations in Police Recruitment and Hiring: Hiring in the Spirit of Service," report completed in 2004, *Community Oriented Policing Service*.

17. "What Is "Problem-Oriented Policing?" citing Herman Goldstein's pioneering work in 1979, as elucidated in his 1990 classic, *Problem-Oriented Policing* (New York: McGraw-Hill, 1979). From Center for Evidence-Based Crime Policy, George Mason University.

18. Ibid.

19. Ibid.

20. Anthony M. DeStefano, "Larry DePrimo, NYPD Cop, Buys Homeless Man Boots," *Huffington Post*, November 29, 2012.

21. Tom Waits, "Warm Beer and Cold Women," from the album *Nighthawks at the Diner*, 1975.

CHAPTER 14

1. Tavis Smiley, "Black Lives Matter Organizer Dr. Melina Abdullah," *The Tavis Smiley Show*, PBS, November 18, 2015.

2. Ibid.

CHAPTER 15

1. Will Bredderman, "De Blasio and Bratton Debut 'Neighborhood Policing' Plan with Beefed-Up NYPD," *Observer*, June 25, 2015.

2. Ibid.

3. "Safe and Fair Everywhere," at http://www.nyc.gov/html/nypd/html/home/poa.shtml.

4. Mychal Denzel Smith, "Abolish the Police. Instead, Let's Have Full Social, Economic, and Political Equality," *Nation*, April 9, 2015.

5. Mitchell O'Neal Mitchell, "Twelve Considerations for Congregational Security," undated, NOVA Security and Defense Concepts, at http://valuespartnerships.com/wp-content/uploads/2015/06/churchsecurity.pdf.

6. Chris Megerian et al., "Americans Who Thwarted Train Attack Now International Heroes," *Los Angeles Times*, August 23, 2015.

7. Joe Palazzolo, "U.S. Leads World in Mass Shootings," *Wall Street Journal*, October 3, 2015.

8. See http://hedricksmith.com.

9. Hedrick Smith, in-person interview, March 14, 2015, Washington, DC.

10. "Community-Oriented Policing Strategies: Meta-Analysis of Law Enforcement Practices," *Journalist's Resource*, March 11, 2015.

11. Anderson Cooper, "Baltimore Mom Who Slapped Son: He Was Embarrassing Himself," *Anderson Cooper 360°*, CNN, April 29, 2015.

CHAPTER 16

1. Deborah Jacobs, in-person interview, Eastsound, Washington, July 12, 2015.

2. Conor Friedersdorf, "A Conversation About Black Lives Matter and Bernie Sanders," *Atlantic*, August 21, 2015.

3. Ian Millhiser, "Big City Sheriff Says Black Lives Matter 'Will Join Forces with ISIS' to Take Down America," *ThinkProgress*, October 28, 2015.

4. Scott Eric Kaufman, "'Fox and Friends' Guest: There Hasn't Been Any Police Brutality in America Since the 1960s," *Salon*, October 26, 2015.

5. Daniel Bice, "Sheriff David Clarke Says Police Brutality and Racism Have Ended," *No Quarter Blog, Milwaukee Wisconsin Journal Sentinel*, October 28, 2015.

6. Nancy McPherson and Barbara Raymond, telephone interview, June 5, 2015.

7. Draft of Institute for Developing Police Leaders proposal.

CHAPTER 17

1. Zusha Elinson and Dan Frosch, "Cost of Police-Misconduct Cases Soars in Big U.S. Cities," *Wall Street Journal*, July 15, 2015.

2. "The Ferguson Report: Department of Justice Investigation of the Ferguson Police Department," *United States Department of Justice, Civil Rights Division*, June 2015.

3. Office of Community Oriented Policing Services, May 2015.

4. Tim Lynch, "President Obama's Task Force on 21st Century Policing," *Cato at Liberty*, June 24, 2015.

FURTHER READING

Adams, Ronald J., Thomas M. McTernan, and Charles Remsberg. *Street Survival Tactics for Armed Encounters*. Villa Park, IL: Calibre Press, 1990.

Alexander, Michelle. *The New Jim Crow: Mass Incarceration in the Age of Colorblindness*. New York: New Press, 2010.

American Civil Liberties Union. "War Comes Home: The Excessive Militarization of American Policing." New York: ACLU Foundation, June 2014.

Argyris, Chris, and Donald A. Schön. *Organizational Learning II: Theory, Method, and Practice*. Upper Saddle River, NJ: Financial Times, 1995.

Balko, Radley. *Rise of the Warrior Cop: The Militarization of America's Police Forces*. New York: PublicAffairs, 2013.

Bratton, William, and Peter Knobler. *Turnaround: How America's Top Cop Reversed the Crime Epidemic*. New York: Random House, 1998.

Caldero, Michael A., and John P. Crank. *Police Ethics: The Corruption of Noble Cause*. London: Routledge, 2010.

Coates, Ta-Nehisi. *Between the World and Me*. New York: Random House, 2015.

Dhywood, Jeffrey. *World War D: The Case Against Prohibitionism, Roadmap to Controlled Re-Legalization*. California, n.p.: Columbia Communications, 2011.

Domanick, Joe. *Blue: The LAPD and the Battle to Redeem American Policing*. New York: Simon and Schuster, 2015.

Drucker, Ernest. *A Plague of Prisons: The Epidemiology of Mass Incarceration in America*. New York: New Press, 2013.

Gilmartin, Kevin M. *Emotional Survival for Law Enforcement: A Guide for Officers and Their Families*. Tucson, AZ: E-S Press, 2013.

Grossman, Dave, and Loren W. Christensen. *On Combat: The Psychology and Physiology of Deadly Conflict in War and Peace*. Millstadt, IL: Human Factor Research Group, 2011.

Kelling, George L., and Catherine M. Coles. *Fixing Broken Windows: Restoring Order and Reducing Crime in Our Communities*. New York: Free Press, 1998.

Kelly, Ray. *Vigilance: My Life Serving America and Protecting Its Empire City*. New York: Hachette Books, 2015.

Kraska, Peter. "Militarization and Policing: Its Relevance to 21st Century Police." *Policing* 1 (4), December 13, 2007.

Leovy, Jill. *Ghettoside: A True Story of Murder in America*. New York, NY: Spiegel & Grau, 2015.

Martín, José. "Policing Is a Dirty Job, but Nobody's Gotta Do It: Six Ideas for a Cop-Free World." *Rolling Stone,* December 16, 2014.

Miron, Jeffrey. "The Budgetary Implications of Drug Prohibition." Department of Economics, Harvard University, December 2008.

Plantinga, Adam. *Four Hundred Things Cops Know: Street-Smart Lessons from a Veteran Patrolman*. Fresno, CA: Quill Driver Books, 2014.

Police Executive Research Forum, Critical Issues in Policing. "Restructuring Police Use of Force Training." August 19, 2015. Available at https://improvingpolice .wordpress.com/2015/08/19/restructuring-police-use-of-force-training.

Police Executive Research Forum, Critical Issues in Policing Series. "Civil Rights Investigations of Local Police: Lessons Learned." July 2013. Available at http://www.policeforum.org/assets/docs/Critical_Issues_Series/civil%20 rights%20investigations%20of%20local%20police%20-%20lessons%20 learned%202013.pdf.

Police Executive Research Forum and Community Oriented Policing Services, Department of Justice. "Implementing a Body-Worn Camera Program: Recommendations and Lessons Learned." 2014. Available at http://www.policeforum .org/assets/docs/Free_Online_Documents/Technology/implementing%20 a%20body-worn%20camera%20program.pdf.

Quinn, Michael W. *Walking with the Devil: The Police Code of Silence: What Bad Cops Don't Want You to Know and Good Cops Won't Tell You*. Minneapolis, MN: Quinn and Associates Publishing and Consulting, 2011.

Schein, Edgar. *Organizational Culture and Leadership*. San Francisco: Jossey-Bass, 2010.

Seattle Police Department. "The Seattle Police Department After Action Report. World Trade Organization Ministerial Conference. Seattle, Washington, November 29–December 3, 1999." April 4, 2000. Available at http://www.seattle .gov/police/publications/wto/wto_aar.pdf.

Senge, Peter. *The Fifth Discipline: The Art and Practice of the Learning Organization*. New York: Random House, 2010.

Simon, David. *Homicide: A Year on the Killing Streets*. New York: Holt Paperbacks, 2006.

Skolnick, Jerome. *Justice Without Trial: Law Enforcement in Democratic Society*. Classics of Law and Society. New Orleans: Quid Pro Books, 2013.

Smith, Hedrick. *Who Stole the American Dream?* New York: Random House, 2012.

Smith, Mychal Denzel. *Invisible Man, Got the Whole World Watching: A Young Black Man's Education*. New York: Nation Books, 2016.

Thompson, George, and Jerry B. Jenkins. *Verbal Judo: The Gentle Art of Persuasion.* Updated edition. New York: William Morrow, 2013.

United States Department of Justice, Civil Rights Division. Introduction by Theodore M. Shaw. "The Ferguson Report: Investigation of the Ferguson Police Department." June 23, 2015.

United States Department of Justice, Civil Rights Division. "Investigation of the New Orleans Police Department." March 17, 2011.

United States Department of Justice, Civil Rights Division and United States Attorney's Office, Western District of Washington. "Investigation of the Seattle Police Department." December 16, 2011.

Walker, Samuel, and Carol A. Archbold. *The New World of Police Accountability.* Thousand Oaks, CA: Sage Publications, 2013.

INDEX

Norm Stamper began his law enforcement career in San Diego in 1966 as a beat cop. In 1994, he was named chief of the Seattle Police Department. Retired in 2000, he now lives in a cabin on a mountain in the San Juan Islands in Washington state. He is the author of *Breaking Rank* and is at work on a novel.